Harnessing Knowledge Dynamics:
Principled Organizational Knowing & Learning

Mark E. Nissen
Naval Postgraduate School, USA

IRM Press

**Publisher of innovative scholarly and professional
information technology titles in the cyberage**

Hershey • London • Melbourne • Singapore

Acquisitions Editor:	Michelle Potter
Development Editor:	Kristin Roth
Senior Managing Editor:	Amanda Appicello
Managing Editor:	Jennifer Neidig
Copy Editor:	April Schmidt
Typesetter:	Amanda Kirlin
Cover Design:	Lisa Tosheff
Printed at:	Integrated Book Technology

Published in the United States of America by
IRM Press (an imprint of Idea Group Inc.)
701 E. Chocolate Avenue, Suite 200
Hershey PA 17033-1240
Tel: 717-533-8845
Fax: 717-533-8661
E-mail: cust@idea-group.com
Web site: http://www.irm-press.com

and in the United Kingdom by
IRM Press (an imprint of Idea Group Inc.)
3 Henrietta Street
Covent Garden
London WC2E 8LU
Tel: 44 20 7240 0856
Fax: 44 20 7379 3313
Web site: http://www.eurospan.co.uk

Library of Congress Cataloging-in-Publication Data

Nissen, Mark E., 1958-
  Harnessing knowledge dynamics / Mark E. Nissen.
     p. cm.
  Summary: "This book provides 30 principles on which to base the most important decisions and actions in an organization pertaining to knowledge management"--Provided by publisher.
  Includes bibliographical references and index.
  ISBN 1-59140-773-7 (hard cover) -- ISBN 1-59140-774-5 (soft cover) -- ISBN 1-59140-775-3 (ebook)
  1. Knowledge management. 2. Organizational learning. I. Title.
  HD30.2.N59 2006
  658.4'038--dc22
                          2005020632

British Cataloguing in Publication Data
A Cataloguing in Publication record for this book is available from the British Library.

Harnessing Knowledge Dynamics:
Principled Organizational Knowing & Learning

Table of Contents

Foreword

"Remember that information flows, but that knowledge grows" is what I once told the graduate students in the PhD seminar on knowledge management that I co-taught at USC with my colleague Dr. Alexander Hars in the late 1990s. How could one possibly apply a transportation or flow metaphor to something as evolving and capricious as knowledge? And everyone seemed comfortable with that. It gave them a way of thinking about knowledge that captured its organic nature and its distinction from information, and perhaps it also had some intellectual playfulness in a memorable one-liner. I had even exported that image to the Swedish School of Business and Economics in Helsinki, Finland where I co-taught the doctoral workshop on knowledge management in 1997. Even the Scandinavians who are culturally and historically the masters of knowledge sharing and participation accepted that distinction. Furthermore, in 2001, I published a book on redesigning enterprise processes for e-business, and, in it, the link between business processes and knowledge was mainly about increasing the knowledge-creating capabilities around a specific business process. Mark Nissen, with this innovative and mold-breaking book, has elegantly shown that my statement and approach around knowledge growing rather than flowing were limiting. Knowledge too can flow — and regarding it as such has many operationally practical benefits to management, decision making, and the execution of business processes. As enterprises grow to be more knowledge-intensive and knowledge permeates all business processes (even the very mundane ones), Dr. Nissen's view is an increasingly useful one.

The concept that organizational knowledge moves and flows from how it exists and where it is located to how and where it is needed in order to enable work and organizational performance is a very powerful idea in this book. It heralds the emergence of a school of knowledge dynamics that combines in an operational manner the capriciousness and elusiveness of tacit knowledge with the down-to-earth phenomena of process flow analysis. It also brings to the attention of both academics and practitioners the notion of the "knowledge divide" in terms of the difference between the "haves" and the "have-nots." The book's driving notion is that there are different kinds and levels of knowledge within an organizational setting, and there is a critical need for a principled way of managing this distribution of knowledge in order to enhance organizational performance. This book is both conceptually elegant and operationally useful and is a much needed contribution.

Dr. Nissen gives us solid principles and techniques that we can use to manage knowledge flows, and the 30 knowledge flow principles are practically useful to anyone who would like to understand how to harness knowledge management as a strategic capability for enhancing organizational performance. The principles lead us through the logic and "how to" that explains the unevenness of distribution of knowledge and how it must flow for organizational performance, the criticality of tacit knowledge, and what drives the flow of knowledge. It unearths some very new and previously untreated issues, such as the tendency of knowledge to remain at rest, the relationship between workflows and knowledge flows, and how knowledge flows lie on the critical path of workflows and, hence, influence organizational performance. The principles take into account how knowledge flows and organizational change are linked in multidimensional ways and the role of information technologies in enhancing and managing knowledge flows. The 30 actionable principles are a treasure chest for understanding, diagnosing, and enhancing knowledge dynamics and organizational performance.

The second section of the book has the application cases that test the mettle of those principles and provide ways of relating to a variety of organizational contexts that help managers apply these principles to their own organization or enterprise setting.

Dr. Nissen weaves the phenomena in this book like a probing doctor who identifies medical pathologies with a knowledge flow stethoscope, and yet he anticipates future issues like a skilled urban planner who needs to better allocate knowledge as a public good. The book brings together the conceptual richness of a new way of diagnosing knowledge flows with the practical operational how-to of linking that to organizational performance and the requisite organizational change for long-term competitive advantage. It identifies archetypes of knowledge flow patterns that help diagnose and uncover problems, but also directly links that with management interventions.

Finally, the book does something that will, in my opinion, becoming increasingly important in the coming years: It sets the stage for better management of real-time organizations. As the environment continues to speed up, techniques for real-time management will increasingly influence organizational performance. Knowledge dynamics is at the heart of managing real-time enterprises and organizations, and Dr. Nissen's book is showing us the way of the future and how we can apply it now.

I think my new pseudo-rhyming one-liner should now be something like, "Comatose knowledge flows help you diagnose where organizational performance goes…"

I am honored and proud to write the foreword to this mold-breaking and immensely useful book.

Omar A. El Sawy
Professor of Information Systems
Marshall School of Business
University of Southern California, USA

Preface

Knowledge is power. Knowledge represents one of the few bases of sustainable competitive advantage available to the modern enterprise, but knowledge is distributed unevenly through most organizations. Rapid and reliable flows of knowledge across people, organizations, times, and places are critical to enterprise performance. Unfortunately, the leader and manager have negligible current guidance for assessing and enhancing knowledge flows in practice. A dearth of contemporary research addresses the dynamics of knowledge, which are fundamental to understanding knowledge flows.

For several instances, epistemology has much to say about the nature of knowledge, but it offers little actionable guidance for the leader and manager; information science and information technologies have much to say about flows of information and data, but knowledge is distinct (e.g., it enables action) and exhibits different dynamic behaviors; knowledge management has much to say about organizing static knowledge, particularly knowledge articulated in explicit form, but it remains largely silent concerning dynamics of tacit knowledge; and strategy has much to say about the benefits of competing on the basis of knowledge, but it offers little in terms of how such benefits can be obtained.

Alternatively, emerging knowledge-flow theory addresses the dynamics of knowledge — as distinct from information and data — directly. It also applies equally well to tacit and explicit knowledge. Techniques associated with knowledge-flow analysis enable the practicing leader and manager to visualize flows of knowledge using a multidimensional framework. Such techniques also facilitate diagnosing an enterprise's knowledge flows for problems such as bottlenecks, clumping, source inadequacies, and short circuits. Archetypal knowledge-flow patterns associated with well-understood management interventions (e.g., training, mentoring, communities of practice, experience, technology) can be matched with diagnosed problems to generate practical plans for enhancing knowledge flows.

The knowledge of how to diagnose and enhance knowledge flows exists today. It is ready to emerge from the lab and to inform the leader and manager in a practical way. However, the practicing leader and manager are unlikely to piece together the numerous elements from academic journals and laboratory research. Knowledge-flow theory is emerging still and only beginning to cohere and coalesce into actionable principles. This book condenses, consolidates, and collimates such actionable principles into articulated form that can enable leaders and managers to depart from the prevalent current practices of trial and error and imitation. Trial and error represents a well-known approach to organizational knowing and learning: It is known well for being very slow and inefficient as well as error-prone. Imitation also represents a well-known approach to organizational knowing and learning: It is known well for copying the many mistakes of others as well as their occasional successes. In contrast, our principled approach to organizational knowing and learning can enable leaders and managers to directly identify and solve problems with knowledge flows. Through such principled intervention, an organization can set the standard to be envied and imitated by its competitors.

This book builds upon theory but targets practice; it takes knowledge known only by a few researchers and shares it with many leaders and managers. It translates what is arcane and controversial today into managerial guidance that is sophisticated yet practical. It complements the many extant management books on strategy, technology, knowledge, and systems while addressing a well-recognized and significant void. This book provides 30 principles on which to base the most important decisions and actions in an organization: harnessing knowledge dynamics. Such principled approach defines a unique place for and contribution of the book. This book also provides 30 leadership mandates to make actionable the principles and applications presented in this volume. Such integration of principles and applications defines another unique place for and contribution of the book.

The overall objective is to inform the practicing leader and manager about the importance of knowledge flows and to provide practical but principled guidance for diagnosing and enhancing such flows. The mission is to condense emerging knowledge-flow theory and to distill it into actionable form of immediate relevance and use by enterprise leaders and managers. The principal audience is the enterprise leader and manager (e.g., in business, government, non-profit) with concerns about organizational knowledge. The book provides a set of actionable principles to understand the phenomenon of knowledge flows, and it includes many concrete examples to help ground such principles in the realities of practice. The book also includes several practical illustrations of key principles and techniques. A variety of organizations from the business, government, and non-profit sectors are selected for examination of their knowledge flows. The application cases in Part II offer detailed yet generalizable examples of how principles apply to operating organizations in practice. Such cases provide opportunities to induce new principles as well. Such induction leads to the 30 leadership mandates noted previously.

The academic is also likely to take interest in the book for use in teaching (e.g., on knowledge management, information systems, strategy, organization) and for research. The concise and articulated set of 30 principles for knowledge dynamics appears to be unmatched today in the scholarly literature. Each chapter also includes exercises to stimulate critical thought, learning, and discussion. These exercises are ready for classroom use and allow ample room for instructors to tailor the associated discussions. The references cited in this book point to a rich and integrated literature that remains fragmented largely among several different scholarly fields at present. Such references point to a substantial, growing intellectual basis for understanding knowledge flows and for harnessing the power of dynamic knowledge.

The book also includes a relatively large glossary of key terms. Each term is defined and includes a pointer to the chapter in which it is discussed. Although universal agreement on the definitions contained in this glossary would not be expected at this time, by including such glossary, we make explicit the meaning and usage of key terms used in the book. This helps to promote a common lexicon in the field of knowledge dynamics, and it enables one to understand, explicitly, what the various terms in this book are intended to mean. This provides a stark contrast with most books today.

The book further includes an appendix that lists the code of a small, simple, illustrative expert system discussed in the knowledge technology chapter. By including the complete code, the book enables an instructor to leverage the expert system discussion and gives students an assignment to develop a small system of their own. Students can learn much from developing expert systems, particularly when assigned to "knowledge engineer themselves"; that is, when the assignment is for students to make knowledge that they possess explicit. This helps students to better understand their own tacit knowledge, and it reinforces numerous important principles about knowledge from the book.

To harness knowledge, one must understand how it flows through the organization; that is, one must understand the dynamics of knowledge flows. The key to such understanding is knowledge: knowledge about knowledge dynamics. Such knowledge represents the focus of this book. Through its principles, the leader and manager can learn to harness knowledge dynamics.

M.E.N.
Royal Oaks, CA

Acknowledgment

As with any undertaking on the scale of a book such as this, the author serves largely as spokesperson for many others who have contributed and helped to refine good ideas. This is certainly the case here. This also explains in part why the words *we* and *our* are used instead of *I* and *my*. The book contains myriad literary citations to acknowledge the sources of good ideas upon which it builds. This represents the standard for acknowledgment in academics. Each of the cited authors should feel proud to know his or her work contributes to an endeavor as important as harnessing knowledge dynamics. Of course, there are others as well. You know whom you are, and I thank all of you, again, warmly. Last and hence first, there could be no book like this without the grace of God, to Whom I am thankful most of all.

M.E.N.
Royal Oaks, CA

Knowledge-Flow Principles and Application Cases

For ready reference and as a précis of subsequent chapters, we summarize here 30 knowledge-flow principles addressed in detail through Section I of the book. Each principle is accompanied by a corresponding implication (**emboldened** for emphasis) for managerial learning and intervention.

1. Knowledge is distinct from information in enabling competitive advantage (see Ch. I). **Shuttling *information* around via computers, networks, reports, and communications does not address the flow of *knowledge*, at least not directly or on the same time scale.**

2. Knowledge is distributed unevenly, hence, must flow for organizational performance (see Ch. I). **Knowledge clumps need to be identified, and knowledge flows need to be enabled through the organization.**

3. Tacit knowledge supports greater appropriability for competitive advantage than explicit knowledge does (see Ch. I). **Knowledge managers may benefit from an emphasis on tacit knowledge flows.**

4. Knowledge flows must balance exploration through learning with exploitation through doing (see Ch. I). **Understanding the kinds of knowledge that are important in an organization's particular environment is essential for promoting the most important knowledge flows.**

5. Enhancing knowledge flows requires simultaneous attention to personnel, work processes, organizations, and technologies (see Ch. I). **The four organizational elements of personnel, work processes, structure, and technology operate as a cohesive system and should be addressed as an integrated design problem.**

6. Knowledge enables action directly, whereas information provides meaning and context for such action (see Ch. II). **Understanding whether flows of data, information, or knowledge are required in a particular situation depends upon what needs to be accomplished (e.g., resolving uncertainty, deriving meaning, or enabling action, respectively).**

7. Data, information, and knowledge flows are interrelated dynamically yet distinct *mental* processes (see Ch. II). **People play the critical role in flows of data, information, and knowledge.**

8. Flows of knowledge require supplementary flows of information, data, and signals (see Ch. II). **Every flow (data, information, and knowledge) from signal interpretation through knowledge creation requires some kind of knowledge.**

9. *Explicitness* represents a very discriminatory dimension for evaluating the uniqueness of knowledge (see Ch. II). **Moving knowledge through tacit vs. explicit flows represents a management decision in many cases, a decision which has implications in terms of power.**

10. Information technology supports principally flows of explicit knowledge (see Ch. II). **The nature of knowledge represents a critical factor for determining where IT can be expected to enhance knowledge flows.**

11. Knowledge exhibits some properties of inertia such as *tendency to remain at rest* (see Ch. III). **Knowledge-flow processes represent direct focuses of leadership and managerial action.**

12. Experiential processes contribute principally toward workflows (doing), whereas educational processes contribute principally toward knowledge flows (learning; see Ch. III). **Changes to workflows demand changes to knowledge flows, and vice versa.**

13. Knowledge flows always lie on the critical paths of workflows, hence, organizational performance (see Ch. III). **Knowledge flows should be planned and managed like workflows are.**

14. Time-critical workflows must wait for enabling knowledge flows to run their course (see Ch. III). **Most knowledge flows must complete their course before critical and dependent workflows can begin.**

15. *Knowledge* is a multifaceted, dynamic, and multidimensional concept (see Ch. III). **Managerial efficacy through intervention can be increased by learning the principles of dynamic knowledge.**

16. Information technology is helpful and necessary but not sufficient for knowledge management (see Ch. IV). **The manager needs to employ non-technological interventions to enhance knowledge flows.**

17. People — not information technology — are central to tacit knowledge flows (see Ch. IV). **One cannot manage tacit knowledge without managing people.**

18. Information technology plays supportive roles in organizational work routines, whereas people play the performative roles (see Ch. IV). **Most IT plays a supportive role in the organization, whereas people play most of the performative roles.**

19. Expert systems, software agents, and like "intelligent" applications address and apply knowledge directly (see Ch. IV). **"Intelligent" applications can play a performative role in the organization.**

20. Simulation technology can enhance knowledge flows in addition to workflows (see Ch. IV). **Simulation represents a different class of IT, one that facilitates learning as well as doing through virtual practice.**

21. Knowing reflects knowledge in action (see Ch. V). **Knowledge must be put to use through action in order to be useful.**

22. Learning reflects knowledge in motion (see Ch. V). **Learning both uses and increases knowledge.**

23. Knowing and learning beyond the individual offer the greatest potential for knowledge superiority (see Ch. V). **The impact of KM increases in direct proportion to the reach of knowledge flows through an organization.**

24. Knowing and learning are dynamic, mutually reinforcing activities (see Ch. V). **Promoting knowing promotes learning, and vice versa.**

25. Knowing and learning are path-dependent, enabling both competencies and rigidities (see Ch. V). **An organization's knowledge inventory both enables and inhibits what actions it can take.**

26. Knowledge management involves organizational change (see Ch. VI). **The knowledge manager has much to learn from business process re-engineering and like change-management approaches.**

27. Knowledge inventory can be used to assess an organization's readiness to perform its work processes effectively (see Ch. VI). **The manager needs to measure the knowledge inventory for every organization.**

28. When estimating the value of knowledge, it is often better to light a candle than to curse the darkness (see Ch. VI). **Knowledge value analysis provides an approach to measuring the relative value of knowledge associated with various organizational processes.**

29. Culture, trust, and incentives affect organizational learning, hence, performance as much as process, technology, and training do (see Ch. VI). **Every organizational process should improve its performance over time.**

30. Computational modeling is useful for knowing and learning about organizational knowing and learning (see Ch. VI). **Computational models of knowledge flows provide an approach to mitigating the risk inherent in KM programs.**

We also list the nine application cases to which such principles are applied in Section II of the book.

1. In the chapter on business organizations, we look first at an advanced-technology company involved with new-product development (see Ch. VII).

2. The discussion turns then to examine an independent production company involved with a feature film (see Ch. VII).

3. The third case involves a technology-transfer project between a university and a microelectronics company (see Ch. VII).

4. In the chapter on government organizations, we look first at a military organization involved with maritime warfare (see Ch. VIII).

5. The discussion turns then to examine a federal government agency involved with a knowledge management program (see Ch. VIII).

6. The sixth case examines a public service organization involved with large-scale IT integration (see Ch. VIII).

7. In the chapter on non-profit organizations, we look first at a national youth soccer organization (see Ch. IX).

8. The discussion turns then to examine a local tennis club (see Ch. IX).

9. The final case examines a nondenominational community church (see Ch. IX).

We list further the set of 30 leadership mandates induced through practical application in Section II of the book.

1. Realistic expectations, shared vision, and appropriate people participating full-time represent the preconditions for success that are absent or insufficient most often in KM projects (see Ch. VI).

2. Reliance upon external expertise, narrow technical focus, and animosity toward staff and specialists represent the preconditions for failure that are present or sufficient most often in KM projects (see Ch. VI).

3. Knowledge representation, attention to tacit knowledge, and focus on organizational memory represent unique considerations that merit particular attention in KM projects (see Ch. VI).

4. Measurements of how people perceive a KM project (e.g., using measures such as *pessimism, affective commitment,* and *normative commitment)* can indicate KM readiness (see Ch. VI).

5. Knowledge audits can help organizations that do not know what they know (see Ch. VI).

6. Knowledge value analysis privileges tacit knowledge appropriately (see Ch. VI).

7. The greater the use of automation at the beginning of a process, the lower the improvement rate (see Ch. VI).

8. Performance improvement reflected by learning curves involves more than just individual knowing and learning (see Ch. VI).

9. Knowledge can be lost and found (see Ch. VI).

10. Trust cannot be bought (see Ch. VI).

11. Using computational models, organizations can be designed and tested virtually, in a manner similar to the design of airplanes, bridges, and computers (see Ch. VI).

12. Specialist and generalist knowledge represent (imperfect) economic substitutes for one another (see Ch. VI).

13. Knowledge-flow vectors can be used to represent dynamic knowledge requirements (see Ch. VII).

14. It is essential to plan how knowledge technologies will be used by people (see Ch. VII).

15. The learning curve measures knowledge flows through OJT (see Ch. VII).

16. Socialization and acculturation represent viable approaches to enhancing tacit knowledge flows (see Ch. VII).

17. Trans-organizational collectives (e.g., communities) may have greater influence over employee knowledge, culture, and performance than leadership and management do (see Ch. VII).

18. Knowledge flows critical to enabling critical workflows center on tacit knowledge (see Ch. VII).

19. An organizational process without consistent improvement over time suffers from knowledge clumping (see Ch. VII).

20. Members of a team must learn to work with one another before knowing how to work together on a project (see Ch. VII).

21. Ten unique knowledge-flow processes are required for military task force efficacy (see Ch. VIII).

22. OJT involves knowledge flowing at two different speeds: knowledge application through doing is fast; knowledge creation through learning is slow (see Ch. VIII).

23. Given the time-critical nature of warfare, most tacit knowledge must already be in place when the officer first reports for duty (see Ch. VIII).

24. Systematic storytelling can increase the reach of this time-honored and effective approach to sharing tacit knowledge (see Ch. VIII).

25. Socialization, teamwork, and acculturation must interconnect to enable healthy knowledge-flow circulation (see Ch. VIII).

26. Leading by example and evangelism represent viable approaches to enhancing acculturation knowledge flows (see Ch. IX).

27. Once one understands a relatively small set of key knowledge-flow processes, he or she can analyze any knowledge flows — healthy or pathologic — in any organization (see Ch. IX).

28. The key to self-organization is having people enjoy what they do together (see Ch. IX).

29. The ability of different people to work together on teams is just as important as the individual skills and experiences they bring individually (see Ch. IX).

30. Leaders who are concerned about acculturation knowledge flows must address participants' beliefs. (see Ch. IX).

SECTION I:
INTELLECTUAL BASIS

True knowledge exists in knowing that you know nothing.

Socrates

Cogito ergo sum.

Descartes

We have much to say about this, but it is hard to explain because you are slow to learn.

Heb. 5:11

The intellectual basis of this book centers on emerging knowledge-flow theory. This involves the growing body of research addressing questions regarding how knowledge "moves" through an organization. Knowledge is required to perform knowledge and information work effectively, and such work drives organizational performance directly. Hence, knowledge drives organizational performance through the work it enables. To the extent that organizational knowledge does not exist in the form needed for application or at the place and time required to enable work performance, then it must flow from how it exists and where it is located to how and where it is needed. This is the concept *knowledge flows*. As explained in this book, the concept *knowledge flows* represents more than just a metaphor: It explains the phenomenon of how knowledge moves through an organization.

In the context of organizational performance, knowledge flows lie on the critical paths of the workflows they enable. Where knowledge-flow problems, such as clotting, poor circulation, or bleeding (metaphorically), may exist, it is important to diagnose such problems and to understand flow principles well enough to identify and implement the appropriate management interventions. Knowledge-flow theory provides the intellectual basis for diagnosis and intervention of problems with knowledge flows. Harnessing knowledge dynamics requires understanding flow principles well enough to identify and correct pathologies. Further, it requires anticipating where future flow problems are likely to occur, and it depends on designing work processes, organizations, technologies, and personnel systems to address such problems before they manifest.

This first part of the book is organized into five chapters. Chapter I — Knowledge Power — focuses on how the power of dynamic knowledge can be harnessed. Chapter II — Knowledge Uniqueness — addresses how knowledge flows differ from flows of information and data, and it indicates where such differences are important. Chapter III — Knowledge Flow — centers on the phenomenology of dynamic knowledge flows. Chapter IV — Knowledge Technology — surveys several classes of technologies, and it indicates which kinds of knowledge flows are enabled and supported relatively better and worse by such technologies. Chapter V — Knowing and Learning — discusses the concepts *knowing*, which involves knowledge in action, and *learning*, which involves knowledge in motion. Together, these five chapters provide the intellectual basis needed for practical application in Part II of the book.

Chapter I

Knowledge Power

This chapter focuses on how the power of dynamic knowledge can be harnessed. We look first at how knowledge enables competitive advantage and then discuss the nature of knowledge flows. The chapter concludes with five knowledge power principles and includes exercises to stimulate critical thought, learning, and discussion.

Competitive Advantage

Organizational strategists have long discussed competitive advantage, generally, in economic terms such as earning superior rents, gaining larger market share, raising barriers to market entry, locking out competitors, and locking in customers. Of the numerous "theories of the firm," the resource-based view is somewhat unique (Barney, 1986). This view articulates that competitive advantage stems from the specific mix of resources an organization is able to appropriate (assert ownership over) in addition to how such resources are used. The latter part of this point is key. If an organization bases its competitive advantage on some resources that can be obtained readily through the market, then there is little to prevent competitors from obtaining the same resources (Dierickx & Cool, 1989). Hence, any competitive advantage effected by the lead firm is destined to be ephemeral at best.

Competitive advantage based on information technology (IT), for the most part, falls into this category. For a period of time in the 1970s, for instance, a few banks offering automated teller machines (ATMs) to customers enjoyed some competitive advantages over those without this technology. But today nearly every bank offers ATMs. Instead of conferring some competitive advantage, ATM technology now represents just another cost of doing business in banking. Computerized reservation systems (CRSs), as another instance, similarly conferred some competitive advantage to the pioneering airlines behind their development and initial deployment in the 1980s. But today nearly every airline uses CRSs. Instead of conferring some competitive advantage, CRS technology now represents just another cost of doing business in air travel. Leading-edge financial investment firms, as a third instance, gained some competitive advantage in the 1990s through computer trading systems for securities such as stocks, bonds, and futures. But today nearly every financial investment firm trades securities as such. Instead of conferring some competitive advantage, this information technology now represents just another cost of doing business in securities financial investment. The list of similar instances goes on.

Indeed, this phenomenon is neither new nor unique to IT resources. The same applies also to other primary resources such as the traditional economic inputs of land, labor, and capital. For instance, in terms of land, for centuries the vineyards of France enjoyed considerable competitive advantage over wine producers in other regions. But today world-class, award-winning wines are produced in California, South America, Australia, and other regions. Fine wines are still produced in France, of course, but the land alone is no longer sufficient for competitive advantage over vintners in other fertile regions of the world.

As another instance, in terms of labor, for decades the relatively low cost and high quality of Japanese workers conferred considerable competitive advantage across numerous durable-goods and consumer-electronics industries (e.g., machinery, automobiles, televisions, radios). Then labor-based advantages shifted to South Korea, then to Malaysia, Mexico, and other nations. Today, China appears to be capitalizing best on the basis of labor. Japanese firms still remain competitive in markets for such durable goods, electronics, and other products, but the labor force alone is no longer sufficient for competitive advantage over manufacturers in other industrializing nations.

Such shifting of labor-based advantage is clearly not limited to manufacturing industries. Today, a huge number of IT and service jobs are moving from

Europe and North America to India, Singapore, and like countries with relatively well-educated, low-cost workforces possessing technical skills. However, as educational levels and technical skills continue to rise in other countries, India, Singapore, and like nations enjoying labor-based competitive advantage today are likely to find such advantage cannot be sustained through the onset of new competitors.

As a third instance, in terms of capital, for centuries the days of gold coins and later even paper money restricted financial flows. Regional concentrations formed where large banks, industries, and markets coalesced. But today capital flows internationally at the speed of electrons. Global commerce no longer requires regional interactions between business people. Regional capital concentrations in places such as New York, London, and Tokyo still persist, of course, but the capital concentrated there is no longer sufficient for competitive advantage over other capitalists distributed worldwide. Only if an organization is able to combine, integrate, and apply its resources (e.g., land, labor, capital, IT) in an effective manner that is *not readily imitable by competitors* can such organization enjoy competitive advantage sustainable over time.

In a knowledge-based theory of the firm, this idea is extended to view organizational knowledge as a resource with at least the same level of power and importance as the traditional economic inputs (Grant, 1996; Spender, 1996). An organization with superior knowledge can achieve competitive advantage in markets that appreciate the application of such knowledge. Semiconductors, genetic engineering, pharmaceuticals, software, military warfare, and like knowledge-intensive competitive arenas provide both time-proven and current examples. Consider semiconductors (e.g., computer chips), which are made principally of sand and common metals. These ubiquitous and powerful electronic devices are designed within common office buildings, using commercially available tools, and fabricated within factories in many industrialized nations. Hence, land is not the key competitive resource in the semiconductor industry.

Likewise, people with training and experience in semiconductor design and fabrication are available throughout the world. Hence, neither is labor the key competitive resource in this industry. Similarly, even though semiconductor fabrication plants must be custom-designed, require over a billion dollars to build, and become obsolete within a few years, a great many nations and large corporations can afford to construct such expensive plants. Hence, capital too fails to qualify as the key competitive resource here. Yet one semiconductor firm is hugely successful in financial terms such as earnings and market share. This firm *knows* how to design, fabricate, and market semiconductors better than its competitors do. Hence, knowledge is the key competitive resource in the semiconductor industry. This knowledge-based competitive advantage has been sustained for several decades now. Similar examples concerning computer operating systems software, networking equipment, and like knowledge-based products serve to reinforce this point.

Two competitors can possess exactly the same kinds of land, labor, capital, and IT but differ in terms of how such resources are combined in the organization, integrated through work processes, and applied to develop products and services. The one with better knowledge can win consistently and through time. Consider military combat (e.g., naval warfare), the history of which is replete with examples of "inferior" forces (in terms of land, labor, capital, and technology) winning battles and even wars. For instance, recall the colorful era of sailing ships with fixed rows of cannons along their sides. The outcomes of naval battles in this era were predictable generally on the basis of the number of ships in a fleet and the number and size of cannons on board ships. The countries whose land, labor, capital, and technology could produce fleets in greater numbers than those of adversaries fared well consistently in battles at sea.

However, such battles were commonly fought through broadside cannon exchanges between ships from opposing fleets sailing past one another in long, straight lines. "Crossing the T" (sailing perpendicular to the line of ships from an opposing fleet) represented a *tactic* (a set of actions based upon knowledge) that conferred competitive advantage even to a smaller fleet of lesser-equipped ships. Because ships of the day had difficulty shooting forward, the "crossing" fleet faced comparatively little cannon fire. Because cannons were relatively inaccurate in those days, the "crossing" fleet also had a long line of opposing ships to target lengthwise, whereas the fleet shooting broadside had comparatively small targets as ships pitched, rolled, and sailed on the high seas. Here tactical knowledge conferred competitive advantage even to fleets lacking material advantage based upon traditional resources of land, labor, capital, and technology. In our current era of network-centric warfare (Alberts, Garstka, & Stein, 1999), knowledge remains a key competitive resource in military combat.

Nonetheless, trying to sustain competitive advantage through knowledge as a resource can suffer the same limitations as noted previously in terms of sufficiency. Where a competitor can obtain the same kind of knowledge and apply it just as well, then any competitive advantage is unlikely to be sustainable. Information — and knowledge made explicit — falls generally into this category. When an organization attempts to take advantage of such information or explicit knowledge, it is required to guard it vigilantly or risk losing any advantage it enables. This is the fundamental motivation for keeping secrets (e.g., military, trade, stock picking) and underlies laws for patent and copyright protection in many countries, as well as espionage and organized intelligence collection. Thus, not all knowledge offers equal potential in terms of competitive advantage. Speaking generally, the more explicit that knowledge becomes, the lower its competitive potential becomes (Saviotti, 1998).

Alternatively, tacit knowledge, particularly knowledge that is specific to a particular organization, market, or domain, is not as susceptible to loss. Gained principally through experience and accumulated over time, organizational capabilities based upon tacit knowledge are difficult to imitate. Hence, knowledge-based competitive advantage can obtain and be sustained. Speaking generally, tacit knowledge offers greater promise in terms of competitive advantage than explicit knowledge does. Such inimitability represents a proverbial double-edged sword, however. Even in situations of planned technology transfer between different units of a single firm, for instance, in which management *encourages* knowledge to flow, such transfers are consistently problematic (Szulanski, 1996). The tacit knowledge is "sticky" (von Hippel, 1994), clumps in the transferring unit, and does not flow freely. Further, even where substantial knowledge has been made explicit (e.g., through drawings, procedures, lessons learned), in many cases, it is not sufficient to write down the work steps and to expect people in different offices, plants, companies, or regions to perform at comparable levels.

For instance, despite overt help and cooperation from Toyota, advantages stemming from producing low cost, high quality automobiles via the Toyota Production System have been elusive for numerous other companies attempting to replicate Toyota's success. As another instance, the U.S. government has encountered similar experiences. Many large contracts to produce weapon systems have required defense firms to provide detailed engineering drawings, manufacturing assembly plans, and production tools to enable competing firms to build the same weapon systems. The rationale was to introduce a modicum of competition in the defense procurement process. However, "second sources," as they are called, are rarely able to compete on a head-to-head basis. Even after being forced to share abundant explicit knowledge, the lead firm retains its knowledge-based competitive advantage. Tacit knowledge, which resists articulation and transfer, accounts in great part for this phenomenon.

Organizations that develop tacit knowledge — at the individual level as well as across groups, teams, and organizations — enjoy much greater power of appropriation and lower risk of imitation than organizations relying upon traditional resources do. The problem is that tacit knowledge requires considerable time (e.g., years, decades) to develop and accumulate into an "inventory" sufficient to enable competitive advantage. Further, an organization's level of knowledge enhances its ability to learn new knowledge. The further behind one organization gets with respect to its competitors in terms of knowledge, the more difficult it becomes to catch up. Notice this represents a dynamic phenomenon. Not only is the *inventory* (knowledge level) important to enable competitive advantage, but also the *learning rate* (knowledge flow) is critical to sustaining any such advantage they may obtain. The more you know, the faster you learn. This maxim applies to organizations as well as to individuals (Cohen & Levinthal, 1990).

Knowledge Flows

Like mineral deposits that are rich in some geographical regions and sparse in others, knowledge is not distributed evenly throughout the world. Different organizations possess different kinds and levels of knowledge. We noted how differential knowledge between organizations can establish a basis for competitive advantage. However, we noted also how tacit knowledge is difficult to imitate, even when corresponding knowledge flows are encouraged by management within a single organization. This sticky nature of tacit knowledge is thus a mixed blessing. On one hand, it supports competitive advantage; on the other, it restricts knowledge flows within one's own organization.

To emphasize this important point, consider an organization that develops a knowledge-based competitive advantage through learning and application of an exceptional team of people in one particular plant, regional office, or product line. This organization would naturally seek to exploit such advantage and to capitalize on its knowledge differential over competitors. Keeping this exceptional team of people together and preventing defections to rival organizations represent two objectives management is likely to pursue to prevent knowledge from flowing out of its prize unit. Capabilities based on the tacit knowledge enabling this organization's competitive advantage will be difficult for competitors to imitate. This contributes toward sustainability of its knowledge-based advantage. But at the same time, this organization seeks to leverage its competitive advantage by transferring key knowledge from its prize unit to other plants, regional offices, and product lines. The same attributes of tacit knowledge that make it difficult for competitors to imitate knowledge-based capabilities make it difficult also for other parts of the same organization to imitate. Such organization seeks methods and technologies to promote knowledge flows internally yet prohibit simultaneously external knowledge flows. This represents a challenging problem of harnessing knowledge dynamics that we address later in the book.

A case study of one successful automobile company in Europe (Loch et al., 2001) illustrates in part this difficulty of promoting internal knowledge flows. The company developed and implemented an effective means of improving research and development (R&D) decision making through the use of mathematical programming techniques. Despite demonstrating performance benefits of such techniques within the adopting unit, however, the company had little success in terms of diffusing the approach through other units within the firm. The manager responsible for the original advance had engaged external academic consultants contractually. Although this manager understood the benefits and overall approach of mathematical programming, he did not possess the detailed expertise to implement it in his unit of the company or in other units. Hence, the company failed to appropriate the mathematical programming knowledge. Rather, it remained dependent upon external consultants. When such consultants were not retained by the company to extend the decision-making techniques into other units, the corresponding knowledge and expertise left the company along with the consultants. Then, knowledge flows associated with the mathematical programming techniques ceased.

It is important to note that the objective of promoting knowledge flows internally within organizations is not restricted to select knowledge that enables competitive advantage. All knowledge required for an organization to perform its work processes and to accomplish its mission needs to flow within such organization. Knowledge lies always on the critical path of work; that is, people must know how to accomplish a job before they can accomplish it. Hence, even routine knowledge necessary to perform ordinary work processes within an organization must flow across numerous dimensions.

For instance, we noted how knowledge flows between different organizational units are desirable where such knowledge enables competitive advantage. Inter-unit knowledge flows are important also for organizations that seek to maintain consistent work processes, technological environments, and product quality levels across units. Whether the products of interest are semiconductors, pharmaceuticals, software applications, or government services, knowledge is required to perform the work processes, and such knowledge must flow between units to ensure consistent organization-wide performance. The aforementioned case of the automobile company illustrates well how failure of interunit knowledge flows can prevent some units within a single firm from enjoying benefits demonstrated in other units.

As another instance, knowledge flows across time are also necessary in addition to flows across different organizations and geographical regions. Consider where one shift replaces another in a factory, processing plant, or military watch. Management is interested in using the knowledge gained during a shift by one group to enhance the performance of the other group. Take a network problem, for example, in a global telecommunications firm. Such firms operate 24 hours a day, yet individual employees work generally only 8 hours at a time. When an individual customer service agent leaves at the end of a shift, it is important for him or her to convey what he or she knows about the network problem to the person taking over. Otherwise, the agent beginning a new shift may not adequately understand the network status to effectively relate with customers or to steer them toward work-around solutions to network problems. Similar examples in other settings (e.g., plant equipment problems in a petroleum-processing operation, health problems of a patient in a hospital intensive-care unit, intentions of commercial aircraft in flight as air traffic controllers change shifts) abound as well. Notice, such knowledge flows — across shift changes — represent dynamics occurring over relatively short periods of time (e.g., hours).

Alternatively, other flows require knowledge to move over extended periods of time. Consider how most organizations expect junior members to develop knowledge and expertise over time. Some aspects of knowledge and expertise can be acquired directly (e.g., through education and training programs), whereas others accumulate indirectly through experience (e.g., working on a particular kind of problem). Some kinds of knowledge are quite general and broadly transferable (e.g., engineering principles and methods), whereas others are specific to a particular company, department, and work assignment, hence, more restricted in terms of opportunities for application and transfer. In some cases, people can begin at a state of ignorance and incompetence yet develop knowledge and expertise through a process of repeated trial and error (e.g., on-the-job training [OJT]), whereas other work contexts require competent performance on the first attempt (e.g., surgery). In other situations, knowledge and expertise apply to individuals (e.g., the previous examples), whereas group, team, and department interaction requires collections of people to learn how to work together (e.g., basketball teams, software development groups, police SWAT teams).

In every case, considerable time is required for learning (knowledge to flow). The amount of time *allocated* for learning represents a management decision. In the research university, for example, assistant professors are given six years to establish a positive national reputation, after which they face an up-or-out staffing decision. However, the kinds of work they perform (e.g., research, instruction) remain the same for the most part throughout this period (and in many cases, for years or even decades beyond). Most research universities have decided that six years of the same work after earning a PhD is enough time to become an associate professor. In a corporate employee-internship program, as a different example, new college hires may be rotated through different departments and jobs every six months. Unlike the research university, the kinds of work new hires perform change with each rotation. Such organizations have decided that six months of the same work after earning a college degree is enough time for rotation to another job. The U.S. Navy, as a third example, rotates its personnel roughly every three years. Here, *all of its people* (e.g., junior and senior, enlisted and officers, sailors and staff) change jobs at three-year intervals. This military organization has decided that three years of the same work after assignment to a new command is enough time for rotation to another job.

Knowledge flows between people denote a related instance. Of course, this transcends the other instances mentioned because, ultimately, nearly all knowledge flows in an organizational context take place between people. In the case of inter-unit transfers, people in the different organizations must learn from one another (e.g., about decision-making techniques). In the case of flows between shifts, people on the different shifts must learn from one another (e.g., about equipment problems). In the case of new employees, people must learn from some combination of the work itself (e.g., trial and error, OJT) and other people (e.g., supervisors, mentors, instructors, peers). Hence, knowledge flows across different organizational units, geographical regions, and points in time involve people and are necessary *just to accomplish the work at hand* (e.g., ordinary work processes), even where such knowledge may not necessarily lead to competitive advantage. This elucidates a critical point in terms of diagnosing knowledge-flow problems. Viewed in reverse, where knowledge fails to flow well, even to enable ordinary workflows, the organization may experience competitive *disadvantage*, as it fails to perform its routine work effectively.

Consider the Business Process Re-engineering (BPR) movement in the 1990s. Conceived originally as an approach for radical change to effect dramatic performance improvements in organizations (see Davenport, 1993; Hammer & Champy, 1993), BPR provided a broad-based impetus and set of techniques to enable organizations to perform better with fewer resources. However, the focus of this approach shifted over time from one of superior performance to one of fewer resources. BPR was employed extensively then as a cost-cutting mechanism. Profits rose at many companies, and competitors followed suit to avoid being left behind. However, in the U.S. alone, many tens of thousands of jobs were eliminated through the process. Many such jobs belonged to knowledge workers and middle managers. After some period of time, it became apparent to several firms that critical organizational knowledge had left the company with the people who were "downsized." Such people had to be rehired—oftentimes as expensive consultants or for far more than their previous salaries. The short-term focus on cost reduction and job elimination took place at the expense of longer term performance and knowledge accumulation.

A similar situation is occurring at the time of this writing for a different reason. People from the Baby Boomers generation are nearing retirement age. Organizations lack the resources and techniques to ensure their knowledge flows effectively to Generations X, Y, and other groups that are performing junior- and mid-level jobs in such organizations. Indeed, the U.S. government estimates that roughly half of its workforce will be eligible for retirement before the end of this decade (Liebowitz, 2004a). This massive governmental organization has little clue as to how the corresponding knowledge can be preserved.

Even within a particular organization, knowledge can be observed to clump noticeably in certain people, groups, locations, and points in time. The phenomenon of knowledge distributing itself unevenly across different people has been studied extensively for years. Researchers have examined the nature of expert performance and tried to draw generalizable comparisons with the performance of novices, for instance. Many studies of leadership fall into this category. A whole industry of expert systems was developed around the idea of capturing expert level capabilities and formalizing them in computers. Indeed, knowledgeable people have been painting caves, chiseling stones, and writing books for millennia in attempts to share their expertise, and society has developed many other techniques for experts to share knowledge (e.g., stories, mentoring, apprenticeships, university courses).

Since expert knowledge is generally tacit, it is sticky (von Hippel, 1994), and the corresponding clumps remain difficult to distribute. For instance, it is recognized widely that roughly 10 years' sustained and dedicated effort is required to become an expert in a particular field with accumulation of some 10,000 chunks of corresponding knowledge (see Turban & Aronson, 1998). Trying to share such expertise encounters the well-understood problem associated with "the fish." Recall the parable of giving someone a fish vs. teaching him or her how to fish. In the former case, one feeds the person for a day, but he or she becomes hungry again the following day. In the latter case, the person learns to feed himself or herself for a lifetime, but such learning takes time. Ask an expert to solve a problem, and he or she solves the problem. This takes care of the situation until its next occurrence. But ask the expert to teach an apprentice how to solve the problem. The problem may go unsolved for some time, yet eventually a capable apprentice can learn how to solve the problem for himself or herself. Teaching how to solve problems is more time consuming than problem solving is. For knowledge to flow at the individual level, the expert (or simply more knowledgeable person) must be willing and able to share; the novice must be willing and able to learn; and the organization must be willing and able to help them do so. Very few organizations accomplish such individual learning well at present. As a general rule, individual knowledge does not flow well through most organizations.

Even more difficult is enabling knowledge flows at other levels. Because groups, teams, departments, firms, and even larger aggregations of people are comprised of individuals, all of the same individual-level problems previously noted are present within such organizations. In addition, knowledge is noted to clump in certain organizations as well as specific individuals. Accounts abound of groups, teams, offices, units, ships, crews, and the like that are practically identical except for the individuals comprising them, yet one organization outperforms the others, oftentimes dramatically. Identifying the sources of performance differences between apparently equivalent organizations is diffi-cult, even though it often reduces to some kind of tacit knowledge that is shared within a particular group. Conceiving mechanisms for such shared knowledge to flow between two groups is very challenging. Because the shared knowledge is tacit, attempting to write it down and disseminate it via books, standard operating procedures, lessons learned, Web portals, workflow systems, and other explicit knowledge approaches offers limited potential for efficacy. This same point pertains to enterprises that are separated across time and space, as well as those separated by organizational boundaries. Think of a new group taking over a work task from a group that has been performing it effectively for some time, or an organization in one geographical region that is able somehow to perform more effectively than its equivalent counterpart in another region. Knowledge flows are essential for power through competitive advantage. But enabling such flows remains a huge challenge for most organizations. This is the case in particular for large and bureaucratic enterprises that rely upon information technologies. We address such challenges in subsequent chapters.

Knowledge Power Principles

Five principles developed in this chapter help shed light on developing knowledge power: (1) knowledge is distinct from information in enabling competitive advantage; (2) knowledge is distributed unevenly, hence, must flow for organizational performance; (3) tacit knowledge supports greater appropriability for competitive advantage than explicit knowledge does; (4) knowledge flows must balance exploration through learning with exploitation through doing; and (5) enhancing knowledge flows requires simultaneous attention to personnel, work processes, organizations, and technologies.

Principle 1. Distinguishing knowledge from information is important. One effective operationalization is that knowledge enables direct action (e.g., correct decisions, appropriate behaviors, useful work), whereas information provides meaning and context for such action (e.g., decision criteria, behavior norms, work specifications). As a Gedanken experiment, consider two people tasked to perform a knowledge-intensive activity. These could be captains on the bridge of a ship, surgeons at the operating table, managers at the negotiating table, professors in a classroom, attorneys in a courtroom, or any similar situations requiring knowledge. Provide these two people with exactly the same information (e.g., books to read, charts and reports to reference, instruments to monitor, direct views and sounds, advisors to consult, etc.). Say one person has 20 years experience, whereas the other has much less experience (or possibly none). Most informed leaders, managers, and scholars would expect differential performance from these two people. Such differential performance can be attributed generally to differences in knowledge. **Hence, shuttling** *information* **around via computers, networks, reports, and communications does not address the flow of** *knowledge*, **at least not directly or on the same time scale**.

Principle 2. Knowledge clumps in particular people, organizations, regions, and times of application. Knowledge power through competitive advantage requires knowledge to flow, but tacit knowledge is sticky, difficult to imitate, and slow to move. This same property, which enables the sustainability of knowledge-based competitive advantage, inhibits simultaneously sharing within the organization. **Hence, knowledge clumps need to be identified, and knowledge flows need to be enabled through the organization**.

Principle 3. The second principle gives rise to a third principle, which is focused on differentiating between kinds of knowledge. In particular, explicit knowledge that can be articulated is distinct in many ways from the kind of tacit knowledge that accumulates, often slowly, through experience. Neither is individual expertise quite the same as knowledge shared across members of a group, team, or other organization. Knowledge can also be quite situated, ephemeral, and local, meaning a person on the "front lines" cannot always communicate the richness of what he or she knows to someone at headquarters. Yet people at headquarters tend to demand abundant information flows to support decision making that is better made on location. Of course, the person on the scene with detailed and local knowledge lacks the high-level integrative understanding of managers at headquarters, and the need for functional specialists to share specific knowledge for complex problem solving is well known. Central to the point of knowledge power is that tacit knowledge supports greater appropriability than explicit knowledge does. **Hence, knowledge managers may benefit from an emphasis on tacit knowledge flows**.

Principle 4. Not all knowledge, not even tacit knowledge, is of equal value. Furthermore, not all knowledge needs to be shared to effect performance. Indeed, there is a classic tension between exploration and exploitation. Because resources such as time, energy, and attention are limited, investing in exploration of new knowledge and opportunities necessarily limits the resources available to exploit the knowledge and opportunities that exist, and vice versa. Moreover, to the extent that an organization focuses solely on exploitation, for instance, it can quickly develop competency traps (Levitt & March, 1988) and suffer from debilitations associated with single-loop learning (Argyris & Schon, 1978); that is, an organization can learn to do the wrong thing very well and not realize that its competency is no longer suited to the environment. In contrast, to the extent that an organization focuses solely on exploration, it can quickly see its demise, as competitors capitalize upon current opportunities and take advantage of the organization's time away from task; that is, the organization can prepare itself well for a future environment but fail to survive until such future arrives. Similar tensions arise between learning and doing, sharing and hoarding knowledge, acquiring general vs. specialized expertise, and similar knowledge-oriented tradeoffs. **Hence, understanding the kinds of knowledge that are important in an organization's particular environment is essential for promoting the most important knowledge flows.**

Principle 5. It is well known that organizational personnel, work processes, structures, and technologies are tightly interconnected and interact closely (Leavitt, 1965). When seeking to redesign and change organizations to identify knowledge clumps and to enhance knowledge flows, it is important to focus simultaneously upon all of these interconnected and interacting elements. Most people can quickly identify a technological "innovation" that failed to produce favorable results when implemented in an organization. Bringing in people or teams with different backgrounds in terms of education, training, skills, and experience represents a similar instance (e.g., conjuring up memories of failed implementation), as does changing work processes or organizational reporting relationships and responsibilities without addressing personnel and technologies. **Hence, the four organizational elements of personnel, work processes, structure, and technology operate as a cohesive system and should be addressed as an integrated design problem.**

Exercises

1. Describe a situation of knowledge enabling competitive advantage in an organization with which you are familiar. Explain how knowledge, and not other resources, is key.

2. Describe how additional knowledge could — but has not — enable improved competitive advantage in the organization of Exercise 1. What would have to be done to effect such improved competitive advantage?

3. Describe a situation of knowledge clumping in an organization with which you are familiar. What was done to address the clumping in such situation? What else could be done?

4. Conceive of an experiment or other empirical test to assess the relative value of two different chunks of knowledge that you possess. Briefly describe how the value of knowledge could be measured.

Chapter II

Knowledge Uniqueness

This chapter focuses on how flows of knowledge differ from flows of information and data. It also outlines where such differences are important. We look
first at the concept *knowledge hierarchy* and then discuss at a high level the
role of information technology in knowledge management projects. The
discussion then turns to examine knowledge explicitness. The chapter concludes with five knowledge uniqueness principles, including exercises to
stimulate critical thought, learning, and discussion.

Knowledge Hierarchy

Many scholars conceptualize a hierarchy of data, information, and knowledge.
As illustrated in Figure 1, each level of the hierarchy builds upon the one below
it. For instance, data can reduce uncertainty or equivocality, and they are
required to produce information. However, information involves more than just
data: the data must be in context to inform (e.g., so someone can ascribe
meaning to a message). Similarly, information can help people make sense of
their environments, and it is required to produce knowledge. Although,
knowledge involves more than just information: It enables direct action (e.g.,
good decisions, appropriate behaviors, useful work — judgment and norms

Figure 1. Knowledge hierarchy (adapted from Nissen, Kamel, & Sengupta, 2000)

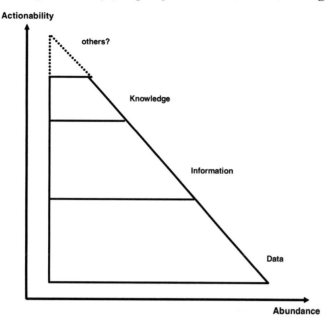

determine what constitutes good, appropriate, and useful). These three concepts are clearly complementary yet are clearly distinct.

Consider this Gedanken experiment. Someone sends you an e-mail message. This person prepares the message meticulously to ensure it is factually correct and delivered immediately. It is sent via Internet routers and arrives in your mailbox within seconds of being sent. The message suffers from no transmission errors and appears on your screen exactly as it was sent. The message is written in Korean. Is this knowledge (e.g., reading the message enables you to take direct action)? Is it information (e.g., you can ascribe meaning to the message content)? Is it even data (e.g., it reduces uncertainty or equivocality)? Unless you can read and understand Korean, the answer is probably "no." In such a case, you would have received visual signals (e.g., symbols on the display screen) that do not even represent data to you. Many otherwise capable intelligence analysts confront this situation daily when searching for clues through communications (e.g., e-mail messages, recorded telephone conversations). Notice here that some knowledge (e.g., of Korean language) would be required to interpret signals into data.

Now say the message is written in a language you can understand (e.g., English). The message is "333/33." Is this knowledge, information, data, or simply signals? Unlike the previous example, in which a lack of language knowledge precludes even the interpretation of signals from conversations into data, here no such language barrier exists. One can say the message provides data; a person can interpret the signal as a compound symbol with three "3s" preceding a "/" and two more "3s," but can we say this data symbol represents information or knowledge? Unless the symbol comes as the specific answer to a factual question (e.g., how can the repeating decimal number 10.$\underline{09}$ be represented by two whole numbers with five digits total, both ending with the digit 3?) or with some comparable context (e.g., mathematical symbols), the answer is probably "no." The symbol constitutes data but not information or knowledge. In other words, the symbol can reduce uncertainty or equivocality if the right question is asked or if appropriate context is communicated. It is unlikely that such symbol alone would enable someone to ascribe meaning to the message (constitute information). Notice here that some knowledge (e.g., of the question being asked or the context associated with the message) would be required for data in the message to inform its recipient (for information to flow). Notice too that such contextual knowledge (e.g., mathematical symbols) differs from the kind of language knowledge (e.g., Korean) from the preceding paragraphs that supports signal interpretation. One should get a sense that different kinds of knowledge (e.g., language, contextual) are required for different kinds of actions (e.g., interpretation, informing) related to the knowledge hierarchy.

Next, say the message includes some context in terms of an English-language clause: "your blood pressure: 333/33." Is this knowledge, information, data, or simply signals? Here we are not constrained by a lack of either language or contextual knowledge. Hence, one should be able to both interpret the signals and ascribe meaning to the content of the message. Indeed, with such context, one can become informed about a blood-pressure measurement; that is, one could say information has flowed. Recall that such ascription of meaning could not be achieved with the same message sent without context. What about knowledge? Absent supplementary physiological knowledge, for instance, it is unlikely that the message would enable direct action (e.g., what, if anything, should be done in response to the blood pressure measurement?). Hence, the message content involves the flow of signals, data, and information but not knowledge. Notice here the message recipient can interpret the signals (i.e., for data) and ascribe meaning (for information) to the message *but cannot take action* (for knowledge) without additional knowledge (e.g., of human physiology).

Finally, say you learn from a physician or health Web site that systolic blood pressure levels — the number listed first (before the /) in blood pressure measurements — above 200 are hazardous, and diastolic levels — the number listed second (after the /) in blood pressure measurements — below 60 are dangerous. At this point, one can understand the health implications of the message: The person is near death! Such understanding enables one to take action such as deciding whether to consult a doctor, take a medication, or change diet and exercise habits. Notice here that a different kind of knowledge (e.g., of human physiology) is required to understand the health implications of the message. Still different knowledge (e.g., of alternate treatment options) is needed to enable action on the basis of the message content. Through the four parts of this e-mail example, it should be clear how knowledge is required for action at every level of the hierarchy and how different kinds of knowledge are associated with different actions at various levels.

Drawing from Nissen (2002a), we notionally operationalize the triangular shape of this hierarchy using two dimensions — *abundance* and *actionability* — to further differentiate between the three constructs *data, information,* and *knowledge*. Briefly, in this view, data lie at the bottom level with information in the middle and knowledge at the top. The broad base of the triangle reflects the abundance of data with exponentially less information available than data and even fewer chunks of knowledge in any particular domain. Thus the width of the triangle at each level reflects decreasing abundance as one progresses from data to knowledge. The height of the triangle at each level reflects actionability (i.e., one's ability to take direct action). Converse to their abundance, data are not particularly powerful for supporting action, and information is more powerful than data. But knowledge supports action directly, hence, its position near the top of the triangle. Interestingly, some models, especially those in the trade press, discuss one or more levels "above" knowledge in the hierarchy (e.g., *wisdom, intelligence, enlightenment,* etc.). This book does not attempt to address wisdom management or engage in similar speculation.

Notice that Figure 1 elucidates a conceptual inadequacy associated with knowledge hierarchy: The hierarchy infers that knowledge — positioned at the top — is somehow "more" or "better" than either information or data. Yet we described previously how knowledge is required for action at every level of the hierarchy (e.g., to interpret signals, ascribe meaning to symbols, understand implications of messages) and how different kinds of knowledge are associated with different actions at various levels of the hierarchy. If knowledge is required to interpret signals into data, then how is it more or better than such data? If knowledge is required to ascribe meaning to symbols, then how is it more or better than the information that results? Hence, it is important to interpret the vertical axis of the hierarchy in a value-free manner: Knowledge is *more actionable* than information or data is, but actionability does not imply a separate judgment such as better.

Further, although knowledge is positioned in the hierarchy at a higher level than data, knowledge without data is frequently incomplete; that is, knowledge often requires data to enable action. In our blood pressure example, an experienced and licensed medical doctor would certainly know the health implications of blood pressure and be able to prescribe several alternate treatments for a diversity of patients and measurements. Without the data (333/33) to reduce uncertainty (e.g., answer the question: What is the patient's blood pressure?), such physiological knowledge could not be put to use directly to prescribe treatment. The point is that knowledge without data is insufficient for action. Knowledge is necessary for action, but it is not necessarily sufficient. Clearly, the interrelationships between knowledge, information, and data are more complex than implied by a simple three-layer diagram such as the one presented in Figure 1. Nonetheless, the knowledge hierarchy provides insight into some unique and complementary characteristics of knowledge, information, and data.

Indeed, many scholars share this simple layered view of the hierarchy, but certainly not all scholars do. For instance, some argue for an inverted hierarchy (Tuomi, 1999), in which hierarchical relationships such as those outlined previously are reversed to reflect data on the "top" and knowledge on the "bottom." The argument is that knowledge is required to establish a semantic structure to represent information, which in turn represents a prerequisite for creating data. With this inverted hierarchy, there appears to be a contradiction with even the basic order of hierarchical levels. Further, in the inverted view, activities performed at different levels of the hierarchy differ from the ones mentioned previously (e.g., "establish semantic structure" and "create data" vs. "interpret signals" and "ascribe meaning"). In other words, the elements of the two hierarchies (data, information, knowledge) appear to be the same, but transitions from one hierarchical level to another (e.g., data to information, information to data) take on different meanings. Plus, if knowledge is required at the base of this inverted hierarchy to represent information and in turn create data, then one must ask, from where does the knowledge derive? When taken together as contrasting views, the two hierarchies present a conundrum.

Figure 2. Knowledge flow directionality (adapted from Nissen, 2002a)

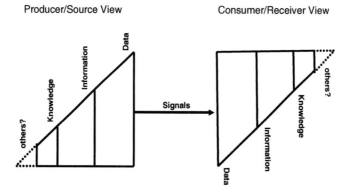

Perhaps this apparent conundrum can be resolved in part by introducing the concept *directionality* in terms of knowledge flow. As depicted in Figure 2, the producer or source of knowledge could indeed view the inverted hierarchy as previously conceptualized — where knowledge is necessary to produce information, which in turn is necessary for data that are conveyed through signals. For instance, say an experienced attorney is confident that his or her client is innocent of some criminal charge. This attorney seeks to convince members of a jury that the verdict "not guilty" is appropriate in the case. The attorney may use his or her experience-based knowledge of how to persuade jurors to outline a set of arguments to make, witnesses to call for testimony, questions to ask, and so forth (make a case for innocence). One could say here the attorney is using knowledge in a manner he or she hopes will influence the meaning ascribed by jurors to various data produced through court proceedings. Then, in turn, by making the arguments, calling the witnesses, and asking the questions, data (e.g., words spoken by the attorney, visual appearances of the witnesses, answers to questions) can reach the jurors via signals (e.g., pressure waves of sound through the air, patterns of light reflecting off people). If jurors ascribe meaning to such data in the manner hoped for by the defense attorney, then they may come to view the defendant as innocent and render a "not guilty" verdict.

Alternatively, the consumer or receiver of knowledge could view the hierarchy from the opposite perspective outlined previously — where data are placed into context to become information, and information enables action through knowledge. Continuing with our courtroom example, say a juror who hears the sound waves and sees the light patterns is able to interpret such signals into data (e.g., words spoken by the attorney, visual appearances of the witnesses, answers to questions). With the courtroom context of such data, a juror would likely be able to ascribe meaning (e.g., the attorney is trying to make a case for innocence) and be informed by the corresponding arguments, testimony, and answers. The juror could in turn come to understand how the relevant matters of fact and law in the case interrelate, which would enable action in terms of rendering a verdict. Of course, whether such verdict coincides with the "not guilty" hope of the attorney becomes a matter of the *juror's* knowledge, not the attorney's. As a consumer or receiver of knowledge, the juror could be viewed according to the former knowledge hierarchy (in which knowledge is positioned on top). This knowledge-consumer or -receiver view is compatible with, and supplementary to, the knowledge-producer or -source view mentioned previously. The key point is that there is directionality to knowledge as it flows from producer or source to consumer or recipient. This concept *directionality* helps explain how both knowledge hierarchies can co-exist and indeed supplement one another, as they correspond to different directions of knowledge flows (e.g., to or from). We revisit knowledge-flow directionality repeatedly in this book.

Information Technology

Many knowledge management projects fail to appreciate the distinction between knowledge and information/data. Project after project in practice implements information technology (IT) applications such as databases, data warehouses, document repositories, search engines, and Web portals when attempting to support knowledge management. Arguably, just looking at the word *data* in the names of many "knowledge management tools," we are not even working at the level of information, much less knowledge. Moreover, although Internet tools applied within and between organizations provide a common, machine-independent medium for the distribution and linkage of multimedia documents, extant intranet and extranet applications focus principally on the management and distribution of information, not knowledge (Nissen et al., 2000).

Consider, for example, a corporate database that is fed by the company's nationwide point-of-sale (POS) system. The POS system records the specific details of every merchandise item purchased by every customer everyday. One may overhear expressions such as, "there's a wealth of knowledge in that POS database." But our previous discussion should stimulate one to question the veridicality of statements along these lines. Specifically, the POS database may contain volumes of data. But the data themselves (e.g., 654321-10987) require something more to enable action. One can argue that metadata (data about the data in a database) allow a person (or machine) to piece together the various data elements and values to make sense of database records. The string of symbols comprising a database record, such as "28 March 2004 Smith Margarie A 654321-10987 2 socks crew white M 6.99," could be ascribed meaning as a customer purchase. Even after being informed that some person named Margarie Smith purchased two pairs of medium-sized, white crew socks for $6.99 on March 28, what action is enabled by such information? Not much without supplementary knowledge. One can argue further that running database queries and performing data-mining analyses across numerous records can reveal insightful patterns (e.g., purchasing habits of customers, sales trends of products) that enable knowledge-based actions (e.g., targeted advertising, coordinated sale pricing). Yet the wealth of knowledge resides within the analyst performing the queries and mining the data, not the database. The actions are enabled by knowledge learned through analysis, not data stored on disk.

Along these same lines, groupware (e.g., e-mail, chat, discussion boards) offers infrastructural support for knowledge work and enhances the environment in which knowledge artifacts are created and managed. However, the flow of knowledge itself remains indirect. For instance, groupware is noted widely as helpful in the virtual office environment (e.g., when geographically dispersed knowledge workers must collaborate remotely). It provides networked tools such as shared, indexed, and replicated document databases and discussion threads (e.g., Lotus Notes/Domino applications), as well as shared white boards, joint document editing capabilities, and full-duplex, multimedia communication features. These tools serve to mitigate collaborative losses that can arise when rich, face-to-face joint work is not practical or feasible. But supporting (even rich and remote) communication is not sufficient to guarantee a flow of knowledge (e.g., consider such technologies used by people who are unable to communicate in a common language, convey context, or enable learning).

Consider, for example, video teleconferencing (VTC) and PC-based collaborative applications (e.g., Groove, NetMeeting, Information Workspace). Such applications are often heralded for supporting rich and synchronous audio and video communication in addition to capabilities for exchanging and working remotely on common documents. The situation, in terms of knowledge, is similar to that discussed through the database example. On a very basic level, one can turn on the VTC and let it run indefinitely, but unless people are using it to communicate, no knowledge, information, or data are flowing (cf. only signal flows). The same can be said for PC-based collaboration tools: people must use them in order for any flows, except for signals, to take place. Even at a higher level, however, having people use such applications to communicate is insufficient for knowledge, information, or data flow. This follows the same set of reasons that were articulated in terms of the e-mail message (e.g., need to understand Korean, context of a message, understanding of its health implications). Alternatively, because people are synchronously connected via rich communication media, they can interact, ask questions, provide examples, inquire about interpretations, question ramifications, propose implications, and perform other typical actions of interlocutors trying to communicate. If, through such communication, the receiver interprets correctly the symbol "333/33," for instance, then one can say data flows have taken place. Likewise, if the receiver ascribes meaning to the symbol as his or her blood pressure measurement, as a related instance, then one can say information flows have occurred. Moreover, if the receiver understands the health implications of such measurement and learns of treatment alternatives, as yet another related instance, then one can say knowledge flows have obtained. The point is that such flows depend upon *the people*, not the technologies.

Knowledge Explicitness

One dimension of relevance in terms of knowledge uniqueness is *explicitness*. The distinction between knowledge and information/data is particularly apparent where tacit knowledge is involved. Tacit knowledge is described generally as being implicit within the knower and inherently difficult to articulate (e.g., through writing, drawing, or discussing). Riding a bicycle, playing chess, raising children, interviewing for a job, interpreting tactical patterns in warfare, diagnosing diseases in patients, and recognizing when students are comprehending principles: these all represent examples of activities (direct actions) that depend upon tacit knowledge for effective performance. In contrast, explicit knowledge is described generally as articulable. Such explicit knowledge exhibits many properties of information that complement yet are distinct from those of tacit knowledge. Notice here we extend our discussion of knowledge uniqueness: not only is knowledge distinct from information and data, different kinds of knowledge (e.g., tacit, explicit) are mutually distinct across multiple dimensions, as well.

However, although explicit knowledge can be articulated (e.g., through writing, drawing, or discussing) and shares properties in common with information, even knowledge made explicit as such enables action (e.g., decisions, behaviors, work). The distinction between explicit knowledge and information is subtle — particularly when compared with tacit knowledge — but informative. Consider a cookbook, for instance. Recipes in a cookbook are generally comprised of two supplementary parts: (1) list of ingredients and (2) preparation procedures. The former is declarative in nature. It represents a set of symbols (e.g., amounts, units of measure, food items) in the context of preparing a meal. As such, it informs the reader about how much of which ingredients go into each dish. In the context of a cookbook, one can ascribe meaning to the list of ingredients, but the list alone is insufficient for most people to use for *preparing* a meal (i.e., the action of cooking). Hence, we would classify the list of ingredients as *information*. Alternatively, the latter is procedural in nature. It represents a sequence of steps for combining and heating different ingredients to prepare a meal. As such, it enables the action *cooking*. Thus, we would classify a cooking procedure as *knowledge*. Nonetheless, such knowledge is explicit, not tacit. It describes explicitly which cooking actions are required.

Notice in this cooking example that both parts of the cookbook are explicit (e.g., written down in a book) and that both parts are necessary for most people to prepare a meal. One part informs a reader about ingredients, whereas the other guides cooking actions. Notice too that neither explicit part of a recipe may be necessary for an expert chef, who may, for instance, be capable of consistently preparing fine meals without ever referring to a written recipe (from cooking principles) and without ever repeating exactly the same recipe twice. Here we elucidate again the contrast between knowledge made explicit (e.g., in a cookbook) vs. its tacit counterpart (e.g., cooking principles in the memory of a chef).

The contrast in terms of explicitness goes much further. For instance, even where a recognized expert is able to articulate his or her knowledge about actions to take (e.g., how to prepare a meal), such articulation is often insufficient to enable a non-expert to perform effectively. Many colorful images of newly married couples experiencing this phenomenon at the family dinner table may come to the reader's mind here. Reading a book about how to ride a bicycle, as a different instance, can inform a person considerably about riding bicycles and even make explicit the actions required for riding safely (e.g., stay balanced, lean into turns, watch for cars). It is unlikely, though, that someone who has never ridden a bicycle would be able to do so based solely upon reading a book about it. Nearly everyone with children who ride bicycles can attest to problems they have with watching for cars, even after "expert" parental instruction. The same holds in the organizational environment. Even if one can "capture" knowledge (e.g., expertise in an organization) in explicit form such as through writings, where tacit knowledge is involved, one is simply accomplishing the organizational equivalent of telling people how to ride bicycles. The same holds true even if one can organize such expertise through a taxonomy or directory of some sort, and even if one can distribute this organizational expertise broadly, say through a searchable, Web-based document repository on the corporate intranet.

Even more troubling, in many domains, experts have repeatedly demonstrated great difficulty articulating their tacit knowledge. The saying is, "experts know more than they can tell." This is the principal problem experienced by developers of expert systems (artificial intelligence applications that include codified expertise) over the past three decades. When someone has developed expertise, particularly through the accumulation of considerable, tacit, experience-based knowledge, it can be exceptionally difficult and time-consuming for another person — or a machine — to develop a comparable level of expertise. This represents a key distinction regarding the explicitness of knowledge flows: tacit knowledge is sticky, clumps locally, and flows slowly. Yet rich, tacit, experience-based knowledge is often the most valuable resource an organization possesses.

Let us reconsider our cooking example. An expert chef possesses considerable tacit knowledge about cooking, enough to enable him or her to prepare fine meals without consulting a cookbook. One could argue that such chef has simply memorized the recipes and could make explicit the corresponding knowledge at any time by writing down the steps or by speaking into a tape recorder while each meal is prepared. Many television shows continue to feature chefs doing just this. However, most experienced chefs will tell you their cooking involves much more than simple memorization. They spend long periods of time in schools and apprenticeships, learning by observation, mentoring, and practice from master chefs to understand the principles of which kinds of foods combine in a pleasing manner and which methods of combination and heating are appropriate for various kinds and combinations of ingredients.

Many such experienced chefs never measure ingredients using devices such as teaspoons, tablespoons, and cups, nor do they monitor preparation and cooking time with clocks, stopwatches, or kitchen timers. Rather, they observe ingredients as they are combined and adjust where they deem appropriate. They watch a meal as it cooks, often judging by taste when various ingredients may need to be added and judging by smell when a meal is ready to be served. This appears to be a different approach to preparing meals (set of actions enabled by knowledge) than following or memorizing a cookbook.

The action of preparing meals through memorization or by following recipes in a cookbook is enabled by explicit knowledge. In contrast, the action of preparing meals by application of principles and by sight and smell is enabled by tacit knowledge. Moreover, many experienced chefs would find it difficult to articulate the latter approach to cooking. Even if such an experienced chef is able to write down in a book — or is able to speak into a tape recorder — guidance such as, "adjust ingredients as necessary to taste," or "heat until the bouquet of the wine wanes," it is unlikely that *an inexperienced cook* would be able to cook well from such guidance. The key point is that *explicitness* represents a very discriminatory dimension for evaluating the uniqueness of knowledge.

Knowledge Uniqueness Principles

Five principles developed in this chapter help shed light on knowledge uniqueness: (1) knowledge enables action directly, whereas information provides meaning and context for such action; (2) data, information, and knowledge flows are interrelated yet distinct *mental* processes; (3) flows of knowledge require supplementary flows of information, data, and signals; (4) *explicitness* represents a very discriminatory dimension for evaluating the uniqueness of knowledge; and (5) information technology principally supports flows of explicit knowledge.

Principle 6. Distinguishing knowledge from information is important. One effective operationalization is that knowledge enables direct action (e.g., correct decisions, appropriate behaviors, useful work). Alternatively, information provides meaning and context for such action (e.g., decision criteria, behavior norms, work specifications). Data reduce uncertainty or equivocality (e.g., supplying parameters to an equation, providing numbers for a formula, specifying states in a relationship). We identify also a fourth level for the knowledge hierarchy previously discussed: signals. One can say with confidence, "only signals flow across time and space," not knowledge, information, or even data. Signals (e.g., light reflecting from objects in the world or computer-generated images; sound waves propagating through a room; electrical currents alternating in discrete and analog patterns) are perceived by people. Where they are interpretable, they can provide the basis for data; where uninterpretable, they constitute noise. Where data are provided in context, they can inform. Where information enables direct action, knowledge exists. **Hence, understanding whether flows of data, information, or knowledge are required in a particular situation depends upon what needs to be accomplished (e.g., resolving uncertainty, deriving meaning, or enabling action, respectively).**

Principle 7. Data, information, and knowledge are dynamically interrelated, yet distinct from one another as mental processes. A number of Gedanken experiments and practical examples can be used to distinguish between the interrelated concepts, but all three involve mental, not physical, processes. Whether interpreting data from signals, deriving information from data, or learning knowledge from information, such processes take place in the minds of people, not in computers, networks, or databases. **Hence, people play the critical role in flows of data, information, and knowledge**.

Principle 8. Knowledge flows require flows of information, data, and signals. Physically, only signals flow. Data, information, and knowledge flow via cognitive processes. Such cognitive processes of different people require communication. For knowledge to flow from a producer or sender, information is required to produce data, which are required to encode signals. In reverse sequence, for knowledge to flow to a consumer or receiver, signals must be interpreted into data, which must be placed into meaningful context to inform. Every conversion (e.g., interpreting data from signals; ascribing meaningful information from data; learning knowledge from information) involves some kind of knowledge (e.g., language, context, physiology). **Hence, every flow (data, information, and knowledge) from signal interpretation through knowledge creation requires some kind of knowledge**.

Principle 9. *Explicitness* characterizes an important dimension of knowledge uniqueness. In particular, tacit knowledge can be distinguished along such a dimension from its explicit counterpart. One's ability to articulate his or her knowledge provides an operationalization for explicitness: Explicit knowledge has been articulated; tacit knowledge has not. Further, some kinds of tacit knowledge can be articulated into explicit form more easily than others can. Some kinds cannot be articulated at all. Most knowledge made explicit loses power in at least two important ways: (1) knowledge made explicit often fails to enable the same levels of performance corresponding to actions enabled by the tacit knowledge from which it is formalized; and (2) explicit knowledge shares many properties with information, which is more difficult to appropriate than tac isit knowledge. **Hence, moving knowledge through tacit vs. explicit flows represents a management decision, in many cases, a decision which has implications in terms of power**.

Principle 10. IT support is principally limited to explicit knowledge flows — and information/data — but enables large amounts of such knowledge to be organized, aggregated, and disseminated broadly and quickly. Where knowledge is explicit — or can be formalized into explicit form — IT offers great power to enhance the corresponding flows. Where important knowledge is tacit — and cannot be readily formalized into explicit form — IT offers less potential to affect knowledge flows. **Hence, the nature of knowledge represents a critical factor for determining where IT can be expected to enhance knowledge flows**.

Exercises

1. Describe a Gedanken experiment that illustrates how knowledge is distinct from information and data in terms of enabling performance. Try to informatively characterize differences between what knowledge enables one to do vs. what benefits information and data provide.

2. Describe some tacit knowledge that you possess. Indicate which aspects of such knowledge you feel can be articulated (i.e., made explicit) and which cannot. Why is this the case?

3. Describe how IT can be used to support: (1) the sharing of your tacit knowledge described in Exercise 2; (2) the sharing of your explicit

knowledge described in Exercise 2; (3) the application of your tacit knowledge described in Exercise 2; and (4) the application of your explicit knowledge described in Exercise 2.

4.   Describe a knowledge management (KM) program with which you are familiar. To what extent does it address explicit vs. tacit knowledge? Cite one or two specific examples of each (if applicable).

Chapter III

Knowledge Flow

This chapter focuses phenomenologically on the dynamics of knowledge flows. We look first at the organizational processes responsible for knowledge flows and then discuss knowledge-flow patterns. The discussion then turns to examining interactions between knowledge flows and workflows, in addition to timing and obstacles of dynamic knowledge. The chapter concludes with five knowledge-flow principles and includes exercises to stimulate critical thought, learning, and discussion.

Knowledge-Flow Processes

Recall from your high school physics the concept *inertia*: Objects at rest tend to stay at rest; and objects in motion tend to stay in motion. Then, of course, you have Newton's famous law: $F = ma$; that is, force equals mass times acceleration. Combine the concept with the law and note acceleration (the change in velocity) is related directly to the force applied to an object and inversely to the object's mass. Even such basic principles from physics have been used successfully for centuries to describe, explain, and predict the dynamics of objects in the world. They enable a person to analyze nearly any physical object (e.g., within the Newtonian realm), given a set of initial conditions (e.g., starting position, velocity, acceleration), and to predict precisely in which direction, how fast, how far, and how long it will move (if at all). Further, for more complex systems of objects and forces, such principles enable the understanding and prediction of intuitive (e.g., ballistic) as well as seemingly random (e.g., chaotic) dynamic patterns. Other factors such as friction, elasticity, energy losses, and the like pertain as well, but we can ignore these for now in our present context.

The science addressing physical flows is very advanced. The corresponding principled knowledge enables sophisticated, precise analysis and prediction of dynamic patterns. Unfortunately, the science addressing knowledge flows has not caught up to physics in terms of understanding dynamics, but several knowledge-flow principles and discernable patterns are emerging from this science: principles and patterns that enable some degree of description, explanation, prediction, and understanding. We begin this discussion by borrowing some concepts from physics for insight through flow metaphors. We then delve into the phenomenology of knowledge flows.

Several principles from physics can be used to conceptualize knowledge flows metaphorically. For instance, knowledge at rest tends to stay at rest. Say some particular knowledge (e.g., a chunk, a fact, a procedure, an association, an inference) is possessed by a single individual in a particular organization at a specific location at a unique point in time. Unless something is done to move such knowledge, it will likely remain confined to that single coordinate (person, organization, location, time). Looking around most organizations today, such confined, single-coordinate knowledge clearly represents a common case. Hence, some kind of metaphorical force is required for knowledge at rest to "move" (we use quotation marks here to indicate knowledge does not represent some tangible physical object that can be rolled around like a ball on the floor).

Further, some aspects of such metaphorical force and the knowledge itself (e.g., organizational analogs to *mass*, *friction*, *energy*) may affect how fast and how far it will move. Borrowing from Newton, if the "force" is strong and the "mass" is light, then the associated knowledge should flow swiftly and broadly. Moving from metaphor to example, a gifted teacher, for instance, may represent the organizational analog of a strong force. A conceptually simple chunk of knowledge, as a related instance, may represent the analog of light mass. Together, the gifted teacher and simple concept may result in rapid and broad knowledge flows. A less-skilled teacher and more complex knowledge, as a counter instance, may result in comparatively slow and confined knowledge flows, or even no flows at all. Hence, we can argue that knowledge at rest tends to stay at rest and that organizational analogs to forces and masses can affect if, how fast, and how far any particular chunk of knowledge may flow. Here the inertia principle and associated flow metaphors appear to apply relatively well in our organizational context.

Alternatively, consider the other part of inertia (an object in motion tends to stay in motion). In the domain of physics, some force is required to stop a moving object or to change its direction. As mentioned, the stronger the force and lighter the mass, the faster an object can be stopped or turned. The organizational analog to this part of the inertia phenomenon is less clear than its counterpart, however. On one hand, consider, for example, management trying to stop an outflow of knowledge from an organization resulting from experienced people leaving to join rival firms (e.g., flows set in motion by the defection of a respected employee). Here one can argue some organizational analog to force (e.g., management action) would be necessary *to stop knowledge in motion* (i.e., via people leaving the firm). On the other hand, in our teacher-student learning example, it is unclear whether or how any particular chunk of knowledge learned by one student (e.g., set in motion through classroom interaction) would continue to flow without some additional effort *to keep it moving* (e.g., to other students). Here the inertia principle and associated flow metaphors appear to break down a bit.

Nonetheless, knowledge can be viewed as exhibiting some aspects of inertia, and it does not appear to flow unless some organizational analog of force makes it move. If we wish to understand knowledge flows better (e.g., to enable rich description, detailed explanation, precise prediction), then we need to develop principles of dynamics that are based upon more than a physical metaphor. Principles can be induced via phenomenology of knowledge flows. Such phenomenology points to the *process* as a focal concept in our present context of organizations. In other words, the knowledge-flow process represents the phenomenological analog to the metaphorical force in a knowledge organization.

We are probably all familiar with processes. For instance, as implied by the name, work processes represent the sets of activities responsible for accomplishing work in an organization. Examples from manufacturing organizations include developing new markets for products, designing product components, planning manufacturing sequences, assembling products, supporting customers, accounting for revenues and expenses, managing the organization, and others. Examples from service organizations include developing new markets for services, designing service activities, planning work sequences, delivering services, supporting customers, accounting for revenues and expenses, managing the organization, and others. Work processes are also found in the public sector (e.g., government organizations perform processes to serve constituents; military units perform processes to wage wars), non-profits (e.g., professional organizations perform processes to serve members; churches perform processes to serve congregations), and practically any other kind of organization one can think of (e.g., families perform processes such as grocery shopping, cooking, and raising children). Hence, *process* represents a general concept to describe how work is accomplished in the organizational context. If an organizational process is not performed (or not performed well), then the associated work does not get accomplished (well).

The same relationship holds for *knowledge-flow processes*. If a knowledge-flow process is not performed (or not performed well), then the associated knowledge does not flow (well). Examples of knowledge-flow processes include *education, training, research, contemplation, discussion, mentoring, observing, reading, trial and error*, and others. Through the education process, for instance, one attends generally some kind of school, completes a curriculum of study, *and learns*. This last activity is key: Where knowledge flows, learning takes place. Hence, the phenomenon of knowledge flows involves learning. Continuing with this education process example, one can view knowledge as moving from instructor to student (e.g., through classroom interaction, through instructor feedback on student points made in class, homework assignments, term papers, and examinations). But one can also view knowledge as moving in other directions (e.g., through peer interaction with classmates and through the student's individual reading of textbooks and completion of homework assignments). Hence, several detailed activities (e.g., classroom interaction, instructor feedback, student reading, homework, and peer interaction) are involved with the knowledge-flow process *education*. Detailed activities such as these can be identified readily for other knowledge-flow processes (e.g., *training, research, mentoring*) as well. Again, some kind of organizational analog to force is required for knowledge to move through an organization. The knowledge-flow process — and its detailed activities — provides a phenomenological explanation for how knowledge moves in the organizational context.

Knowledge-Flow Patterns

Knowledge flows are dynamic. As such, they form distinctive patterns. Several scholars are working to model the dynamics of knowledge flows and to help understand such flows by interpreting their patterns. One of the best-known models to describe the knowledge-flow phenomenon stems from the work of Nonaka (1994) and various colleagues (e.g., Nonaka & Takeuchi, 1995). This model describes a "spiral" pattern of knowledge flows through the organization. It also characterizes recurring patterns of interaction between explicit and tacit knowledge. Recall in Chapter II that we used the explicit-tacit distinction as one dimension (*explicitness*) to help characterize knowledge uniqueness. Here we use the dimension *reach* — which pertains to the level of social aggregation (e.g., individual, group, organization) associated with knowledge — also to describe different kinds of knowledge flows that are unique and mutually distinct. These two dimensions derive directly from Nonaka's model. Only the names are changed here for clarity (i.e., Nonaka uses the term *epistemological* to characterize explicitness and the term *ontological* instead of reach).

Later research by Nissen (2002a) extends Nonaka's two-dimensional model to integrate two complementary dimensions: *life cycle* and *flow time*. *Life cycle* refers to the kind of activity (e.g., creation, sharing, application) associated with knowledge flows. *Flow time* pertains to the length of time (e.g., minutes, days, years) required for knowledge to move from one person, organization, place, or time to another. These four dimensions for characterizing knowledge flows can be employed collectively to visualize the kinds of patterns associated with Nonaka's model. In addition, we elucidate and map in subsequent paragraphs a wide variety of knowledge flows from practice that are otherwise nearly impossible to discern and visualize.

Drawing from Nissen (2005), in Figure 1, these dimensions are used to delineate one "loop" from the spiral knowledge-flow pattern described by Nonaka. Each part of this loop corresponds to one of four knowledge-flow processes articulated in the model (*socialization, externalization, combination, internalization*). The figure illustrates how our four dimensions can be combined to visualize a representative knowledge flow from this well-known theory. The explicitness dimension is shown as the vertical axis with tacit and explicit endpoints. The reach dimension identifies different levels of social interaction (e.g., individual, group) on the horizontal axis. The life cycle dimension is plotted as a third axis labeled with six KM activities (e.g., create,

Figure 1. Multidimensional knowledge-flow visualization (adapted from Nissen, 2005)

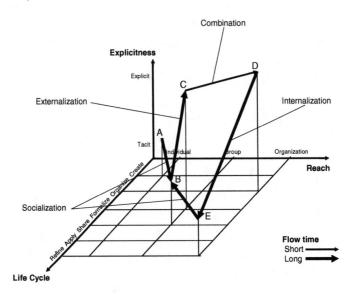

share, apply). To incorporate the flow time dimension, we use arrows of different thickness (e.g., thin for fast flows, thick for slow flows) when delineating various segments of the flow pattern. Notice how the organizational dimension *flow time* relates directly to the physical concept *acceleration* discussed previously.

We begin at Point A, representing tacit knowledge created by an individual; Nonaka (1994) suggests tacit knowledge held by individuals is central to knowledge creation (p. 20). The socialization flow (A to B) reflects a movement of tacit knowledge across the reach dimension. We depict a representative flow from the individual to the group level in the figure. This kind of socialized flow is classified best as "share" in terms of the life cycle dimension (e.g., Nonaka notes "shared experience" (p. 19) as important to socialization). The externalization flow (B to C) reflects a movement from tacit to explicit knowledge. We depict a representative flow at the group level in the figure. The formalize life cycle stage corresponds best to this kind of movement (making knowledge explicit).

The combination flow (C to D), in turn, reflects a movement of explicit knowledge across the reach dimension. We depict a representative flow from the group to the organization level in the figure. The organize life cycle stage appears to correspond best to this kind of movement (e.g., Nonaka notes as examples: sorting, editing, recategorizing, and recontextualizing explicit knowledge). We also use a thinner arrow to represent this flow, as only explicit knowledge is involved. This is consistent with von Hippel (1994) (e.g., tacit knowledge is related to stickiness) and Nissen et al. (2000) (e.g., the organize life cycle stage is supported well by IT). Finally, the internalization flow (D to E) reflects a movement from explicit to tacit knowledge. We depict a representative flow at the organization level in the figure. The refine life cycle stage corresponds best to this kind of movement (e.g., learning organizational routines).

Notice we also include a socialization flow from Points E to B (tacit knowledge moving from the organization to the group level) to complete the one loop. Individuals and groups learn many organizational routines, cultural norms, and objectified ideas (Czarniawska & Joerges, 1996) that remain tacit. This is essentially socialization in reverse. Other loops from the spiral model (e.g., extending beyond the organization level along the reach axis) could also be included, as could various knowledge flows from other models (e.g., life cycle, knowledge transfer). But this single loop is representative, and it provides an illustration of how the four dimensions of our analytic framework can be integrated into a single figure for knowledge-flow visualization.

In light of our discussion, the knowledge flows delineated in this figure can be interpreted in part through some organizational analogs to physical principles. For instance, recall only one knowledge-flow vector in the figure (C to D, corresponding to the process *combination*) is depicted by a thin arrow to denote relatively short flow time. In graphic contrast, all four of the other knowledge-flow vectors are depicted by thick arrows to denote comparatively long flow times. One organizational implication is that something is different about the knowledge associated with the combination process. In particular, notice only explicit knowledge is involved. Considering organizational analogs to forces and masses, one could posit here that explicit knowledge corresponds to relatively "light mass" in the context of knowledge flows, hence, contributes toward rapid flows (short flow time).

In contrast, each of the other four knowledge-flow processes involves tacit knowledge to some extent, with the socialization flows (A to B, E to B) involving *only* tacit knowledge. Accordingly, tacit knowledge would correspond comparatively to "heavy mass" in the context of knowledge dynamics, hence, contributes toward slow flows (long flow time). The key point is that the nature of the knowledge-flow process (e.g., *combination* vs. *socialization*) and associated knowledge (e.g., explicit vs. tacit) affects how rapidly knowledge will flow (e.g., short vs. long flow time). Similarly, notice only this vector representing the knowledge-flow process *combination* extends outward beyond the group level along the reach dimension. One could posit also that the nature of the knowledge-flow process and associated knowledge affect how broadly knowledge will flow (e.g., narrow vs. broad reach) as well. Here we are beginning to develop some principles that may prove useful for describing, explaining, and even predicting a variety of knowledge flows.

Knowledge-Flow and Workflow Interactions

Notice several of the knowledge-flow processes described in this chapter appear also to involve the performance of work. For instance, many of the activities associated with education involve work by student and instructor alike. Students engage in "coursework," perform "homework," and "work diligently" to prepare for examinations. In this case of education, however, all such "work" applies directly and almost solely to the learning process. We say "almost" here to accommodate applied class projects that may result in useful work (e.g., in support of some university sponsor). Nonetheless, while the student is participating in educational activities, he or she is generally not participating in other activities such as working at a fast-food restaurant, at least (hopefully) not at the same time.

Likewise, while such person is busy accomplishing work by flipping hamburgers, he or she has little opportunity for university learning. Here the distinction between a knowledge-flow process such as education and a workflow process such as flipping hamburgers should be relatively clear: Learning through the knowledge-flow process *education* and doing through the workflow process *flipping hamburgers* represent mutually exclusive activities. Any time and energy devoted to one activity necessarily takes away from the other, and vice versa. This explains in part why many students who work part-time while in college take longer to complete their degrees than full-time students do. It may also explain in part why such working students tend to have more spending money than their more studious counterparts do.

We graphically depict this interaction between knowledge flows and workflows in Figure 2. The vertical axis represents the relative contribution of some process activity toward knowledge flows, and the horizontal axis represents the

Figure 3.2. Knowledge-flow and workflow contributions (adapted from Nissen, 2004a)

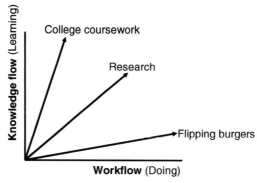

relative workflow contribution. One vector (labeled "College coursework") delineates the relative contribution of the education process activities mentioned previously. Another (labeled "Flipping burgers") delineates the contribution from the work process of flipping hamburgers in a fast-food restaurant. Notice the college coursework vector is nearly vertical — but not quite — and the flipping burgers vector is nearly horizontal — but not quite. This depicts graphically the aforementioned relationship: Education contributes principally toward knowledge flows (learning) and negligibly toward workflows (doing); work in a fast-food restaurant has inverse contributions with respect to learning vs. doing.

The two vectors are depicted as not quite vertical or horizontal, respectively, to illustrate that some useful work can emerge from college coursework (e.g., via practical application project) and that some learning can result from flipping burgers (e.g., cooking techniques). Clearly, a great many diverse processes can be depicted graphically in this manner. Such depiction helps elucidate the relative contributions of various process activities toward knowledge flows and workflows. The two examples illustrated here represent relatively pure cases (contributing almost exclusively toward one flow vs. another).

What about an alternate process such as research, the activities of which contribute differently? Many people such as professors, attorneys, and product development engineers conduct research as their principal job (doing activity). They also develop new knowledge through research (learning activity). Clearly there is learning as well as doing taking place. Flows of knowledge and flows of work both obtain through the single process *research*. Consider the research performed by a university professor, for example. He or she may conduct research to understand some phenomenon better. Such process activity to improve one's understanding is intense in terms of learning but contributes negligibly toward productive output (doing). Hence, the activity contributes strongly toward knowledge flows and weakly toward workflows. Alternatively, research also provides the intellectual and empirical basis to write papers for publication in academic journals, write textbooks for use in courses, and prepare lecture notes for class instruction. Such process activities are more intense in terms of doing but contribute negligibly toward one's own knowledge (learning). Hence, the activities contribute weakly toward knowledge flows and strongly toward workflows.

Taken individually, the learning component of research would plot similarly to the vector in Figure 2 for college coursework, and the doing component would plot similarly to the flipping burgers vector. When taken together, however, the learning and doing components would combine to delineate an intermediate vector such as the one labeled "Research" in the figure. This method of graphical depiction enables quick visual classification of processes in terms of their relative contributions toward knowledge flows and workflows. We return to utilize such method for classification and visualization later in the book.

Knowledge-Flow Timing

Beyond the phenomenology of knowledge flowing through an organization by way of processes, terms such as *flow* and *move* imply dynamic action; that is, flows and movements take place through time. Flows of water, for example, from the physical world, move through finite and measurable periods of time. Indeed, it can take a particular volume of water several months to make its way down the Mississippi River, for instance, and one can measure the flow time of such water volume (e.g., with a dye marker). Flows of water and other fluids also vary with different conditions of their conduits. Where the banks of a river narrow and the bottom steepens, for instance, the flow rate of river water increases consistently at such points. Flows of electricity take place much faster, of course, than water flows do, but their flow times are finite and measurable also, and they vary according to the nature of and conditions in the conduit (e.g., conductivity, temperature, size). Flows of electromagnetic radiation (e.g., light, radio waves) are similar (finite, measurable, vary according to different conditions). Flows of containers along the conveyors of a bottling plant are similar too, as are flows of packages being delivered by mail carriers. They all take place through finite and measurable periods of time and are all affected by various conditions. Knowledge flows are no exception.

Consider, for instance, our example of a student participating in an educational program. Focus in particular on interaction between the professor and the student. The professor presumably knows the material associated with a course, and the student presumably does not (or at least not well). If this is not the case, then why would such professor teach the course, and why would such student enroll in it? As part of the professor's work process, say he or she prepares for and leads a one-hour class session, in which the student participates. In terms of timing, perhaps several hours are required for the professor to prepare for the class session, and exactly one hour is required to lead it. The knowledge that flows during this period (as a result of the processes *class preparation* and *class discussion*) does so quite quickly (e.g., in a matter of hours) by knowledge-flow standards.

Now consider some related processes that need to be completed before the professor can prepare for a class session. Depending upon the nature and level of material taught in the course, one could argue the professor has to earn a PhD and to research the subject matter discussed in the course, among others (e.g., get a teaching job at the university). The knowledge flows associated with such latter processes take place quite slowly (e.g., in a matter of years) by comparison with those mentioned previously. Notice the variation associated with the time required for knowledge-flow processes such as *class preparation* and *earning a PhD* is huge (e.g., many orders of magnitude). The key point is that knowledge flows are dynamic, and such flows can be measured.

Additionally, various knowledge flows are tightly interrelated through precedence relations; that is, some chunks of knowledge must complete their flows before others can begin effectively. Consider further the example of a professor leading class discussion. We noted how the class preparation process must (or at least should) be completed prior to the beginning of class discussion. Otherwise, the professor may come to class poorly prepared for the discussion, hence, may fail to anticipate and answer students' questions well. This indicates a precedence relation between these two knowledge-flow processes, a relation which we note symbolically: *class preparation* → *class discussion*. Flow times for these two processes are noted previously as relatively short.

Conversely, flow times for the latter processes such as earning a PhD and researching subject matter are considerably longer. Notice further such latter knowledge-flow processes also exhibit precedence relations, between themselves as well as with the former processes. For instance, say earning a PhD is prerequisite to effectively researching the subject matter of a course. Using our previous notation, we could write: ***earning a PhD → researching subject matter***. Notice we highlight these knowledge-flow processes with bold font to denote their relatively long flow times. This shows the precedence relation between these two relatively slow processes.

But the precedence linkage extends farther, as researching the course subject matter is prerequisite to class preparation. Hence, our notation could be extended further: ***earning a PhD → researching subject matter → class preparation → class discussion***. Precedence chains as such can be of arbitrary length, depending upon how many different knowledge-flow processes are interrelated as prerequisites, for instance. Notice a precedence chain such as this also represents a rudimentary plan; that is, it specifies which flows need to be completed and in which order.

With the identification of precedence relations as such, one can begin to make useful inferences about knowledge flow times. For instance, when asked about how much time is required to prepare for a class discussion, the answer would clearly depend upon the states of the prerequisite knowledge-flow processes (e.g., *earning a PhD and researching subject matter*). If such prerequisite processes had completed their flows, as one case (e.g., a professor with a PhD had already conducted research on the course subject matter), then one could answer that class preparation should require time on the order of a few hours to complete. In this case, only the class preparation and class discussion processes would require performance.

If such prerequisite processes had not completed their flows, however, as a contrasting case (e.g., a graduate student had just begun working toward a PhD and accomplished no research to date on the course subject matter), then one may have to answer that class preparation could require time on the order of *several years* to complete! In this latter case, the class preparation and class discussion processes would have to wait for knowledge flows associated with earning a PhD and researching the subject matter to complete. The point is that by identifying and linking precedence relations between diverse knowledge-flow processes, one can develop an understanding of process interrelations and begin to appreciate issues associated with timing and sequencing among various knowledge flows.

Knowledge-Flow Obstacles

Drawing from our discussion of inertia, we noted one obvious obstacle to knowledge flows: inactivity. Unless a process is performed to move knowledge, there is little reason to believe such knowledge will flow. Drawing from research to date on knowledge flows (e.g., Dierickx & Cool, 1989; Nissen, 2002a; Nonaka 1994), another important consideration pertains to the nature of knowledge. In general, tacit knowledge flows more slowly (has longer flow time) than explicit knowledge does. Likewise, tacit knowledge flows more locally (has narrower reach) than explicit knowledge does. Knowledge creation generally requires longer than its application does (along the life cycle dimension). Hence, the various dimensions we use to characterize different kinds of knowledge provide insights into the dynamics of knowledge flows (e.g., flow time).

For instance, where some kind of important organizational knowledge is tacit and clumped within a single person or organization, the leader or manager wishing for such knowledge to flow quickly across many people and across several organizations faces a daunting obstacle. Of course, other obstacles to knowledge flows obtain as well: A person must be competent at learning before knowledge creation can take place reliably; a person must be willing to share knowledge before it can be transferred effectively; a person must have internalized knowledge before it can be applied well. A plethora of different obstacles to knowledge flows have been reported and described in the academic literature as well as the management press.

How would a leader or manager work to overcome obstacles to knowledge flows? First, one needs to recognize the need for knowledge to flow. Despite our understanding about knowledge power, not every organization is concerned equally with knowledge flows. Indeed, some organizations may find it important to *restrict* flows of knowledge. Consider, for example, an organization that bases much of its competitive advantage on keeping secrets within the enterprise. Many commercial firms and military units attempt to compete on the basis of privileged information, trade secrets, and appropriable knowledge, for instance. In such organizations, there are clearly limits to the kinds of knowledge flows managers are willing to accept, and there are many kinds of knowledge flows managers work actively to prevent. Even for organizations facing limits along these lines, however, effective performance of work processes still depends upon knowledge. To the extent that such knowledge is not located how, where, and when, it is needed to support workflows, then the knowledge must be induced to flow. Hence, the leader or manager is faced with the prospect of trying to restrict some flows of knowledge while trying to enhance other flows in a single organization.

Second, one needs to understand the kind of knowledge involved with flows. Using the dimensions of our framework (e.g., *explicitness*, *reach*, *life cycle*) provides a good start. The kinds of managerial, organizational, and technological changes likely to be effective and to induce or enhance knowledge flows depend directly upon the nature of the knowledge. Recall our organizational analogs to inertia, force, and mass: A heavy mass requires a proportionately stronger force to effect the same acceleration created by a weaker force applied to a lighter mass. In the organizational context, moving tacit knowledge requires a different set of knowledge-flow processes than those required for explicit knowledge to flow. For instance, where knowledge is tacit, held individually, and associated solely with creation, there is little point to investing in Web portals with the hope of disseminating such knowledge. The knowledge-flow processes associated with such portals (e.g., *explicit knowledge dissemination*) do not induce tacit knowledge to flow well. Likewise, where knowledge is explicit, distributed widely, and used for application to work processes, there is little reason to collocate people with the hope they will share such knowledge. The knowledge-flow processes associated with such collocation have their greatest effect on tacit knowledge.

Third, one needs to understand the timing of, and workflow interactions with, knowledge. Where work needs to be accomplished in a time-critical manner, then generally all of the required knowledge flows must be completed before such workflow begins. Otherwise, people performing the work may not be fully qualified (e.g., not know what to do or how to do it). Further, workflows and knowledge flows alike may have precedence relations between them (e.g., certain work activities must be completed before others can begin effectively or certain learning activities must be completed before others can begin effectively). Project managers and like professionals who plan and schedule work activities for others have developed a robust set of tools and techniques (e.g., Gantt Charts, PERT networks; see Cleland & Ireland, 2002) to identify, align, and plan precedence relations among *workflow* processes. This is where the term *critical path* comes from, for instance, the sequence of work activities that determine the shortest possible project completion time.

However, such tools and techniques do not address precedence relations among *knowledge-flow* processes. This remains the case today, even though precedence relations among such processes must be identified, aligned, and planned in a manner comparable to that for workflows. Recall the earlier example of the university professor preparing for class discussion. The length of time required for such preparation could vary by several orders of magnitude, depending upon which of the prerequisite knowledge-flow processes (e.g., earning a PhD, researching the subject matter) had been completed. Moreover, the class preparation workflows must be completed before the work process *class discussion* can begin fruitfully. Indeed, where workflows depend upon knowledge flows for effective performance, *flows of knowledge lie always on the critical paths of workflows*. In other words, in nearly every domain of work, people must know what to do and how to do it before they can effectively accomplish a knowledge-based activity.

Fourth, one needs to place a relative premium on workflows vs. knowledge flows — or vice versa — in the organization. Different processes contribute in different magnitudes toward the relative flows of work and flows of knowledge. We illustrated this concept previously through the contrast between process activities such as *college coursework, research,* and *flipping burgers.* A related example from the domain of organizations can be seen with formal classroom training vs. on-the-job training (OJT). The former often accomplishes no useful work yet achieves focused learning in a relatively short period of time. The latter generally accomplishes useful work directly but has a relatively small and slow learning component. A focus on knowledge flows vs. a focus on workflows reflects a leader's or manager's relative concern for learning vs. doing, respectively. Indeed, the approach selected by a leader or manager (e.g., formal training, OJT) will contribute differently toward learning vs. doing. Hence, such an approach constitutes an important decision variable for consideration.

Fifth, one needs some kind of model to pull together the various factors, considerations, and alternatives associated with workflows and knowledge flows and to help support informed decision making. Which managerial, organizational, or technological changes would be most appropriate in a given situation? This represents the kind of question a leader or manager needs to have answered. Unfortunately, at present, the state of the art has yet to develop a reliable model to support such decision making well. Even models such as Nonaka's Spiral are purely descriptive and offer little decision support at present. This remains an active topic of current research, however.

Knowledge-Flow Principles

Five principles developed in this chapter help shed light on knowledge flows: (1) knowledge exhibits some properties of inertia such as *tendency to remain at rest*; (2) experiential processes contribute principally toward workflows (doing), whereas educational processes contribute principally toward knowledge flows; (3) knowledge flows lie always on the critical paths of workflows, hence, organizational performance; (4) time-critical workflows must wait for enabling knowledge flows to run their course; and (5) effectively intervening to dissolve knowledge clumps requires understanding the dynamic nature of knowledge.

Principle 11. We noted how knowledge at rest tends to stay at rest. If a leader or manager seeks to have knowledge flow, then something must be done to induce it to flow (e.g., formal training, OJT). Further, knowledge in motion tends to stay in motion in some cases (e.g., via employee defections). If a leader or manager seeks to cease or restrict knowledge flows in such cases, then something must be done to stem the flows. In contrast, if the leader or manager is content with such flows, then no action is required. In other cases, however, knowledge in motion (e.g., student learning through classroom interaction) appears to require additional action just to keep it in motion. If a leader or manager seeks to cease or restrict knowledge flows in such cases, then no action is required to stem its flow. In contrast, if the leader or manager wants such flows to propagate further, then something must be done to continue the flows. The *organizational process* represents the phenomenological analog to physical force in overcoming knowledge inertia. **Hence, knowledge-flow processes represent direct focuses of leadership and managerial action**.

Principle 12. Workflows and knowledge flows interact, and various processes contribute in different magnitudes toward doing vs. learning. If a leader or manager is interested in promoting knowledge flows in the organization, then it will be important for him or her to understand how the specific knowledge flows of concern interrelate with workflows of value to the organization. In some cases, workflows and knowledge flows are independent, so one can be changed without affecting the other. In other cases, however, workflows and knowledge flows are interrelated tightly, so altering one will affect the other directly. **Hence, changes to workflows demand changes to knowledge flows, and vice versa**.

Principle 13. The activities associated with organizational processes are responsible for the phenomenon of knowledge flows. Knowledge-flow processes represent the organizational analogs to physical forces. The different kinds of knowledge represent the organizational analogs to physical masses. Together, the two determine the direction, rate, and extent of knowledge flows. If a leader or manager is interested in inducing, enhancing, restricting, or ceasing knowledge flows, then he or she should examine the associated organizational processes. Because processes are composed of activities, which have long been the focus of leadership and managerial attention, such a process focus should be quite natural. Also, there appears to be considerable opportunity for such a process focus to be supported by the same kinds of tools and techniques for the planning, organizing, monitoring, and control of work (e.g., Gantt Charts, PERT networks, work/knowledge specifications). Indeed, in every case of knowledge-based action, knowledge flows lie on the critical paths of workflows and the associated organizational performance. **Hence, knowledge flows should be planned and managed like workflows**.

Principle 14. Knowledge flows and workflows vary in terms of timing. Some workflows require quick, precise, and thorough activities that can be performed only by knowledgeable people. In such cases, the enabling knowledge flows are prerequisite to their corresponding workflows. Other workflows afford greater tolerances in terms of performance, which can be performed by people who learn over time and by trial and error. In such cases, the enabling knowledge flows can be concurrent with their corresponding workflows. Indeed, in many cases such as OJT, the learning associated with knowledge flows takes place *through* the doing associated with workflows. Before deciding upon and implementing a particular approach to inducing, enhancing, restricting, or ceasing knowledge flows, the leader or manager needs to consider how the target flows interact temporally with corresponding workflows of importance. **Hence, most knowledge flows must complete their course before critical and dependent workflows can begin**.

Principle 15. *Knowledge* is not a single, static, monolithic concept. Rather, it is multifaceted, dynamic, and multidimensional. Different kinds of knowledge behave in different ways, exhibit different properties, and manifest different dynamic patterns. Such differences present various obstacles and imply alternate approaches to overcoming them. The leader or manager interested in overcoming obstacles to knowledge flows in his or her organization should understand the nature of the knowledge associated with such flows and should use such understanding to identify the most appropriate managerial, organizational, and technological interventions. **Hence, managerial efficacy through intervention can be increased by learning the principles of dynamic knowledge**.

Exercises

1. Describe a knowledge-flow process in an organization with which you are familiar. Indicate what its constituent activities are and how this knowledge-flow process interacts with one or more workflow processes.

2. Describe a critical part of a job you have or have had that requires knowledge. How is such knowledge acquired? To what extent do you devote your time in the organization to learning vs. doing (i.e., knowledge flows vs. workflows)?

3. Describe the temporal interaction between the knowledge flows and workflows from Exercise 2. To what extent must knowledge flows precede the enabled workflows vs. occurring contemporaneously?

4. Describe a clump associated with flows of the knowledge from Exercise 2. Indicate the nature of such knowledge. Propose at least two alternate approaches to dissolving the clump and to enhancing the corresponding knowledge flow.

Chapter IV

Knowledge Technology

This chapter surveys several classes of technologies and indicates which kinds of knowledge flows are enabled and supported relatively better and worse by such technologies. We look first at common problems associated with the most prevalent and prominent KM technologies and then discuss interactions between such technologies and the knowledge life cycle. The discussion then turns to examine expert systems technology, which addresses knowledge directly. This is followed by a discussion of simulation technology, which enables the development of tacit knowledge through practice in virtual environments. The chapter concludes with five knowledge technology principles and includes exercises to stimulate critical thought, learning, and discussion.

Knowledge Technology Problems

Have you ever worked with technology in an organization that failed to produce the intended results? Technology — particularly information technology (IT) — forms the foundation of many KM projects in practice and offers great potential in terms of enhancing knowledge flows. As has been noted repeatedly, however, few *information* technologies even address *knowledge* as the focus or object of flow. Over-reliance on IT has sounded the death knell for myriad KM projects.

Ask yourself why most IT fails to support KM well. We have learned that knowledge is distinct from information. Yet we have also learned that knowledge builds upon information (and vice versa). It appears that flows of information are necessary to support flows of knowledge, but such former flows are *insufficient* to enable the latter ones. In this way, IT to enable flows of information may be necessary to support flows of knowledge, but many KM programs rely naively upon such technology as sufficient to effect knowledge flows. IT is capable of transmitting signals (e.g., electrical waves and pulses across networks, photonic patterns from displays, acoustical patterns from speakers), but conversion of such signals into data, information, or knowledge takes place within the minds of people receiving such signals, not the electronics of IT systems. To ensure flows of knowledge, one must do more than deliver signals. Thus, *knowledge flows require more than just IT*.

Next, ask yourself how some kinds of IT support KM better than others. Some technologies claim to automate work processes. Many people think of automation as the ultimate in terms of IT evolution. The word processor application automates many document processing tasks such as formatting, spell checking, and filing, for instance. The workflow application automates flows of documents through an organization, as another instance. Intelligent software agents can search networks autonomously and retrieve information automatically from distributed and disorganized sources (e.g., the Internet), as a third instance. Related shopping "bots" can identify and automatically select certain products and services based on lowest price, as a fourth instance.

However, people are still required to create the messages that become documents and to complete the work as it flows into their workspaces. People are required also to read and understand documents that are created and to cumulatively build upon the work of others in workflows. People are further required to determine which information retrieved by agents is relevant and to decide whether non-price product and service attributes are sufficiently compelling to override bots' purchase recommendations.

In each of these instances and as a general rule, technologies automate some activities within workflows but not all of them. The people in an organization perform most workflow roles requiring knowledge — particularly those involving experience, judgment, and like capabilities dependent upon tacit knowledge. This leaves IT to largely systematic, clerical, and procedural roles, for which requisite knowledge can be formalized explicitly (e.g., via computer software). Hence, we see again, as in Chapter II, how knowledge uniqueness and IT are tightly intertwined.

Other technologies such as computer databases and online repositories are excellent at organizing, storing, manipulating, and facilitating the query and retrieval of data and documents, but we know that data must be placed in context and used to enable direct action to become knowledge. Likewise, documents must be read, understood, and used for action before they can be considered to represent knowledge. As noted previously, such technologies are clearly important in, and in many respects necessary for, supporting knowledge work in the organization, but they are not sufficient to enable knowledge flows. Again, the people in an organization maintain responsibility for most workflow activities requiring knowledge, particularly tacit knowledge.

Moreover, recall the discussion pertaining to interaction between workflows and knowledge flows. The kinds of KM-prominent technologies described here are largely neutral in terms of supporting processes for learning vs. doing. To reiterate briefly, learning has most to do with flows of knowledge, whereas doing has more to do with flows of work. If a particular technology focuses principally on supporting workflows and not knowledge flows, then one should question the value of such technology to a *knowledge* management effort. For instance, a set of documents from a searchable intranet repository may be used to support knowledge flows (e.g., via a formal training course) or workflows (e.g., via a standard operating procedure) equally well. Hence, the key is how a technology is used (e.g., to support learning vs. doing), not the technology itself.

A great many KM programs are meticulous about the technologies they implement, only to then leave people in the organization unguided and uninformed about how such technology can be used to enhance knowledge flows. Indeed, most KM projects that focus on technology miss and neglect the most important resource: people. In the document example given previously, for instance, it is the person who finds, selects, and reads the documents — and the organizational context of his or her activities (e.g., learning vs. doing) — that determines whether the repository is used for learning or working. This point may appear a bit tangential at first look, but it cuts away at the widely perceived primacy and privileged nature of *information* technologies for *knowledge* management. For instance, one can make many of the same points about how other "technologies" — such as office chairs, pencil sharpeners, filing cabinets, and similar artifacts of both knowledge-flow and workflow processes — can be used equally well to support learning as well as doing. Yet what intelligent knowledge manager would base an organization's KM program on advanced office chair technology?

Now ubiquitous computer networks share many of these same properties with respect to knowledge. They appear to be present in most KM programs and are, in many cases, both important and necessary. But networks shunt signals around and connect various other IT applications. To a large extent, we can label technologies such as these "infrastructure." As an analogy, trains, depots, tracks, trucks, warehouses, and highways support interstate commerce in the U.S., but they only help to move commercial products around the country — from producers to consumers. Such commercial infrastructure is important for commerce and can improve the distribution of physical goods. But having them in place, and even using them, does not constitute commerce. Many other processes must also contribute in order to leverage the transportation infrastructure (e.g., product development, marketing, manufacturing, retailing). Likewise, IT infrastructure is important to KM and can improve the distribution of information. But much more is required to manage organizational knowledge and the associated work.

Still other technologies such as Web portals and search engines contribute more directly to managing knowledge than infrastructure tools do. The same caveats apply, and whatever knowledge is embedded in such technologies is principally explicit. For instance, people use Web portals to organize and distribute information and to point to other resources where knowledge can be found. Such portals only *point to* tacit knowledge (e.g., people, organizational routines). Whatever knowledge they help organize and disseminate (e.g., via electronic documents, graphics, movies) is explicit (e.g., written down, delineated, spoken). Likewise, with search engines, people use them to find information in disorganized and distributed sources. Beyond the people who create and maintain the kinds of explicit resources that can be indexed and searched via this technology, there is no tacit knowledge involved.

Communication technologies such as e-mail, chat, video teleconferencing, telephone, and radio enable people to communicate in a distributed manner across time as well as space in some cases (e.g., asynchronous tools). Such technologies support conversations and interactions between people and can be used to convey information as well. Communication is important for knowledge flows, and one can argue that it is necessary, but it is not sufficient. Recall the example from Chapter II in which the message "333/33" is placed into context as a blood pressure reading. Even when the communication itself is flawless (e.g., no transmission errors, negligible latency, legible message, interpreted correctly by receiver), medical and physiological knowledge are required as well to enable appropriate action based upon such communication.

Figure 1. Knowledge life cycle (adapted from Nissen et al., 2000)

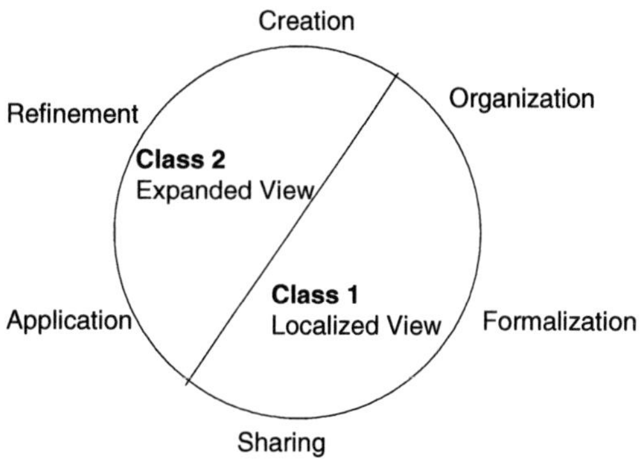

A KM program that includes technologies such as these may be able to improve flows of knowledge, but it cannot guarantee them. Alternatively, "technologies" such as face-to-face meetings, socialization, and mentoring often have no prominent place in KM programs today. Yet many experts identify interpersonal interaction as a central vehicle for learning and the flow of knowledge, particularly tacit knowledge.

Technology and Life Cycle Interaction

Relationships between diverse classes of information technologies and knowledge flows can be understood more systematically in terms of our 4D framework. In particular, the life cycle dimension can be used to divide technologies into two broad classes. First, look more closely at the various phases of the knowledge life cycle. We represent these phases as a cycle in Figure 1. As with life cycle models used commonly in the design of information systems and other complex systems — and as with our mutually inverted knowledge hierarchies — this dimension gives a sense of directionality to knowledge flows.

Drawing briefly from Nissen et al. (2000), the creation phase begins the life cycle, as new knowledge is generated within an enterprise; similar terms from other models include *capture* and *acquire*. The second phase pertains to the organization, mapping, or bundling of knowledge, often employing systems such as taxonomies, ontologies, and repositories. Phase 3 addresses mechanisms for making knowledge formal or explicit; similar terms from other models include *store* and *codify*. The fourth phase concerns the ability to share or distribute knowledge in the enterprise; this also includes terms such as *transfer* and *access*. Knowledge use and application for problem solving or decision making in the organization constitutes Phase 5. A sixth phase is included to cover knowledge refinement and evolution, which reflects organizational learning — and thus a return to knowledge creation — through time. It is important to note, as in the familiar life cycle models used in IT design (e.g., System Development Life Cycle), progression through the various phases of this life cycle model is generally iterative and involves feedback loops between stages. All steps need not be taken in order, and the flow through this life cycle is not necessarily unidirectional.

Notice in Figure 1 the three knowledge activities noted previously (i.e., organize, formalize, share) that are adjacent on the right-hand side of the cycle. These activities are supported relatively well by extant information technologies. They represent something of a localized view of knowledge management — hence, the grouping under the "Class 1" heading in the figure. We note such localized knowledge management systems are inherently supportive in nature. This class of implementations to organize, formalize, and share knowledge in the enterprise *supports* people who perform knowledge-flow and workflow process activities. The people in turn also apply, refine, and create knowledge in the organization. This represents a common theme that runs through all of the technology examples discussed previously.

Alternatively, notice the three activities that are adjacent on the left-hand side of the cycle. In contrast with their counterparts, these activities are supported quite poorly by extant information technologies. They represent an expanded view of knowledge management — hence, the grouping under the "Class 2" heading in the figure. We note such expanded knowledge management systems are inherently performative in nature. This class of implementations to apply, refine, and create knowledge in the enterprise *performs* (e.g., automates) knowledge management activities, either in conjunction with or in lieu of people in the organization.

Unlike the many supportive technology examples discussed thus far in the book, we have said almost nothing about counterpart technologies that perform process activities associated with knowledge creation, application, and refinement. The reason is simple: Very few technologies are performative in nature (cf. workflow systems, software agents, shopping bots, expert systems) and capable of doing so. Moreover, in this section, we focus principally on the most prevalent and prominent technologies used in KM today, making no claims that the discussion is exhaustive or complete. Such discussion is, alternatively, representative of contemporary KM practice. Even the few performative technologies that exist at this time are neither prevalent nor prominent in KM projects. We thus observe a relative abundance of technologies associated with the three supportive phases of the KM life cycle and a dearth associated with the three performative phases.

Expert Systems Technology

From the previous discussion, IT plays a supportive role in most KM programs. People play the performative role. This is largely because knowledge is required to perform knowledge work. Few information technologies address knowledge directly. In addition to some automation technologies such as word processing, workflow, and software agent applications, which perform certain activities associated with documents and information in the organization, the expert system represents another class of IT that offers performative capabilities. Although far from a "silver bullet" or cure-all for KM programs, the performative capability of expert systems makes them informative to examine in our present context. Many other applications based on artificial intelligence (AI) (e.g., software agents, case-based reasoning, intelligent tutoring, qualitative reasoning, Semantic Web) possess similar performative properties and can be considered together as a class with expert systems representing both exemplar and prototype of such class.

The term *expert system* was coined in the 1970s within the AI field. As implied by the name, this technology seeks to use computers to emulate the expertise of human experts. The process for developing expert systems relies upon someone, generally other than the expert, conducting interviews and observing expert behavior. This "knowledge engineer" then formalizes the basis of expertise in the computer via heuristic rules, frames, scripts, and other techniques for knowledge representation. Returning to our 4D framework, developing an expert system represents a knowledge-flow process, through which knowledge moves between two coordinates. It begins as tacit knowledge (i.e., in terms of *explicitness*) within an individual (i.e., in terms of *reach*) that is applied (i.e., in terms of *life cycle*). Through development of an expert system, it moves to explicit knowledge (e.g., heuristic rules of thumb), available

Figure 2. Knowledge-flow vectors for expert system development and use

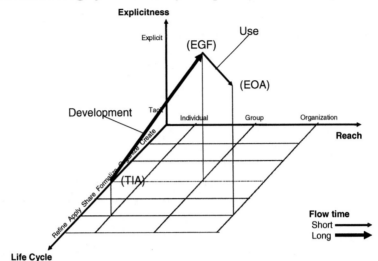

beyond the individual (e.g., group), through formalization (e.g., using predicate logic for representation).

Introducing coordinate shorthand to characterize such knowledge movement in terms of our framework, a flow vector can be viewed as extending from one coordinate point to another. In the case of expert system development, one can use the framework to visualize knowledge moving from one coordinate—at which knowledge is Tacit, at the Individual level, and Applied (TIA) — to another — at which knowledge becomes Explicit, at the Group level, and Formalized (EGF). These coordinate points and the corresponding vector are delineated in Figure 2 (associated with the knowledge-flow process labeled "Development"). We use a relatively thick arrow for such knowledge-flow vector because developing expert systems is often a time-consuming process; that is, the knowledge flow time associated with expert systems development is often quite long.

We also include a second knowledge-flow vector associated with expert systems in the figure. This second vector corresponds to *using* such technology once it has been developed. Notice this latter vector starts from where the former vector terminates (a precedence relation links expert systems development and use) and is delineated via a relatively thin arrow to depict comparatively short flow time. Notice also that the use vector extends Explicit knowledge out to the Organization level in terms of reach and back to Application in terms of life cycle (to coordinate EOA). This latter coordinate indicates that knowledge formalized via expert systems, once developed, can be distributed organization-wide for application. Moreover, experience over the past three decades indicates such application *often reflects the same level of performance* as demonstrated by the individual human experts.

Indeed, where knowledge can be formalized to support computer inference as such, expert systems have demonstrated many times that they are capable of matching, and in many cases exceeding, the performance of human experts. Hence, expert systems take on a performative role by employing (explicit) knowledge to enable direct action (e.g., making decisions, enacting communication behaviors, performing useful analytical work) in the organization. Notice this role is different from those played by most other classes of IT: performative vs. supportive. Further, once developed, expert systems can be distributed broadly across the organization and used simultaneously in massive parallel to address many different knowledge-work tasks and problems by *novices*. The ability to augment the capabilities of multiple novices and raise their performance to levels exhibited by experts represents a powerful contributor to competitive advantage. Contrast this with a single human expert who at any one time cannot generally work in more than a small number of organizations or on more than a few work tasks and problems.

This is the promise of AI. Unlike most technologies, expert systems address knowledge directly in addition to information and data. They offer an approach to formalizing tacit knowledge, distributing broadly the associated power for action, and applying it directly through the organization. None of the more prevalent and prominent technologies stated previously offer this capability. Alternatively, expert systems technology entails difficulty. Many people continue to view AI as over-hyped and unfulfilled even after several decades of active research and commercial work. As noted previously, expert systems development can be time-consuming and expensive. Many industrial expert system projects have failed to realize positive returns on investment. Not all experts are able or willing to articulate their expertise. Numerous application domains do not lend themselves well to formalization via expert system technology. Hence, we reiterate that expert systems technology is far from a "silver bullet" or cure-all for KM programs, but the performative capability of expert systems — and similar "intelligent" applications from the same class of technologies — makes them informative to examine in our present context.

"Expert" System Illustration

It is important to note that one need not be an expert to build or capitalize on the benefits of expert systems. Indeed, *any* knowledge (even novice-level) that a person possesses offers potential for formalization into an "expert" system. The key is that one must be able to articulate his or her knowledge in terms that can be applied directly by computer. Take, for example, designing an asynchronous (e.g., Web-based, interactive, online) course on knowledge management. What kinds of technologies should you consider to support such a course? Can such a course even be offered in asynchronous mode? If you are not an asynchronous instructional designer and have never developed an asynchronous course before, you would probably have to call in an expert to assist you. Or you may simply elect to develop the course through a process of trial and error. But what if all of the available experts were busy, and you could not afford the time and expense associated with trial and error? Perhaps you could consult a relatively simple expert system to point you in the right direction.

Take, as a different example, something from your own professional work that you know how to do better than anyone else. It does not have to be glamorous or sophisticated: just something that no one but you knows how to do well. Say that you wanted to share your expertise. Suppose your supervisor indicates you will not be eligible for promotion or transfer until someone else can do your job as well as you can. You could spend time mentoring one or more possible personnel replacements to help them learn what you do. You could spend time developing and teaching a training course to help them learn what you do. You could gloat — and wait — as others struggle through trial and error to learn what you do. You could do many different things to help others learn what you do. You — even you — could also develop an expert system and use it to distribute your unique work knowledge in a manner that others — who are not as good as you — can use to perform your job as well as you can.

How could you codify and distribute your own knowledge using an expert system? Shell tools such as KnowledgeWright (2004) enable you to serve as your own expert. Even if you do not know a lot about some particular problem area or knowledge domain — and you know nearly nothing about knowledge engineering — you may be able to use expert systems technology to formalize and distribute much of what you know. By interacting with such a shell tool, you can work to articulate your own knowledge and to formalize it via a rule-based expert system, for instance. If you are successful, you could then employ the

Figure 3. Rules for simple expert system

```
rule_set(access, /, [
    description = "",
    type = single_value,
    rules = [[conditions, value], [student_access = "modem", text("low bandwidth")], [student_access = "DSL
or cable", text("high bandwidth")], [student_access = "T1+", text("high bandwidth")], [student_access =
"other", text("low bandwidth")], [student_access = "none", text("no bandwidth")]]
    ]).

rule_set(technology, /, [
    description = "",
    type = single_value,
    rules = [[conditions, value], [feasible = "feasible" and access = "low bandwidth", text("use minimal
graphics & interaction via technology")], [feasible = "feasible" and access = "high bandwidth", text("use full
graphics & interaction via technology")], [default, text("current technology does not appear to support your
plan")]]
    ]).
```

resulting expert system to make decisions and solve problems — automatically and in your absence — that formerly required your personal tacit knowledge and involvement. Plus, many copies of such expert system could be distributed to make decisions and solve problems — again, automatically and in your absence — by people who lack your level of expertise in the area of interest.

As an illustration, we developed a small and simple expert system to help instructors design asynchronous courses. We say "small and simple" because such system attempts to address only one specific aspect of asynchronous instructional design: content delivery mode. Of the myriad design aspects that should be considered when developing an asynchronous course, our tiny expert system focuses on only this one very specific consideration. Also, this system does not necessarily represent the knowledge of an *expert*. A "reasonably knowledgeable professional" represents a more-suitable label. Moreover, this system was developed only for illustration and to help elucidate how an expert system works. Hence, it lacks both the power and sophistication of a system developed for "industrial strength" application. Nonetheless, the principles of system development and use are roughly the same. More powerful, production-grade expert systems generally reflect only larger scales, not different approaches and techniques.

Figure 3 presents two of the rules used for inference in this simple expert system. They are reproduced directly from the shell application used to develop the systems. Hence, their format may appear a bit odd to the reader who is unfamiliar with computer code. Alternatively, the Structured English representation should make the rules intelligible. Briefly, the first rule (labeled "rule_set(access,/,[") pertains to the kind of computer and network access that may be available to potential students who are interested in taking an asynchronous course. The knowledge embedded within this rule begins on the fourth line (labeled "rules = [[conditions, value], …") and illustrates some considerations this expert system will include in its reasoning. For instance, the "condition" (i.e., possible state of the world) examined by this rule is "student access." One possible state of the world included in the rule is "modem"; that is, the rule is considering what to do if a potential student will be accessing an asynchronous course via modem. This represents the "IF" part of this first IF-THEN rule.

The first "value" (i.e., conclusion based on the condition) in this rule is "low bandwidth." This is a label the system is associating with access via modem. Such association will be used in conjunction with different conditions and values embedded in other rules. The other condition = value pairs considered within this rule include: "DSL or cable" = "high bandwidth"; "T1+" = "high bandwidth"; "other" = "low bandwidth"; and "none" = "no bandwidth." Hence, this rule considers technologies ranging from no network access through low-bandwidth access to high-speed Internet access via digital subscriber lines, cable modems, and T1 connections. All of the conditions, values, technologies, and associations reflected by such rules represent the domain knowledge of a professional who is experienced with asynchronous instructional design. This professional's knowledge is made explicit through formalization into rules and encoded in an expert system.

In short, based on the manner in which a knowledgeable, professional (human), asynchronous instructional designer would reason about how to deliver course content to distributed students (who cannot participate in face-to-face classroom sessions), this first rule considers several possible states of the world pertaining to network access (e.g., modem, DSL, cable), and it associates connectivity inferences (e.g., high bandwidth, low bandwidth) to the various states. Other rules in this simple expert system are similar, but they consider different conditions and associations gleaned from the (human) instructional design professional. Examples include equipment needs, cost-effectiveness, student demographics, and similar considerations (not shown).

The second rule shown in Figure 3 represents knowledge used to recommend the approach to and technology for delivery of course content. This rule uses the associations made by other rules as the basis of its conclusions. For instance, as previously, knowledge embedded within this rule begins on its fourth line (labeled "rules = [[conditions, value], …"). Notice the conditions (again, possible states of the world) include labels such as "access," which is considered by the rule mentioned earlier. Specifically, one condition = value pair in this latter rule relates directly to the former rule: "access" = "low bandwidth." This means that our second rule is using the output of our first rule as input. If the first rule were to conclude "access = low bandwidth," for instance, then the expert system would consider such *conclusion from Rule 1* as input to make an *additional conclusion in Rule 2*. Hence, one rule can leverage the inference of another and produce relatively complex and sophisticated chains of reasoning. Such leveraging is termed *chaining* together various rules for inference.

The other condition considered by this latter rule pertains to feasibility. Values associated with both conditions *feasibility* and *access* are used by the system in this rule to recommend technology approaches. For instance, the first recommendation within this rule can be interpreted as: IF the project appears "feasible," AND access is limited to "low bandwidth," THEN the recommended design approach and content delivery mode is "use minimal graphics & interaction via technology." In other words, the system recognizes that potential students in this condition have or can obtain network access but that such access is via low-speed connections. Hence, the recommendation encourages the course designer to minimize the use of graphics and interaction technologies. Both require much greater bandwidth than text does, and both cause delays for low-bandwidth users.

Because an expert system can *perform* activities such as decision making (e.g., selecting course delivery technologies) and problem solving (e.g., designing asynchronous course content for students with low-bandwidth connections) that require knowledge, the system itself can be said to address knowledge, not just information. Notice this differs from sending information to a knowledgeable person (e.g., professional instructional designer) and expecting him or her to use such information for some decision making or problem solving. By sending an expert system, *even an unknowledgeable person* can make such decisions or solve such problems. In the case of asynchronous course design, at one time, such unknowledgeable persons included the author of this book!

Simulation Technology

Simulation technology is not new. People have been conducting Gedanken (i.e., thought) simulations for possibly as long as our species has existed.

Indeed, the ability to contemplate one or more alternate actions — *before* selecting and committing to any particular one — and then pursue the one that appears to suit one's situation best probably represents humans' most powerful competitive advantage over other animals. Beyond such thought experiments, people have also engaged in iconic simulations for many millennia. For instance, using small symbols or pieces to represent Army, Navy, and other battlefield forces — before committing such forces to battle — has been an instrumental part of warfare since the ancient Chinese began writing about it thousands of years ago. Architects that develop multiple alternate perspectives of different building designs can be viewed as helping clients to visualize alternate possibilities for an edifice of interest — before committing to one particular design — hence, engaging in a type of simulation. The key is that some kind of simulation is conducted using representations of the real world—in advance of committing to decisions affecting outcomes in the real world.

Today, of course, simulations can be conducted by computer in addition to the use of thought, icons, drawings, and similar approaches. This enables a great many different elements and relations to be modeled (e.g., many more than can be accommodated by the minds of most people) via computer. Hence, computer simulations can be more complex than those enabled by other approaches. For instance, a battlefield simulation can represent the positions, movements, and interactions between millions of people, weapons, and related equipment for warfare. Computer simulations can also be conducted very quickly, often on timescales many thousands or millions of times faster than the phenomena of interest in the real world. For instance, in the time it would take for a large office building to be designed and constructed, many millions of simulations could take place. Simulations are used routinely in the organizational context to facilitate decision making (see Law & Kelton 1982; Turban & Aronson, 1998). Such simulations are conducted generally to support workflows (e.g., associated with waging war, designing buildings, business operations), hence, are associated most closely with doing.

Alternatively, the same technology can also be used to support knowledge flows, hence, can be associated more closely with learning. This represents the central idea of *microworlds* (Senge, 1990): simulations that are undertaken for the purpose of *learning* about certain systems and processes of interest in the world. One key is to simulate the real world with sufficient fidelity that decisions and actions within the simulation produce the same kinds of results and consequences that would be expected in the real world. Another key is to abstract from the details and complexities of the real world and to concentrate on the most important elements and relations. Clearly, a tension exists between fidelity and abstraction in simulation models. Moreover, through simulation, a person can learn by trial and error but not suffer the consequences of making real mistakes. For instance, it has long been standard procedure for pilots to have a portion of their training conducted using flight simulators. When pilots train to manage particularly dangerous or unlikely circumstances (e.g., severe weather, catastrophic equipment malfunctions, unintended uses for aircraft), they generally do so via simulation. Should a pilot "crash" because of a mistake during a simulation, for example, he or she can learn from such mistake, reset the simulator, and try again, as many times as it takes to master the intended piloting skills or maneuvers. When flying aircraft in the real world, by contrast, one generally has but one "opportunity" to crash, hence, zero opportunity to learn from the corresponding mistakes. In many circumstances including nuclear accidents, terrorist strikes, and epidemic infections, simulation represents the only practical approach to training for such disasters.

Returning to the point about trial and error, this approach to learning is often referred to pejoratively. But trial and error is quite natural for people (e.g., consider how an infant learns most concepts and cause-effect relationships). Without more advanced approaches (e.g., leveraging theory and decision-making tools) at hand, there may be few alternatives. The key to simulation is that one person can repeat the same event many times (altering his or her approach each time and observing the results) in a relatively short period of time (e.g., hundreds or thousands of repetitions of an event can be simulated within the time required for one unfolding of the real-world event). Each repetition represents a learning opportunity. Hence, a person may be able to learn quite quickly via simulation. This is why we include simulation technology here in a book on harnessing knowledge power: It can support learning activities and enhance knowledge flows.

Indeed, recent research includes the use of simulation technology to represent and emulate the performance of organizations that take alternate approaches to enhancing knowledge flows. Hence, this approach uses a technology to enhance knowledge flows (i.e., simulation) to help people learn how to enhance knowledge flows. Consider this illustration (Figure 4) described by Nissen and Levitt (2004) using simulation technology associated with the Virtual Design Team (VDT) research project (VDT, 2004). Using a relatively simple work process for exposition, an overview of a correspondingly simple VDT model for IS design is illustrated through the screenshot presented in Figure 4.

Figure 4. VDT IS design model (adapted from Nissen & Levitt, 2004)

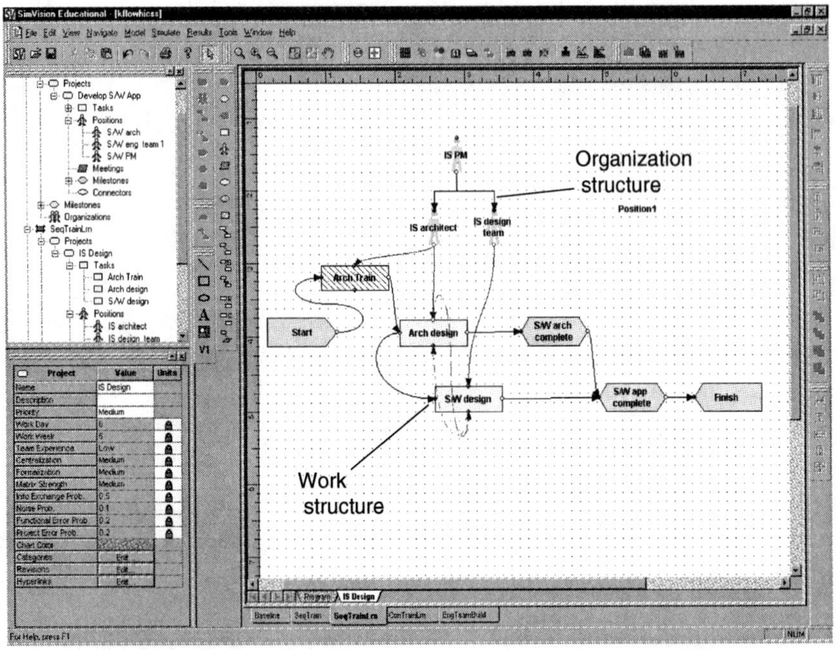

The organization structure is comprised of three elements: (1) a knowledge worker (person icon at the top of the diagram labeled "IS architect") with skills in IS architecture development; (2) a team of software designers (person icon at the top of the diagram labeled "IS design team") with skills in software analysis, design, and programming; and (3) a project lead (person icon at the top of the diagram labeled "IS PM") with skills in project planning, supervision, and IS design. The task structure is comprised of two work elements: (1) architecture design (rectangular icon in the middle of the diagram labeled "arch design") and (2) software design (rectangular icon in the middle of the diagram labeled "S/W design"). The four milestones shown (project start, architecture complete, application complete, project finish) serve as markers of progress against schedule but do not involve work. The diagram in this figure illustrates, for a small and simple project, how models developed in the VDT environment may appear. Of course, the diagram itself is clearly static, but by linking to a simulation engine, the extended representation becomes dynamic: time-varying states, conditions, and results can be projected for the model. We note here for reference that very large and complex models can and have been developed to capture the scale, richness, and detail of numerous diverse organizations in practice (see Kunz et al., 1998). The model discussed here, by contrast, is small, simple, and for illustration only.

Now consider the software design work task from the VDT model. Say that a new technology for developing software architectures is to be used on this project. The problem is that none of the people who will be designing the software architecture is familiar with this new technology. Should management send its software architect to a (formal training) class to learn how to use the new technology, or should it expect this key actor to learn such technology on the job (OJT) while working on the architecture? Drawing from the previous discussion, the formal training alternative would contribute principally (if not exclusively) toward knowledge flows and minimally (if at all) toward workflows while the IS-architect actor was away participating in the training course. Alternatively, the OJT approach would contribute symmetrically (principally toward doing and minimally toward learning).

Notice the inclusion in Figure 4 of a specific task for this knowledge-flow activity (labeled "arch train"). Say the IS architecture actor would require three months of formal training to learn how to use this new tool. Assume further that any formal training would start at project inception and have to be completed before the IS architecture task could begin. In the case of a formal training course, the IS-architect actor would participate in the course first and then begin work on the architecture itself. In the case of OJT, the IS-architect actor would skip such training and begin working (learning by doing) immediately. Which represents a better approach?

Intuitively, if the IS-architect actor participates in a three-month formal training course, then one would expect the entire schedule for the IS design project to simply extend by a period close to this three-month time span. Alternatively, an experienced leader or manager would also expect the IS-architect actor to learn valuable knowledge that enables better work performance following the formal training course. Clearly, this situation represents a tradeoff that confronts nearly every leader or manager who must balance knowledge flows and workflows in an organization. After verifying model fidelity and simulating both cases 100 times each, the project duration in the former case (attending the three-month formal training course) turns out to be considerably less than that of the latter (OJT) approach. The explanation is consistent with our experience. After completing the training course, the IS-architect actor brings an increase in skill level to bear on the workflow and performs substantially better on the architecture task than its OJT counterpart. Further, such performance gain is sufficient to overcome the three-month delay in starting the project while the architect actor is away at school. Simulation of this actor's learning and doing reflects the higher skill level associated with learning from the training class and quantifies the corresponding schedule effect.

We then return to the VDT model, change some factors (e.g., actors' skill levels, course length and difficulty, project requirements), and run it repeatedly until we *learn some general relations* pertaining to the organization modeled and simulated. We learn that other conditions could exist in which formal training would represent an inferior alternative, for instance, if the training course requires six months to complete instead of three; if the IS-architect actor lacks sufficient background knowledge to effectively learn through the course; if the new architecture-development tool is similar to the existing technology it replaces; if the architecture-development part of the project is relatively short and minor with respect to the other project tasks; and so forth. The key point is that through running and experimenting multiple times with the simulation model — a virtual trial-and-error approach to learning — we identify several cause-effect relations associated with this system of interest in the real world. We also stimulate knowledge flows pertaining to how a leader or manager can enhance knowledge flows associated with IS architecture development in the project. Such learning would be difficult to accomplish through trial and error and certainly could not be completed as quickly in the real world as in simulation.

Further, such learning is accomplished *before having to commit time and money* toward a decision (i.e., to send the IS-architect to formal training class or to endure the effects of OJT with the new system). This learning is accomplished also *without having to bear the consequences* of some faulty decisions made while learning about the organization. For instance, we can learn — in a virtual world — that OJT represents an inferior alternative without having to endure the schedule penalty resulting from a decision — in the physical world — to go with such OJT alternative.

This technology enables us to *repeat the simulation* many hundreds of times, all well within the time associated with either the training course or software project in the real world. Such learning bears directly upon our knowledge flows at several phases of the knowledge life cycle. For one, we are using simulation to *create* new tacit knowledge pertaining to the organization and its dynamics. For another, we can also use simulation to *share* such knowledge by distributing copies of the simulation model to enhance the learning of others. For a third, we are further using simulation to *apply* such knowledge to decisions regarding whether to send the IS-architects to the formal training course.

Knowledge Technology Principles

Five principles developed in this chapter help shed light on knowledge technology: (1) information technology is helpful and necessary but not sufficient for knowledge management; (2) people — not information technology — are central to tacit knowledge flows; (3) information technology plays supportive roles in organizational work routines, whereas people play the performative roles; (4) expert systems, software agents, and similar "intelligent" applications address and apply knowledge directly; and (5) simulation technology can enhance knowledge flows across several phases of the life cycle.

Principle 16. We noted how IT plays an important role in supporting knowledge flows. In many cases, IT is even necessary for knowledge to flow, but there is more to flows of knowledge than processing and flowing information, which is the principal domain of IT. **Hence, the manager needs to employ non-technological interventions to enhance knowledge flows**.

Principle 17. We noted previously how problems abound in terms of KM programs that rely heavily upon IT. Many leaders and managers expect naively that IT will improve knowledge flows. Looking at the "I" in IT, however, and understanding the distinctions and relationships between knowledge and information, it should be apparent why such expectations can be considered naive. In particular, people — not information technology — are central to tacit knowledge flows. **Hence, one cannot manage tacit knowledge without managing people**.

Principle 18. The life cycle involves different kinds of knowledge activities, grouped broadly into classes to represent localized and expanded views of KM. We noted previously how IT supports activities in these two classes differently. For the localized activities, IT plays a supportive role well. For the expanded activities, however, a performative role is called for, but few extant IT applications are capable of — or used for — playing such a role. **Hence, most IT plays a supportive role in the organization, whereas people play most of the performative roles**.

Principle 19. Expert systems, software agents, and similar "intelligent" applications address knowledge directly in addition to information and data. They also enable direct action, hence, can play some of the performative roles called for previously. Specifically, once developed, an expert system can apply knowledge directly to perform knowledge work. Expert systems can also be distributed broadly through the organization and used in parallel, even by novices who can sometimes raise their performance to expert levels. **Hence, "intelligent" applications can play a performative role in the organization**.

Principle 20. We noted previously how simulation technology can be used to enhance knowledge flows in addition to workflows. By using simulation models to learn about some systems or processes of interest in the real world, one can create new knowledge relatively quickly and safely. Knowledge associated with a simulation model can also be shared and applied, corresponding with multiple phases of the knowledge life cycle. **Hence, simulation represents a different class of IT, one that facilitates learning as well as doing through virtual practice**.

Exercises

1. Identify the two kinds of IT that you use most often in your current professional occupation or student activities. Briefly describe how each supports knowledge flows and how each supports information flows. What is the primary distinction between the support of knowledge flows vs. information flows?

2. Identify two performative roles that you play in your current professional occupation or student activities and two supportive roles that you play. Describe the impact each role has in terms of how well IT supports your performance.

3. Describe how simulation technology could play a supportive role in your current professional occupation or student activities and how it could play a performative role.

4. Develop a small expert system that codifies your knowledge of this learning module (knowledge technology). Download and use an expert system shell tool (e.g., KnowledgeWright) to articulate and formalize a relatively small number (e.g., 25 to 50) of rules into a computer application that could be used by someone without your level of expertise about

knowledge technology to make decisions or to solve problems that would otherwise be difficult for such person to accomplish. Feel free to incorporate aspects of the decision-making and problem-solving context of your professional organization into the expert system if that proves helpful to you. Or, instead, develop the system in a context-free manner comparable to that of this learning module.

Chapter V

Knowing and Learning

This chapter discusses the concept *knowing*, which involves knowledge in action, and *learning*, which involves knowledge in motion. We look first at knowing and learning in the organization and then examine the tension between learning and doing. The discussion then turns to dynamic interaction between knowledge-enabled action and potential. The chapter concludes with five knowing and learning principles and includes exercises to stimulate critical thought, learning, and discussion.

Knowing and Learning

Knowing and learning are tightly interrelated knowledge-based activities. They are connected strongly by the knowledge-based activity *doing*. We introduce each concept separately but weave together many of their dynamic interrelations.

Knowing

Knowing refers to knowledge in action. This term is used often to differentiate knowledge-based action from the knowledge that enables it. Such differentiation is referred to as epistemology of practice vs. epistemology of possession (Cook & Brown, 1999). The former manifests through what is done. Pragmatism (e.g., as articulated by Dewy) provides a philosophical basis for understanding epistemology of practice. Tacit knowledge practiced in group settings is privileged often in this former view. The latter manifests through what is known. Cartesianism (e.g., as articulated by Descartes) provides a philosophical basis for understanding epistemology of possession. Explicit knowledge possessed by individuals is privileged often in the latter view. Both views can obtain simultaneously and complementarily.

The classic example involves riding a bicycle (Polanyi, 1967). Through the action of riding a bicycle, a person demonstrates knowing how to do so. The knowledge associated with such riding can be tacit as well as explicit. For instance, an effective bicycle rider will certainly be able to balance on two wheels while moving and to turn by leaning into corners. However, if one asks such a rider in which direction he or she turns the handlebars when falling off balance, it is unlikely that the rider will be able to answer the question (see Cook & Brown, 1999, p. 384). Alternatively, if one asks such a rider in which direction he or she leans when turning through a corner, it is very likely that such rider will be able to answer the question.

In the former case of turning the handlebars, a rider is able to employ such knowledge effectively but unable to articulate it (the knowledge remains tacit). The rider knows how to balance but cannot explain the process to others. This phenomenon is common across a diversity of knowledge-based activities. It characterizes well the nature of tacit knowledge. In the latter case of leaning into a corner, the rider is able to both employ and articulate the enabling knowledge (the knowledge is made explicit). The rider knows how to turn and can explain the process (at least in part) to others. This phenomenon is also common across a diversity of knowledge-based activities. It characterizes well the nature of explicit knowledge.

In both cases, the rider is able to demonstrate knowing how to ride a bicycle, and the rider has knowledge of how to ride bicycles. In other words, when a person rides a bicycle, he or she knows how to do so. Such person retains knowledge of how to ride even when not riding actively. Thus, knowing and knowledge can both obtain simultaneously. Yet they are different: one involves manifest action, whereas the other involves potential for action. Knowing and knowledge are also complementary: the action of knowing cannot obtain without the enabling knowledge; and the enabling knowledge cannot be put to use except through the action of knowing.

Additionally, this simultaneous and complementary relationship between knowing and knowledge is dynamic and can be mutually reinforcing. Continuing with the bicycle example, a beginner may find it productive to read a book or like artifact of explicit knowledge about how to ride bicycles. Here theoretical knowledge about riding can reinforce practical knowing through riding. Many similar knowing activities (e.g., flying an airplane, solving differential equations, playing a musical instrument) involve theory as well as practice. Established theory can often be learned through interaction with explicit knowledge sources such as books. In contrast, practice involves experience in the real world. Nonetheless, books about the real world can serve to inform practice, and practice in the world can serve as the basis for writing books. Hence, theoretical knowledge about how to ride can facilitate knowing through riding. Yet the person still needs practice — hence, to experience direct interaction with a bicycle in the world — in order to know riding. Likewise, a proficient rider may be able to experiment while riding — for instance, leaning purposefully in a particular direction and noting in which direction he or she turns the handlebars to maintain balance — and make explicit some knowledge that formerly remained tacit.

Recall our previous discussion of simulation technology. Notice that interacting virtually falls somewhere in between these two cases of theoretical knowledge and practical knowing. Theoretical knowledge (e.g., dynamics and control laws for bicycles) is required to develop a simulator. Even a beginner can learn knowledge about how to ride bicycles through such theory. Likewise, practical knowing (e.g., leaning one's body) can be learned through interaction with a simulator. A person can engage — virtually in a simulated world — in actions that are very similar to those associated with physically riding a bicycle in the real world. Further, through interaction with a simulator, a person can practice riding without encountering the mortal hazards (e.g., maneuvering through automobile traffic) and physical restrictions (e.g., adverse weather) of physically riding. However, even the best simulators are nothing more than sophisticated dynamic models of reality. Using a simulator is never exactly the same as practicing in the real world.

These relationships between knowing and knowledge (e.g., simultaneous and complementary interrelations, mutually reinforcing effects) are not limited to physical activities such as riding bicycles. For instance, they pertain as well to decision making, speaking in front of people, solving calculus problems, and others. Nor are they limited to individuals. For instance, they pertain as well to groups, organizations, and whole societies knowing how to do something and possessing knowledge of how to do it.

An organizational example of this phenomenon pertains to management. Nearly every organization requires management (e.g., of people, assets, projects) activities and has people assigned to managerial roles. Different people clearly vary in their management efficacy, but most people would argue that practical experience (knowing) represents a critical element of being a proficient manager. Likewise, nearly every university offers courses, certificates, and degree programs in management and has students learning about managerial activities. Different students clearly vary in their scholastic efficacy, but most people would argue that knowledge learned (e.g., through study) represents a critical element of graduating from a management program.

Further to the point, many people consider education in management (knowledge) to enhance a person's managerial efficacy (knowing). This accounts in part for the reason that many MBAs, for instance, are able to obtain management positions in organizations, even when they have no prior managerial experience. Alternatively, prior experience often represents a necessary prerequisite for someone without management education to obtain such employment. This accounts in part for the reason that many organizations encourage their managers to pursue management courses, certificates, and degrees.

Hence, there appears to be widespread belief that management education is helpful to managerial practice. If this was not the case, then so many management education programs would be unlikely to persist through time. Experience is believed to enhance management education, too. Indeed, many of the better graduate management education programs prefer to admit students who have acquired several years of work experience, with managerial experience considered even more of a plus. Thus, management knowledge acquired through education appears to enhance managerial knowing, and managerial knowing associated with experience appears to enhance management education.

Doing

Doing refers to knowledge-based work. People must know how to do what they do. Hence, doing represents one kind of knowing activity. The differentiation between knowing and knowledge can be viewed in terms of a knowing-doing gap (Pfeffer & Sutton, 1999). A knowing-doing gap manifests itself in part when organizations "know better" than to do what they do. For instance, an organization with expertise and experience in a certain line of work may repeat past mistakes (e.g., marketing, engineering, manufacturing), even though knowledge of such mistakes — and conceivably how to prevent them — may be possessed by the organization. Such possession could be in terms of management knowledge learned by one or more managers through MBA degree programs (e.g., organizational mistakes that are common across enterprises), direct experience by managers with past mistakes and their corresponding solutions, formal documentation of past mistakes and solutions stored in a lessons learned archive, and others. By any account, such knowledge is possessed by the organization, but it is not put to use.

Organizational memory (Stein & Zwass 1995; Walsh & Ungson, 1991) appears to play an important role in explaining gaps like these. Where an organization learns from education or experience, for example, it relies upon storage, access, and recall processes to preserve, locate, and retrieve the knowledge associated with its experience. Many organizations do not know what they know (e.g., knowledge of employees with MBA degrees). Hence, managers with problems do not bother to ask managers with solutions before repeating past mistakes. Similarly, many organizations fail to make applicable lessons learned reports easy to locate and interpret. This is despite enforcement of formal procedures for writing and filing them. Also, as with riding a bicycle, reading an explicit document about how to avoid repeating a past mistake may not be sufficient for avoiding such mistake in practice.

A knowing-doing gap also manifests itself in part when organizations "know how" to do something they do not do. For instance, one particular unit of an organization may have demonstrated superior performance pertaining to some important work process, product, or service, even though other seemingly identical organizational units remain unable to replicate its high-performance knowing. Such replication could be approached through personnel changes (e.g., assigning people from the high-performance organization to the average ones), organizational routines (e.g., writing work procedures for the average organizations that describe the processes performed by the high-performance one), hiring expertise through external consultants, and like approaches practiced widely under the rubric *knowledge transfer*. Clearly, the relevant knowledge needs to flow from one coordinate (e.g., individual person, organizational unit, work location, application time) to another, and such knowledge must be put to use. Hence, a knowing-doing gap can stem from problems with knowledge flows as well as memory aids.

Knowing further relates to the appropriability of knowledge. Recall our previous discussion, in which we contrast knowledge and information in terms of enabling competitive advantage. Knowledge — particularly tacit knowledge

— is difficult to imitate, hence, can be used as a sustainable basis of competitive advantage. In contrast, information represents a public good that is difficult to keep private over time. Such contrast has to do with the *kind* of knowledge (e.g., tacit, explicit) and its appropriability. Alternatively, knowing has to do with the *use* of knowledge — regardless of kind — and its appropriability. Both explicit knowledge about riding bicycles and tacit knowledge about balancing, for instance, can help enable knowing through riding. Likewise, both explicit knowledge acquired via management education and tacit knowledge derived from managerial experience, as another instance, can help enhance knowing through managing. The key is that where knowledge remains latent in stocks (e.g., as knowledge inventory; consider explicit and tacit knowledge possessed but not put to use), it offers *potential* for action (Dierickx & Cool, 1989). But where knowledge manifests through dynamic action (knowing), the associated action drives performance (Saviotti, 1998). Although latent knowledge stocked in an organization has value, such knowledge also entails an investment in its acquisition and storage (e.g., to create, organize, share). Until an organization can put such knowledge to use, it cannot expect to generate positive returns from its knowledge investment. Hence, appropriability depends upon the use of knowledge (knowing) as well as the type of knowledge (e.g., tacit, explicit) acquired and possessed.

For instance, consider a musician specializing in the piano. Learning to play a musical instrument such as this requires an investment of many years or possibly even decades of time, energy, and money into lessons, equipment, and practice, in addition to some natural musical ability. Such investment increases a musician's knowledge inventory and enables increasingly better action in terms of playing the piano. The investment increases a musician's potential to play well. Without action, however, no amount of piano knowledge left stocked as such can generate a return on the musician's investment in piano practice. Even the best piano player in the world is unlikely to earn a living based upon piano-playing knowledge unless he or she performs for or instructs others (puts knowledge to use through action). Likewise, the organization that invests in knowledge but fails to put it to use will encounter comparable difficulty "earning a living" (e.g., realizing a pecuniary return on its investment). Learning and increasing stocks of knowledge inventory are valuable and necessary to enable productive work in an organization, but performing the associated work processes is what generates returns on organizational investments in knowledge.

Knowing can take place at many levels of analysis, from the individual to groups of organizations. Individual knowing is probably the simplest to understand because we all do it everyday. Indeed, the reader of this text is already knowing how to read and understanding new intellectual material. Riding bicycles, playing chess, solving analytical problems, negotiating contracts, searching for information, and many other individual activities require knowledge for action, hence, constitute knowing when such knowledge is put to use. Organizational routines such as establishing policies, developing products, training personnel, competing in markets, influencing political-legal-economic environments, attracting capital, and many others likewise require knowledge, hence, constitute knowing as well—when put to use—but at a higher level of social aggregation.

Of course, no practical organization can function without the individuals and groups of people in it. Yet there is more to what organizations do than can be accounted for by the activities of its individuals and groups at any point in time. For instance, most organizations continue to function effectively even if one individual calls in sick for a day. The same cannot be said generally about the sick individual. As another instance, organizational routines involving many different people can effect useful actions (e.g., product innovation) even when none of the individual participants knows all of the activities of the routine. Organizational routines can also continue long after all of the original individuals have been replaced by other people. This point regarding level of social aggregation is important. Knowing can reach well beyond the knowledge and actions of individuals in an organizational context. Indeed, the power of knowledge put to use for action is said to "amplify" (Nonaka, 1994, p. 20) through increases in organizational reach.

For instance, consider a skilled soccer player who stands out as a star on the team and is possibly even an all-star in whatever league the team associates with. Soccer is a sport that requires considerable investment in knowledge about scoring tactics, physical conditioning, ball-handling techniques, and other topics, in addition to some natural athleticism. As with the musician example also noted previously, such learning and investment increases an athlete's knowledge inventory and enables increasingly better action in terms of playing soccer. The investment increases an athlete's potential to play well. As with the musician example, without action, no amount of soccer knowledge left stocked as inventory can generate a return on the athlete's investment in soccer learning.

Additionally, soccer is a team sport. Clearly a skillful individual player is likely to perform well—by putting knowledge to use through knowing—in most soccer games, but depending on the skill levels of the various other players, the superior knowledge and knowing of an individual star may or may not be sufficient for *the team* to play well. A musical analog to this would follow where an individual pianist (e.g., even a virtuoso) plays as part of a (perhaps mediocre) jazz band or symphony orchestra.

Now consider if every player on the soccer team has superior skill at the level of this star. Such a team is likely to play well — again, by putting knowledge to use through knowing — and accomplish more than could be done through a single player. For instance, passing the ball between different players clearly represents a critical part of soccer. No single player is likely to take the ball in an unassisted manner (e.g., without passing) past all players on an opposing team. Likewise, with a band or orchestra, an ensemble of skilled musicians is likely to play well — through knowing — and accomplish more than could be done by a single player (e.g., playing many instruments simultaneously). One can see by example how both musical and soccer knowledge that reaches beyond the individual can amplify performance through skillful knowing of multiple players.

Nonetheless, our discussion thus far has ignored that a key aspect of organizational performance involves coordination of diverse individuals' knowledge and performance. Even replicating individual knowledge and knowing through multiple players may be insufficient to amplify performance across broader reaches of social aggregation. People as individuals in groups, teams, and organizations must know who is responsible for which activities at what times, for example, which involves knowledge beyond their individual skills. However, people also need to know how to work with one another and how to coordinate their mutual actions for organizational performance, sometimes even suboptimizing or sacrificing their individual performance in the process. Indeed, assisting others with the performance of their activities represents a critical part of soccer. Most goals on winning teams are scored via "assists" (e.g., passing to the center) from teammates. Likewise, with jazz bands and other collections of musical performers, many members take turns soloing and playing rhythms, thereby enriching the combined performance. Examples from manufacturing organizations pertain as well. Few engineers are able to mass-produce the devices they design, for instance, and few machine operators are able to design the devices they mass-produce.

Here a noticeable difference between music and soccer (and manufacturing) becomes apparent. Soccer is a competitive sport, in which performance depends upon how well one team competes against another. Hence, an additional element of knowing beyond the individual — and even coordinated group action — is notably critical: how to play against others. Similar examples of organizational knowing in a competitive or adversarial manner arise in business, war, politics, and like domains. They take on a game-theoretic aspect of analysis.

A business firm, for instance, must know more than designing and mass-producing quality devices. To compete effectively in business, the firm also needs to develop products that meet consumer demands (e.g., in terms of product features, quality, price) *better than its rival firms do*. A military unit, as a similar instance, must know more than operating weapons and coordinating forces. To compete effectively in war, it also needs to battle (e.g., in terms of attacks, defenses, logistics) *better than its rival armies do*. Political knowing in terms of organizing, fundraising, and communicating follows accordingly. Such knowing must be accomplished better by one politician than by rivals in an election or on an issue. In other words, one must consider the knowing by all competitors, and relative performance considerations pertain as much as or more than absolute ones do.

Indeed, any seasoned coach can tell stories about individual, star athletes not knowing how to play well against others on an opposing team, and many teams comprised of star, individual players have failed to win games, even against teams comprised of "inferior" individuals. Experienced leaders and managers have similar stories about knowledge put into action (knowing) at the team level (e.g., innovation projects, territorial battles, political campaigns). This same principle applies organization-wide as well, with even greater opportunities for knowledge-based performance to be amplified.

Learning

Learning refers to knowledge in motion. It is used most often to characterize the creation or acquisition of new knowledge, but the movement of knowledge (flows) between coordinates (e.g., people, organizations, places, time) need not be "new" (we use quotation marks here because the question of whether any knowledge can ever be new remains a topic of epistemological debate) to the entire world (e.g., knowledge developed through scientific discovery). Rather, such knowledge needs only be new in the context of its coordinates (e.g., to an individual or organizational acquirer at a particular point in space or time).

Classroom instruction represents a clear example at both the individual and group levels. In the majority of circumstances, an instructor already knows the subject matter of a course, but a student acquires "new" knowledge through learning. Such a student may, for instance, learn about a particular class of design mistakes that are common across many enterprises. In this case, knowledge moves from one coordinate (e.g., instructor, university, classroom, class time) to another (e.g., *student*, university, classroom, class time). The knowledge flow corresponds to learning at the individual level.

Moreover, this same knowledge can flow to groups of students (e.g., in class after class) over time. Say a large number of former students learn over time to recognize this particular and common class of design mistakes. As these students graduate and become employees of firms that engage in design processes, design groups in many such firms can learn — through the former students — how to address such mistakes. In this case, knowledge moves from one coordinate (e.g., instructor, university, classroom, *many class times*) to *several* others (e.g., *many students*, *many enterprises*, *many design processes*, *many product-development projects*). The knowledge flow corresponds to learning at both the individual and group levels.

Like knowing, learning is action oriented. A student may know how to learn course material through study, for instance, but that student is unlikely to learn and perform well (e.g., on an examination) unless such learning knowledge is put to use through homework, for example. Also like knowing, learning is enabled by knowledge. A student of advanced mathematics, for example, needs to learn the fundamental concepts and techniques upon which such advanced coursework builds before progressing to more advanced mathematical concepts and techniques. Indeed, the more that is known in a particular domain, the easier it is to learn something new in that same domain (see Cohen & Levinthal, 1990). Hence, learning represents a particular kind of knowing that is focused on moving knowledge between coordinates.

This applies to larger social aggregations (e.g., groups, organizations) as well. An organization may know how to learn about producing electronic products, for instance, but it is unlikely to perform well (e.g., in a product market) unless such learning knowledge is put to use through iterative design and prototyping. Also like organizational knowing, organizational learning is enabled by knowledge. A manufacturer of high-performance electronic products, for example, needs to learn the basic product designs and manufacturing methods upon which such high-performance electronics build before progressing to more sophisticated approaches. Indeed, the more that is known in a particular industry, the easier it is to learn something new in that same industry (see Cohen & Levinthal, 1990). Hence, learning represents a particular kind of knowing that pertains to organizations as well as to individuals.

We also noted previously how knowing relates most closely with knowledge stocks or inventories and how learning relates more closely with knowledge flows. In particular, knowing is enabled by stocks of knowledge, and, generally, greater inventories of knowledge enable correspondingly greater performance through action. This relationship is illustrated by our examples from music, sports, electronics, and other domains. These examples further illustrate how knowing requires learning—often in substantial amounts over extended periods of time—for the accumulation of such knowledge stocks. This pertains to musicians learning to play instruments, athletes learning to play sports, managers learning to supervise employees, warriors learning to fight battles, politicians learning to raise funds, and, quite generally, to nearly every knowledge-based activity.

Three important ramifications obtain: (1) the more learning, the greater the knowledge inventory; (2) the greater the knowledge inventory, the better the knowing, hence, performance through action; and (3) the greater the knowledge inventory, the faster the learning. Hence, knowing and learning are interconnected tightly in a mutually reinforcing manner. Such mutually reinforcing processes contribute to the sustainability of competitive advantage based on knowledge. Specifically, the further ahead one competitor can get in terms of knowledge, the faster such competitor can learn and increase knowledge accumulation. This makes it increasingly difficult for rival competitors to catch up should they fall behind.

The dynamic effect on knowledge and performance is illustrated in Figure 1. Here we include three axes. The cumulative stock, or inventory of knowledge, is represented by the vertical axis. Time is represented by the horizontal axis. The third axis represents organizational performance. As noted, flow time of knowledge is represented by the thickness of arrows used to delineate flow vectors in the figure. Say some important new organizational knowledge is developed (through learning) in a particular domain, somewhere in an organization. Developing this knowledge adds to the stock level for this domain as denoted by the point labeled "C_1" in the figure. By developing new knowledge as such, notice this point is positioned above the origin in the figure ($C_1 > 0$). Knowledge stocked to this level enables the organization to accomplish some new, corresponding knowing activity (through doing). Accomplishing this new activity effects initial organizational performance at the level labeled "A_1" in the figure. Notice this vector is represented by a relatively thick arrow. This denotes proportionately slow flow of knowledge.

Now say the organization uses this new knowledge, learns through experience, and develops additional new knowledge. This additional knowledge adds

Figure 1. Amplifying dynamic organizational knowledge and performance

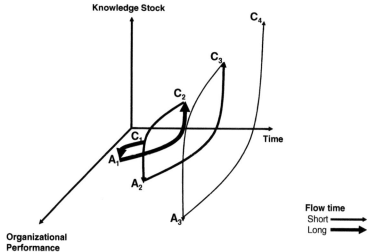

further to the stock level as denoted by the point labeled "C_2" in the figure. Notice this latter point is positioned higher up along the *Knowledge Stock* axis than the former point is ($C_2 > C_1$). Knowledge stocked to this higher level enables the organization to perform its activities more effectively as denoted by the point labeled "A_2" in the figure. Notice this latter point is positioned farther out along the *Organizational Performance* axis than the former point is ($A_2 > A_1$). Notice also that the flow vector is represented by a thinner arrow. This denotes relatively faster flows of knowledge that result from the increased knowledge stock.

This pattern continues: greater knowledge and better performance (at the levels denoted by points C_2 and A_2, respectively) lead to progressively faster learning (e.g., thinner flow vector arrows) and commensurately greater accumulation of knowledge stock (at the level denoted by point C_3); this greater knowledge stock enables proportionately better performance (at the level denoted by point A_3), faster learning (e.g., even thinner flow vector arrows), and greater accumulation of knowledge stock (at the level denoted by point C_4); and so forth. A competitor that does not learn as rapidly as our focal organization does not perform as well, learns less rapidly over time, and is left ever further behind.

To reiterate, learning — like knowing — can take place at many levels of analysis, from the individual to groups of organizations. Individual learning is probably the simplest to understand because we all do it everyday. Indeed, the reader of this text is learning new intellectual material. Riding bicycles, playing chess, solving analytical problems, negotiating contracts, searching for information, and many other individual activities require knowledge, hence, involve learning. Organizational routines such as establishing policies, developing products, training personnel, competing in markets, influencing political-legal-economic environments, attracting capital, and so on likewise require knowledge, hence, constitute learning as well — when put to use — but at a higher level of social aggregation. Learning also plays a central role in the previous examples concerning music, sports, electronics, and others. We indicate too how competition in diverse organizational domains such as business, war, and politics relies critically upon learning. Hence, learning — like knowing — can amplify knowledge as it reaches beyond the individual level of social aggregation.

Learning-Doing Tension

We noted how knowledge put into action represents *knowing*. We identify *doing* as one particular form of knowing and *learning* as another. Because people's time and energy are generally constrained, a tension exists between knowing in terms of learning and that associated with doing. To the extent that someone spends all of his or her time learning, little time is left for doing. This is why most people do not get paid a salary for attending school, for instance. Likewise, to the extent that someone spends all of his or her time doing, little time is left for learning. This is why most people do not work while going to school, as a related instance. To the extent that someone combines learning and doing, then the time and energy spent learning take away from that available for doing, and vice versa. The specific mix of the two knowing activities represents an important decision — the criteria, demands, and efficacy of which will vary from context to context.

Where successful performance is generating rich rewards, for instance, and a stable environment provides negligible threat or reason for change, then learning activities may be de-emphasized appropriately with respect to their doing counterparts. In the case of an individual manager, for example, he or she may be managing effectively in an organization and receiving frequent promotions and salary increases as rewards. Such manager may see little value in pursuing graduate education in management. Indeed, he or she could legitimately envision the associated educational coursework detracting from his or her managerial performance and conceivably even jeopardizing proximate rewards. A similar example pertains to a manufacturing firm with a successful product that is earning high margins for the company and has growing market share in its competitive arena. Such firm may see little value in augmenting research and development (R&D) efforts to enhance this product. Indeed, it could legitimately envision the associated R&D investment reducing margins and a redesigned product conceivably jeopardizing market share.

Alternatively, where current performance is viewed as unsuccessful, the environment is unstable and threatening, or similar conditions suggest an individual or organization may not be satisfied with current goal achievement, then learning activities may be re-emphasized appropriately relative to doing. A manager who is passed over repeatedly for promotion, or is not receiving salary increases, provides an example at the individual level. An employee who has been laid off, or whose skills no longer appear to be highly valued by employers, provides a similar example. A manufacturer that is not earning margins on products, or that is losing market share, provides an example at the organizational level. The firm whose technology becomes dated, outmatched, or even obsolete provides a similar example.

This tension between learning and doing can be characterized in terms of exploration vs. exploitation (March, 1991). On one side, individuals, groups, and organizations can spend time and energy exploring new opportunities, seeking new knowledge, and experimenting with different approaches to current activities. Such exploration is focused on learning and can lead to improved performance over time through new customers and markets, new product discoveries, and new work processes. Without such exploration, performance over time tends to remain static and may decline eventually, as markets become depleted, existing knowledge falls behind the state of the art, and work processes ossify.

Consider an individual pianist, for instance, who learns to play only one song. This pianist may become exceptionally proficient at playing that specific song, but experience suggests playing only this one musical piece may become quite boring over time to the individual musician. And audiences are unlikely to repeatedly pay to see the same performance. A similar observation likely applies to the individual soccer player who learns only a single skill (e.g., dribbling, place kicking, throwing in the ball). Over time, the individual player is likely to become bored with practicing and performing the same skill repeatedly. This player may not be able to remain with a competitive team if other players know multiple skills. The manager who fails to keep pace with advancing information technology may similarly not find much excitement through working with dated systems. This manager may not remain employable if such systems are replaced by newer technology. Other comparable examples apply here, too.

This observation likely applies further to bands and orchestras as well as individual musicians. This explains in part why most players, groups, and symphonies invest considerable time and energy learning and practicing a diversity of songs and musical scores. Likewise, with the soccer team that learns only one way to get the ball downfield into an opponent's area (e.g., a long-ball kick), it is unlikely to succeed by repeatedly using the same approach against opposing teams. The same can be said for a business, military, or political organization that focuses exclusively on one technology, tactic, or issue that becomes dominated by another in a corresponding market, battle, or election, respectively. This phenomenon relates to the concept *competency traps* (Levitt & March, 1988), which describes how organizations can become exceptionally proficient at certain work processes that fail to ensure performance (e.g., in product markets) over time.

On the other side, individuals, groups, and organizations can spend time and energy exploiting current opportunities, using existing knowledge, and fine-tuning institutionalized approaches to current activities. Such exploitation is focused on doing and seeks current performance by tapping existing customers and markets, delivering existing products, and routinizing extant work processes. Without such exploitation, current performance can suffer and decline, as market opportunities are missed, existing knowledge is not applied productively, and work processes are not accomplished effectively. Here we re-emphasize the need for a pianist to perform (put knowledge into action) in order to generate returns on investments made in knowledge. The same applies to the musical group or orchestra as well as the soccer player or team. The same can also be said for exploitation in business, warfare, politics, and other knowledge-based endeavors. Without exploitation of existing knowledge, few organizations (or organisms) are viable. Given limited time and energy, however, a focus on exploration requires some reduction in focus on exploitation, and vice versa. The specific mix of exploration and exploitation employed represents an important decision. Moreover, a tension between learning and doing persists at all levels of social aggregation. Selecting a specific mix of the two foci represents a context-dependent decision to make, whether by individuals, organizations, or entire societies.

Knowledge-Based Action and Potential

A duality of perspectives exists in terms of knowledge-based action and potential. Such duality links dynamically knowing through the forms of doing and learning. We noted how knowing refers to knowledge in action, how doing refers to knowledge-based work, and how learning refers to knowledge in motion. In order to put knowledge to work through action (doing), the knowledge must be acquired. In other words, the potential for action must be developed before such action can manifest. Learning increases the range of potential actions enabled by knowledge. This implies that learning feeds doing, but action can produce new knowledge (e.g., via experimentation). In other words, action through doing involves some component of learning as well as work. Doing provides opportunities to increase knowledge that enables potential actions. This implies that doing can feed learning.

Consider, for instance, a government agency that seeks to replace all paper forms with electronic documents and to perform online all processes that require citizen interaction. In order to put knowledge to work through action, the technological knowledge associated with electronic forms, online repositories, and network communications, for instance, the agency must first acquire the relevant knowledge. In other words, the potential for e-government must be developed before the corresponding e-government processes can manifest. Learning about IT can increase the range of potential actions enabled by e-government. Hence, here we have an example of how learning feeds doing. Similarly, using paperless forms and online communications can produce new knowledge about e-government through experience. In other words, e-government action involves some component of learning as well as work. Such e-government doing provides opportunities to increase technological knowledge that enables potential actions. Hence, here we have an example of how doing feeds learning.

The dynamic cycle of doing and learning was exemplified previously in terms of mutual reinforcement and highlighted in terms of enabling competitive advantage to be sustained through time. Innovation, for instance, involves applying current knowledge to enable novel action (Hargadon & Finelli, 2002, p. 292). A person, group, or organization must acquire knowledge in some domain before realistically expecting to become innovative. Hence, learning represents a necessary precursor to doing through the action of innovation. At the same time, innovation provides opportunities to increase the range of potential actions. A person, group, or organization can learn from failure as well as success to improve the process of innovation. Hence, doing through innovation can powerfully augment actions associated with learning how to innovate. Doing and learning represent important, complementary *enablers* of doing and learning: the more doing, the more learning opportunities; and the more learning, the more doing opportunities.

Consider, for instance, a group that forms to market a new financial product. Say the members of this group are experienced with marketing consumer products but inexperienced with financial products. This group must acquire knowledge in the financial domain before realistically expecting to market such product effectively. Hence, learning represents a necessary precursor to doing through the action of marketing financial products. At the same time, the doing of marketing provides opportunities to increase the range of potential actions. The marketing group can learn from failure as well as success to improve the process of marketing the new financial product. Here doing through marketing a new financial product augments actions associated with learning how to market such product. In this example, the more doing through marketing the new financial product, the more learning opportunities; and the more learning about such marketing, the more doing opportunities.

However, doing and learning also represent important, complementary *inhibitors* to doing and learning. This phenomenon goes by several names (e.g., "skilled incompetence" or "single-loop learning"; see Argyris & Schon, 1978). The learning that has been accomplished at any point in time determines what knowledge an individual, group, or organization possesses at that time. Hence, the potential range of actions available for doing is *limited* by the knowledge possessed. Whereas such knowledge enables a certain set of actions that require knowledge that was learned previously, this same knowledge also inhibits another set of actions that require knowledge that was not learned previously. Likewise, the doing that is performed over any period of time influences what knowledge an individual, group, or organization learns. Hence, the universe of experiences available for learning is limited by the actions undertaken. Whereas such doing affects a certain set of actions from which learning through experience can obtain, it also inhibits learning from another set of actions that have yet to be experienced.

Consider further the new financial product instance, previously discussed. The learning that has been accomplished at the time of product launch determines what knowledge the group possesses at that time. Hence, the potential range of actions available for marketing is limited by the new-product knowledge possessed. Whereas such knowledge enables a certain set of marketing actions that require the product knowledge that was learned previously, it also inhibits another set of actions that require knowledge that was not learned previously. Likewise, the doing that is performed over any period of time influences what knowledge the group learns. Here the universe of marketing experiences available for learning is limited by the actions undertaken toward the new financial product. In this example, such doing affects a certain set of marketing actions from which learning through experience can obtain, but it also inhibits learning from another set of actions that have yet to be experienced.

In particular, to the extent that individuals, groups, and organizations tend to repeat and refine the actions they do well (e.g., which are rewarded in a particular goal and environmental context), a tendency exists for such individuals, groups, and organizations to concentrate their doing on this set of actions by exploiting extant knowledge. In this sense, the "core competencies" (capabilities that can enable competitive advantage through knowing) of an individual, group, or organization can become "core rigidities" (Hargadon & Finelli, 2002, p. 292) where opportunities for exploring new knowledge sources are missed. Hence, doing and learning are path-dependent: Each is linked closely with the time-based behavior of the other.

Continuing with the new financial product instance, to the extent that the marketing group tends to repeat and refine the actions it does well (e.g., consumer products which have been rewarded in the past), a tendency exists for such group to concentrate its doing on consumer-product marketing by exploiting extant knowledge. Such a tendency over time precludes the marketing group from learning about financial products. This group develops a core competency by exploiting its knowledge through marketing consumer products, but the same path-dependent behavior also establishes a core rigidity, as opportunities for exploring new knowledge about marketing financial products are missed.

With this, we establish links between knowing and learning, exploitation and exploration, doing and learning, and action and potential. Each of these links appears to be dynamic, with some involving mutual reinforcement (e.g., knowing and learning, action and potential) and others illuminating tension (e.g., exploitation and exploration, doing and learning). By understanding such dynamics, one can better harness the power of knowledge in an organization.

Knowing and Learning Principles

Five principles developed in this chapter help shed light on organizational knowing and learning: (1) knowing reflects knowledge in action and is required to realize a return on investment; (2) learning reflects knowledge in motion and is required for knowing; (3) amplifying knowing and learning beyond the individual offers the greatest potential for knowledge superiority; (4) knowing and learning are dynamic, mutually reinforcing activities; and (5) knowing and learning are path-dependent, enabling both competencies and rigidities.

Principle 21. Knowing reflects knowledge in action. It is knowledge manifested through practice and involves doing (knowledge-based work). In most circumstances, it is insufficient to simply know something. Whether to convince someone else that you know, to accomplish some objective associated with knowledge, or to otherwise make knowledge useful, some kind of action is required. **Hence, knowledge must be put to use through action in order to be useful**.

Principle 22. Learning reflects knowledge in motion. It represents the action associated with acquiring "new" knowledge (e.g., through scientific discovery or knowledge moving from one coordinate to another). Learning requires knowledge and is action oriented, so it constitutes a form of knowing, but the focus on acquiring knowledge distinguishes learning quite generally from other knowing activities (e.g., doing). **Hence, learning both uses and increases knowledge**.

Principle 23. Knowing and learning both take place at multiple levels of analysis. Individuals, groups, organizations, groups of organizations, and so forth can know and learn. Whereas individuals can know and learn without being affiliated with groups or organizations, groups and organizations require individuals for knowing as well as for learning. Individuals are indispensable to groups and organizations, but there is more to groups and organizations than the collection of associated individuals. The phrase, "the whole is greater than the sum of its parts," applies well here. Indeed, performance effects of knowledge flows can be amplified as they reach broadly through the organization. **Hence, the impact of KM increases in direct proportion to the reach of knowledge flows through an organization**.

Principle 24. Knowing and learning are interrelated. Knowing requires knowledge, which must be learned. Learning involves knowing focused on acquiring new knowledge. Knowing can also involve learning. Knowing contributes to learning, and learning contributes to knowing. Further, learning and doing involve tension and require decisions. Learning is associated with exploration and focuses on knowledge flows. Doing is associated with exploitation and focuses on knowledge stocks. Both serve important purposes, but constrained time and energy impose some degree of tradeoff between them. To the extent that an individual, group, or organization focuses on one, then to some extent the other must suffer. **Hence, promoting knowing promotes learning, and vice versa**.

Principle 25. Knowing and learning involve action and potential. Knowing reflects knowledge put to use through action, which requires knowledge to be acquired before such use. Learning reflects knowledge acquisition, which increases the potential range of actions enabled. Learning from experience (from action) represents a primary contributor to new knowledge and stems directly from knowing. Knowing is inhibited by what has been learned, and learning is inhibited by what experiences have been known. **Hence, an organization's knowledge inventory both enables and inhibits what actions it can take**.

Exercises

1. Describe how a group within an organization with which you are familiar can exhibit knowing independently from, or over and above, the collective knowing of the individuals comprising the group. Provide an example. Does it matter whether what is known constitutes tacit vs. explicit knowledge?

2. Describe how the group from Exercise 1 can exhibit learning independently from, or over and above, the collective learning of the individuals comprising the group. Provide an example. Does it matter whether what is learned constitutes tacit vs. explicit knowledge?

3. Describe an event from your own life in which the amount of your prior knowledge influenced how well you learned something new. Be specific.

How could you tell whether you learned better because of the prior knowledge?

4.   Describe an event from your own life in which the nature of your prior knowledge inhibited you from learning something new. Be specific. How could you tell that your learning was inhibited?

SECTION II:
PRACTICAL APPLICATION

The practical application part of this book builds upon the knowledge-flow theory presented in Part I. Knowledge-flow theory provides the intellectual basis for diagnosis and intervention of problems with knowledge flows. Knowledge-flow application provides tools and techniques for diagnosing problems with knowledge flows and for identifying appropriate management interventions. Notice this deductive approach mirrors that of medical practice. A theoretical basis supports principles used to diagnose pathologies and to identify appropriate interventions. Some medical diagnostics and interventions are quite general and apply across several broad classes of patients, whereas others are very specific and employed only in particular settings. The same applies to knowledge-flow diagnostics and interventions. Hence, we include general as well as specific tools and techniques for practical application.

This second part of the book is organized in terms of five chapters. Chapter VI — Assessing Knowledge-Flow Performance — focuses on tools and techniques for identifying problems with flows of knowledge and includes a general set of management interventions that apply across several broad classes of organizations. Chapter VII — Application Cases in Business — concentrates on knowledge-flow diagnosis and intervention in the private, for-profit sector. Chapter VIII — Application Cases in Government — concentrates on knowledge-flow diagnosis and intervention in the public sector, including the military. Chapter IX — Application Cases in Non-Profits — concentrates on knowledge-flow diagnosis and intervention in the private, not-for-profit sector.

Chapter X — Forward! — includes guidance for learning from this book and for continuing to develop new knowledge about principled organizational knowing and learning. Together, these five chapters illustrate the practical application needed to inform organizational leaders and managers.

Chapter VI

Assessing Knowledge-Flow Performance

This chapter focuses on assessing organizational performance with respect to knowledge flows. We look first at several theoretical and practical bases for assessment and then discuss both knowledge value analysis and learning curves in some detail, including examples for illustration. The discussion then turns to examine computational modeling of knowledge flows, which includes a detailed example for practical illustration. The chapter concludes with five knowledge-flow assessment principles and includes exercises to stimulate critical thought, learning, and discussion.

Theoretical and Practical Bases for Assessment

In this section, we review several theoretical and practical bases for assessment of knowledge flows. We select only a few, diverse representative approaches for discussion, leaving more comprehensive research for the interested reader to pursue via the references cited here.

Change Management Approaches

In terms of theory and practice alike, KM is not as unique as many people assert. For instance, KM is viewed by numerous scholars as fundamentally oriented toward managing change (Davenport, De Long, & Beers, 1998). Business Process Re-engineering (BPR) research has addressed several important questions pertaining to managing change. For example, we have the benefit of results such as "tactics for managing radical change" (Stoddard & Jarvenpaa, 1995), revelations of "reengineering myths" (Davenport & Stoddard, 1994), insight into implementation problems (Clemons, Thatcher, & Row, 1995; Grover et al., 1995), measurement-driven process redesign methods (Nissen, 1998), and many others. Research on BPR has also produced numerous analytical frameworks such as those articulated by Andrews and Stalick (1994), Davenport (1993), Hammer and Champy (1993), Harrington (1991), and Johansson et al. (1993). Many cases of large-scale change have been studied (Goldstein, 1986; Kettinger, Guha, & Teng, 1995; King & Konsynski, 1990; Stoddard & Meadows, 1992; Talebzadeh, Mandutianu, & Winner, 1995) as well. Hence, KM has much to learn from BPR.

Preconditions for Success

Here we describe one BPR assessment approach — which is quite applicable to KM — centering on "preconditions for success" (Bashein, Markus & Riley, 1994). Through research on numerous re-engineering projects, three obstacles to large-scale change are noted (pp. 7-8): (1) lack of sustained management commitment and leadership; (2) unrealistic scope and expectations; and (3) resistance to change. Examine any KM project today, and you are very likely to encounter these same obstacles. Hence, the preconditions for success developed from investigation of BPR projects are very likely to apply also to KM projects. Eight preconditions for KM success are summarized in Table 1 for reference. Most such preconditions are likely to be self-explanatory and intuitive.

Experience to date suggests that preconditions 2, 5, and 7 (Realistic expectations, Shared vision, Appropriate people participating full-time) represent those absent or insufficient most often in KM projects. In terms of expectations (Precondition 2), KM is not a "silver bullet" and will not cure all organizational ills. However, enhancing knowledge flows can enable sustainable competitive

Table 1. Preconditions for KM success (adapted from Bashein et al., 1994)

Precondition	KM Implication
1. Senior management commitment	Change of any magnitude requires commitment by senior managers. KM should be considered change of substantial magnitude.
2. Realistic expectations	Expecting too much, too fast, can deflate support for change. Change takes time to implement and refine in KM as in other areas.
3. Empowered and collaborative workers	People doing organizational work are the ones who will make KM effective or not. Knowledge workers need some empowerment for exploration and learning, not just exploitation and doing.
4. Strategic context of growth and expansion	Enthusiasm and optimism can pervade a change project and contribute to toward its success, whereas negativity and pessimism can kill it. Setting goals for growth and expansion, through sustained competitive advantage, can facilitate KM change.
5. Shared vision	A vision of how knowledge flows can be enhanced must be conceived and shared broadly in order for empowered people to understand how to change.
6. Sound management processes	The better organized an enterprise is to begin with, the better its chances for successful change via KM.
7. Appropriate people participating full-time	Successful change requires talented people devoting their attention and effort toward enhancing knowledge flows. Assigning slack, part-time resources is unlikely to produce successful KM change.
8. Sufficient budget	Successful change costs money and requires time. Competitive advantage enabled by knowledge is not free. The KM budget should reflect this reality.

advantage, which provides a substantial source of power. Hence, realistic expectations — particularly in terms of how much progress can be made and how quickly — are key to successful KM implementation. In terms of vision (Precondition 5), not everyone views KM in the same manner or can envision equally well how organizational knowledge can flow better through change. Yet all involved knowledge workers need to change their behaviors (e.g., in terms of sharing, searching, learning). A common vision can provide necessary cohesion to their disparate change activities. In terms of staffing (Precondition 7), successful change requires thought and action, planning and doing, patience and persistence. Talented people need to be assigned to conceive, plan, and implement KM projects. They need to both commit and devote themselves to such projects as well.

We use this to induce our first leadership mandate from the practical application section of this book. *Mandate 1. Realistic expectations, shared vision, and appropriate people participating full-time represent the preconditions for success that are absent or insufficient most often in KM projects.*

Preconditions for Failure

We include also nine preconditions for KM failure in Table 2. These represent "negative preconditions," which can adversely affect a KM project if present. As with the previous preconditions for success, most are likely to be self-explanatory and intuitive. Experience to date suggests preconditions 10, 12, and 17 (Reliance upon external expertise, Narrow technical focus, Animosity toward staff and specialists) represent those present and sufficient most often in KM projects. In terms of reliance (Precondition 10), many organizations that stand to benefit from enhanced knowledge flows lack the expertise necessary to plan and implement a successful KM project. Hiring external consultants represents a common tactic used by such organizations, but external expertise is generally expensive and often leaves the organization before the requisite knowledge can be absorbed to sustain whatever KM changes are conceived and/or implemented.

In terms of focus (Precondition 12), a narrow technical emphasis pervades most KM projects. This precondition is discussed at length in the chapter on knowledge technology. Successful KM projects require more than just technology. People, organizations, work processes, and technologies must all change — together — in a co-evolutionary manner to enhance knowledge flows. This applies in particular to flows of tacit knowledge. In terms of animosity (Precondition 17), most leaders and line managers remain very busy and are consistently proud of the organizations they lead and manage. Staff members and specialists are often viewed with contempt and animosity by such leaders and managers, who may perceive them as disruptive at best and as threats at worst. Middle management represents the place in which resistance to successful KM implementation is likely to be greatest.

We use this to induce our second leadership mandate from the practical application section of this book. *Mandate 2. Reliance upon external exper-*

Table 2. Preconditions for KM failure (adapted from Bashein et al., 1994)

Precondition	KM Implication
9. Wrong sponsor	Some characteristics of a "wrong sponsor" include too low in management ranks, too technically focused, getting ready to retire or change jobs, and lacking credibility and leadership.
10. Reliance upon external expertise	Reliance upon external talent may be necessary to initiate a KM program, but such talent leaves the organization, often before the requisite expertise can be absorbed. This leaves the KM project without sufficient knowledge for sustainment.
11. Cost-cutting focus	People do not react well to change when they feel threatened. A focus on downsizing effectively killed the BPR movement in the 1990s.
12. Narrow technical focus	People, organizations, work processes, and technologies must all change—together—for successful KM. A single-minded focus on technology is hazardous.
13. Consensus management	Collaboration without leadership is problem-prone. Tough decisions about KM alternatives are required but unlikely to be resolved well by consensus.
14. Unsound financial condition	Many organizations attempt KM out of desperation. When management is desperate, realistic expectations, patience, and sufficient budget are unlikely.
15. Too many improvement projects under way	Successful change requires focus. If everyone in an organization simultaneously changes everything they do, then chaos is likely. Organizations are advised to focus on one or perhaps a few KM initiatives at any one time.
16. Fear and lack of optimism	This is the counterpart to the cost-cutting focus. People associated with change need to believe they are working to improve their own work environment in addition to that of others.
17. Animosity toward staff and specialists	Many leaders and line managers view specialists with contempt and perceive change efforts as disrupting their work processes. Middle management is the place in which resistance to change is likely to be greatest on a KM project.

tise, narrow technical focus, and animosity toward staff and specialists represent the preconditions for failure that are present or sufficient most often in KM projects.

KM-Specific Factors

Unlike the preconditions for success and failure, which derive from the literature on change management, other sets of success factors have been developed specifically for KM projects. For instance, Jennex and Olfman (2004) survey research on KM systems (including but not limited to IT) and identify factors such as incorporation of KM into everyday work tasks, senior management support, and employee training. Other factors cited in this survey include user commitment and motivation, knowledge representation, organizational and cultural issues, leadership and top management support, attention to tacit knowledge, promoting a culture of knowledge sharing, focus on organizational memory, and others.

Clearly, several such factors (e.g., commitment and motivation, leadership and top management support, promoting a culture of knowledge sharing) are included in the previously stated preconditions. Others (e.g., knowledge representation, attention to tacit knowledge, focus on organizational memory), however, are unique to KM and merit additional attention. In terms of knowledge representation, this highlights an important issue. AI researchers and practitioners have worked for decades on how various kinds of knowledge can be represented. Recall we include in the knowledge technology chapter an example of using heuristic rules. Representing knowledge is particularly difficult where such knowledge is tacit. Many organizations satisfice by mapping where (e.g., in which people) such tacit knowledge resides. But much work remains to be accomplished in this area. In terms of tacit knowledge, we devote considerable attention to this phenomenon throughout the book. Such tacit knowledge flows differently than its explicit counterpart does. The appropriability of tacit knowledge also provides an attainable basis for sustainable competitive advantage. Hence, tacit knowledge merits separate treatment. In terms of organizational memory, we devote attention to this phenomenon in the book also, but we do so in the context of knowledge stocks or inventories. It is important to re-emphasize that such inventories complement knowledge flows in a complex, dynamic manner. Hence, organizational memory represents one of several important success factors and must be addressed in concert with knowledge flows.

We use this to induce our third leadership mandate from the practical application section of this book. *Mandate 3. Knowledge representation, attention to tacit knowledge, and focus on organizational memory represent unique considerations that merit particular attention in KM projects.*

Related research has addressed KM readiness (Holt et al., 2004). Readiness in this context is equivalent to preconditions for success. The focus of this work is on KM implementation. Over 30 instruments (guidelines for assessment) are identified for evaluating an organization's readiness for change. Then using a survey of KM practitioners, these researchers identify measures such as *pessimism, affective commitment,* and *normative commitment* as statistically significant indicators of KM readiness. Notice such measures pertain to *how people perceive* a KM project. This is consistent with several of the preconditions noted previously, and it reinforces the importance of leadership and management.

We use this to induce our fourth leadership mandate from the practical application section of this book. *Mandate 4. Measurements of how people perceive a KM project (e.g., using measures such as pessimism, affective commitment, and normative commitment) can indicate KM readiness.*

Knowledge Audit

Other related research involves a knowledge audit (Liebowitz et al., 2000). This represents a diagnostic activity focused on identifying potential problems to be addressed via KM. Such problems include inability to keep abreast of relevant information, "reinventing the wheel," and not knowing where to go for expertise. Notice each of these problems involves "how-to" knowing (e.g., how to keep abreast of information, how to avoid task duplication, how to locate experts), hence, bears directly on knowledge flows. As outlined by the authors, "a knowledge audit assesses potential stores of knowledge and is the first part of any knowledge management strategy" (p. 3). Notwithstanding this assertion, however, if the kinds of preconditions for success mentioned previously are absent from a project, or the kinds of preconditions for failure are present, one would be well advised to address such preconditions before investing in a knowledge audit. Six steps associated with a knowledge audit (p. 5) are summarized in Table 3. They are intuitive but easier said than done.

These researchers also present a survey instrument for auditing knowledge. It includes some of the items summarized in Table 4. It should be clear that such a survey is intended for external consultants who do not understand the knowledge inventories and flows of an organization. However, we noted previously that many organizations do not know what they know. An instrument such as this can be used — in conjunction with employees' knowledge of what

Table 3. Steps of a knowledge audit (adapted from Liebowitz et al., 2000)

Step
1. Determine existing and potential knowledge sinks, sources, flows, and constraints.
2. Identify and locate explicit and tacit knowledge.
3. Build a map of the stocks and flows of organizational knowledge.
4. Perform a gap analysis to determine what knowledge is missing.
5. Determine who needs the missing knowledge.
6. Provide recommendations to management regarding necessary improvements.

Table 4. Sample knowledge audit survey questions (adapted from Liebowitz et al., 2000)

Question
What categories of knowledge are required for your job?
Which knowledge categories are available currently?
How is this knowledge used?
Who else uses this knowledge?
Who are the experts in terms of this knowledge?
In what form is the knowledge of these experts?

knowledge is important and of who knows what — to identify key aspects of knowledge in the organization.

We use this to induce our fifth leadership mandate from the practical application section of this book. *Mandate 5. Knowledge audits can help organizations that do not know what they know.*

An unintended additional benefit involves stimulating people in the organization to think more about the knowledge that is important to them. For instance, by completing a survey along these lines, many people in an organization may think explicitly about knowledge and flows that had never surfaced beyond implicit understanding and tacit execution. Nonetheless, many people find such surveys time-consuming to complete and difficult to answer. Yet the results can provide a rough gauge of knowledge in an organization. Still, surveys are likely to be most valuable to external consultants who do not understand the organization well.

To summarize the approaches described in this section, assessing knowledge-flow performance is addressed by theory and practice alike. Most work along these lines involves the development of preconditions for success and failure, evaluation of readiness factors, and conduct of knowledge audits. In each case, one is trying to identify problems with knowledge flows and to match such problems with the capabilities of KM projects. In each case also, one is striving to address the management of change. A KM project involves substantial change, which must be managed to enhance the likelihood of success. The key problem with all of the approaches in this class is that they describe what to do but not how to do it. In other words, preconditions, readiness factors, audit steps, and like approaches are prescriptive and articulated at a high level, but they are difficult to operationalize and implement.

Perhaps the greatest potential in terms of a knowledge audit lies in the prospect of measuring *knowledge inventory*. Measures of knowledge inventory may be useful to assess an organization's readiness to perform its work processes effectively. At this point, however, *knowledge inventory* represents a non-operationalized concept also, one likely to manifest its own implementation difficulties. We address this later in greater depth.

Knowledge Value Analysis

Research and practice of a different nature departs from these high-level, non-operationalized approaches via a focus on measurement. Knowledge value analysis (KVA) (see Housel et al., 2001) is rooted in Complexity theory and thermodynamics. This approach employs principles such as *information entropy* to measure the return on knowledge (return on investments in productive assets such as employees and technology at the subcorporate level). "KVA provides a methodology for allocating revenue and cost to company's core processes based on the amount of change [change in entropy] each produces" (Housel & Bell, 2001, p. 92).

The idea is to identify the relative returns of processes that employ resources (e.g., employees and technology) to produce their outputs. This is accomplished via a ratio: return on knowledge (ROK). ROK is a surrogate for return on investment. The revenue allocated to a given process (and its resources) is the numerator in a ROK calculation. The cost to use those resources to produce the process outputs is the denominator. Providing leaders and managers with such information can help them to make resource-allocation decisions using logic similar to that of ratio analysis in managing investment portfolios.

The authors describe KVA as "an analytic tautology.... [It assumes that] all of the knowledge required to execute processes is known and ... is a surrogate for the economic value it produces" (p. 100). The reader can judge for himself or herself the value of a tautology and reasonableness of these assumptions. To estimate the amount of knowledge contained within an organizational process, this approach prescribes assessing how much time is required by an "average person" to learn how to produce the outputs of a process. The assumption underlying this prescription is that the amount of time it takes for the average learner to acquire a given amount of knowledge is proportional to knowledge. Here the concept *knowledge* is used as a surrogate for the (change in information entropy and) value added by a process. Hence, learning time is argued to be value-proportional.

Again, the reader can assess the reasonableness of this assumption, but notice this is a knowledge-flow proposition that involves the knowing activities of both learning and doing. If some activity requires a relatively long amount of time to learn, then it would be considered more valuable than an alternate activity requiring less learning time. This would clearly privilege tacit knowledge — which flows more slowly than explicit knowledge — and encourage investments in the associated processes. This is consistent with our previous discussion on the appropriability of tacit knowledge and its contribution toward competitive advantage.

We use this to induce our sixth leadership mandate from the practical application section of this book. *Mandate 6. Knowledge value analysis privileges tacit knowledge appropriately.*

Practical Illustration

The example summarized in Table 5 can help us appreciate this approach. This example is adapted from Housel and Bell (2001), the book in which the KVA method is explained in great detail. Briefly, the first column (labeled "K Area") lists three areas (labeled simply "A," "B," and "C") of knowledge that are deemed important in this organization. Such areas could include knowledge of customers, knowledge of internal operations, knowledge of management procedures, and like areas that would clearly vary across organizations. These represent the important things to know about — at a high level of abstraction — in the organization. The second column (labeled "Learning Time") lists the amount of time (in months) required for the "average person" to become proficient in each knowledge area. For instance, the average person requires roughly 20 months to become proficient at the tasks associated with Knowl-

Table 5. KVA example (adapted from Housel & Bell, 2001)

K Area	Learning Time	Knowers	IT %	Auto K	Total K	K %	Revenue	Expense	ROK
A	20	855	80	13680	30780	34.2	82.7	75.0	110%
B	45	600	60	16200	43200	48.0	116.1	175.5	66%
C	35	255	80	7140	16065	17.8	43.2	49.5	87%
Total					90045	100.0	242.0	300.0	

edge Area A, 45 months for Area B, and so forth. The third column (labeled "Knowers") lists the number of people associated with each knowledge area. For instance, 855 people participate in tasks associated with Knowledge Area A, 600 with those in Area B, and so forth.

The fourth column (labeled "IT %") lists the estimated fraction of knowledge embedded within IT artifacts for each knowledge area. For instance, estimates indicate 80% of knowledge in Area A is embedded in IT, 60% in Area B, and so forth. The estimate represented in this column is not intuitive and requires some explanation. It represents a fraction that is used to calculate the amount of knowledge embedded in IT automation. This latter amount is listed in the fifth column (labeled "Auto K") for each knowledge area. For instance, 13,680 knowledge units are associated with Knowledge Area A, 16,200 with those in Area B, and so forth. Figures in this column are calculated as the product of estimates in columns 2 through 4 (e.g., in Area A: 20 months learning time × 855 knowers × 80% IT fraction = 13,680 knower-months). The sixth column (labeled "Total K") lists the total knowledge associated with each knowledge area. This represents the sum of automation knowledge (calculated in column 5) and human knowledge. For instance, 30,780 knowledge units are associated with Knowledge Area A, 43,200 with those in Area B, and so forth. Figures in this column are calculated as the sum of automation knowledge and product of columns 2 through 3 (e.g., 13,680 knower-months of automation knowledge + [20 months learning time × 855 knowers] = 30,780 knower-months).

The seventh column (labeled "K %") lists the fraction of total knowledge associated with each knowledge area. For instance, 34.2% of total knowledge is associated with Knowledge Area A, 48.0% with Area B, and so forth. Figures in this column are calculated as the ratio of total knowledge in each area to the total knowledge summed across all areas (e.g., 30,780 knower-months for Area A divided by 90,045 knower-months for the total organization = 34.2%). The eighth column (labeled "Revenue") lists the revenue allocated to each knowledge area on the basis of its knowledge. For instance, of the $242.0M total revenue for the organization in the period of interest, 34.2% ($82.7M) is allocated on the basis of knowledge to Knowledge Area A, 48.0% ($116.1M) to Area B, and so forth. Figures in this column are calculated as the product of the knowledge fraction from column 7 and the total revenue summed in column 8 (e.g., 34.2% for Area A × $242.0M total revenue for the organization = $82.7M for Area A). The ninth column (labeled "Expense") lists the expense incurred by each knowledge area (e.g., as recorded via activity-based costing). For instance, of the $300.0M total expense for the organization in the period of interest, $75.0M is incurred for Knowledge Area A, $175.5M for Area B, and so forth.

Finally, the tenth column (labeled "ROK") lists the "return on knowledge" computed for each knowledge area on the basis of the revenue allocation in column 8. For instance, the return on knowledge is shown at 110% for Area A, 66% for Area B, and so forth. This is calculated as the ratio of knowledge-allocated revenue from column 8 to expense from column 9 (e.g., $82.7M allocated revenue for Area A divided by $75.0M expense = 110% ROK). The intent of this final calculation is to show the relative contribution of the three knowledge areas to the organization's economic value. For instance, a relatively high ROK for Knowledge Area A (110%) would be interpreted as indicating this area contributes well to the economic value of the organization. Not only does it contribute relatively better than Knowledge Area B (66% ROK) and Area C (87%), but it contributes more via allocated revenue than its expenses.

One could make an argument that knowledge associated with Area A contributes to an economic profit for the organization, whereas knowledge associated with Areas B and C contribute instead to economic losses. A manager might seek in turn to further exploit the knowledge associated with Area A while exploring ways to ameliorate the knowledge clumps inhibiting performance in Areas B and C. In one case described separately by T. J. Housel (personal communication, August 2004), the billing process of a telecommunications company showed the lowest return of the multiple processes examined via KVA. However, because the case company represented a new subsidiary and because it was stuck for the time being with the current billing process, the executive group decided to invest in a customer-relationship management system to boost sales. Therefore, the numbers alone need not lead to a given knowledge investment decision any more than they do with financial investment decisions made by portfolio managers.

This approach offers a technique to conduct an analysis (e.g., as outlined in the example) for any organization that maintains records and has people willing to make the estimates required to complete a table such as the previous one. However, the approach has several problems. One problem, of course, stems from the inherent subjectivity and possible inaccuracy of estimates required for columns 2 through 4 of the Table 5, in addition to the potential difficulty with obtaining expenses for each knowledge area. For instance, many organizations do not use activity-based costing and do not collect expenses by knowledge area. However, other expenses (e.g., General and Administrative, Operations, Management) are reported routinely or can be derived from financial statements.

Another problem lies in the possibility of excluding from the analysis one or more important knowledge areas. Even relatively informed leaders and managers may be unaccustomed to conceptualizing their organizations in terms of knowledge areas. Hence, they may overlook important areas when asked to help build a ROK table. However, skilled interviewers offer techniques for ameliorating some limitations along these lines, according to T. J. Housel (personal communication, August 2004).

One major problem with this approach is that it reduces to an allocation formula. Where someone has resources to invest among competing process activities, this approach provides a mechanism for making such allocation. However, the approach does not claim any superiority over other allocation formulae (e.g., strategic importance, expected return on investment, expected risk/return ratio). Moreover, the logic of basing investment allocations on the amount of time required for average people to learn various activities is not entirely cogent. This approach provides a means to measure the putative value of knowledge, but the ideas remain a bit inchoate. Further, the approach is still gaining acceptance theoretically. Its employment in practice to date has been positive but limited.

Learning Curves

Similar to the previous approach with its focus on measurement, learning curves provide a technique that blends theory with practice to measure knowledge flows. Unlike the previous approach, however, learning curves are very well accepted and established, both theoretically and empirically. Learning curves have been used for many decades to measure knowledge flows. Born during the World War Era in the aerospace industry, formal techniques were developed to assess organizational learning in terms of the time required to repeat aircraft-assembly tasks successively (Wright, 1936). Briefly, a general relationship can be observed and measured between the cumulative number of times a task is repeated and the time required for each repetition. This relationship has been observed and validated across myriad industries and types of tasks (Yelle, 1979). It appears to represent a fundamental behavior in terms of organizational learning (Argote, Beckman, & Epple, 1990). In words, this relationship indicates that the unit time required to complete a task declines as a predictable percentage with each doubling of task repetitions. Mathematically, the relationship is logarithmic and often expressed as:

$$Y = Ax^b$$

Where:

Y is the unit time required to complete a task after x repetitions

A is the time required to complete a task the first time

x is the cumulative number of task repetitions

b is the learning factor (generally: $-1 < b < 0$)

Consider a task that requires 100 hours to complete the first time ($Y = A = 100$; $x = 1$; terminological note: the first time a task is accomplished is termed *repetition 1*, even though, technically, it has yet to be "repeated"), with a learning factor ($b = -0.3219$) that reflects a common improvement rate. Improvement rates such as this are often expressed in percentage terms (e.g., 80%). Improvement rates can be equated to learning factors (e.g., at 80% improvement: $b = -0.3219 = \log .80 / \log 2$) and are widely considered more intuitive. For instance, the second time this "100-hour" task is performed ($x=2$), the learning curve would predict the time required to be only 80% of that of the first ($Y = 80\%$ of $100 = 80$). The next time the cumulative number of repetitions doubles ($x=4$), the learning curve would predict the time required to be only another 80% ($Y = 80\%$ of 80% of $100 = 80\%$ of $80 = 64$), and so forth. Notice after only eight repetitions ($x=8$) that the unit time declines to approximately half the time required at first ($Y = 51$). In other words, at an 80% improvement rate, only eight repetitions are required for performance of a task to double!

Some General Rules of Thumb

Several general rules of thumb have been developed through experience with learning curves over the years. One is that the greater the use of automation at the beginning of a process, the lower the improvement rate. The reason is that automation generally improves a process via quantum jump, so cumulative improvement following such jump is very moderate. For instance, whereas an 80% improvement rate is common for people performing manual tasks (e.g., assembling airplanes), the improvement rate corresponding to highly automated tasks (e.g., numeric controlled machining) would be only 95% (b = -0.0740) or so. Notice, the faster the rate of improvement, the *lower* the percentage used to depict it. For instance, an 80% improvement rate reflects *faster* learning than a 95% rate does. The exponents are clearly different (cf. b = -0.3219 vs. -0.0740), with larger negative values corresponding to faster improvement. A helpful way to think about this relationship is in terms of how much time is saved on each repetition. For instance, at an 80% improvement rate, each doubling of repetitions saves 20% in terms of time, whereas at a 95% rate, each doubling saves only 5%. Recall our discussion of the tension between learning and doing. The learning rate quantifies the slope of the learning-by-doing (e.g., OJT) vector. The faster the learning (larger negative value of the exponent b), the larger the learning component.

We use this to induce our seventh leadership mandate from the practical application section of this book. *Mandate 7. The greater the use of automation at the beginning of a process, the lower the improvement rate.*

Figure 1 delineates 80% and 95% learning curves for further comparison. Notice both curves start at the same point (x = 1, A = 100) and decrease logarithmically with cumulative repetition. The 80% curve decreases much faster than the 95% curve does. For instance, the former curve reaches the 80-hour point in terms of unit time on the second task repetition (x = 2), whereas the latter curve does not cross this point until the twenty-first repetition (x = 21). Notice also that both curves decrease more rapidly in the beginning than they do as the number of repetitions increases. Mathematically, the second derivatives of these functions with negative values for exponents (b < 0) indicate this must be the case. In words, the more that performance of a task improves through repetition, the less room that remains for subsequent improvement. This makes intuitive sense, given that people tend to make more mistakes when first learning a task than after having mastered it. The learning curve quantifies such intuition.

Figure 1. Learning curves at 80% and 95%

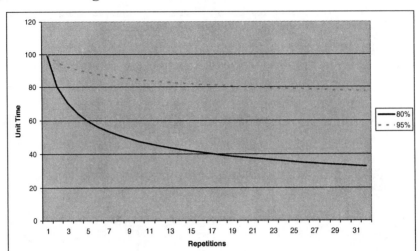

Another rule of thumb pertaining to learning curves involves the nature of "learning." Recall earlier that we describe the use of such curves to depict *organizational* learning. This includes but is not limited to the learning of people accomplishing a task (see Epple, Argote & Devadas, 1991). In the case of aircraft assembly, for instance, people riveting aluminum panels improve individually as they develop increased competence, for example, using the rivet gun; timing and sequencing the holes and rivets they insert; positioning and moving their bodies; and like factors associated with individual learning. Groups of individual riveters learn also, for instance, how to work simultaneously on a large panel without getting in one another's way; how to decrease the amount of rework required by inserting rivets symmetrically around a panel; how to communicate when problems or delays on one person's work affect the work of others; and like factors associated with group learning. The assembly unit responsible for assembling aircraft panels learns too, for instance, as it develops plans for building and sequencing panels; assigns and trains individual people to various assembly jobs; improves work processes; introduces improved tools; and like factors associated with unit learning. Hence, performance improvement reflected by learning curves involves more than just individual knowing and learning.

We use this to induce our eighth leadership mandate from the practical application section of this book. *Mandate 8. Performance improvement reflected by learning curves involves more than just individual knowing and learning.*

Factors other than cumulative repetition can affect organizational learning as well. Learning curves can be adapted to accommodate many such factors. For instance, calendar time spent in a particular industry or line of work can substitute as a proxy for cumulative number of repetitions (Ingram & Simons, 2002). Assuming that people and organizations follow similar organizational processes and learning trends, then an organization that has been doing some set of tasks for a longer period of time than another one would be expected to perform better at such tasks. The learning curve can quantify this dynamic using the same logic and logarithmic form as discussed previously in terms of learning rate. Using a 90% learning rate, for example, one firm that had been in a line of business for twice as long as another firm would expect an approximate 10% performance advantage. Clearly, the larger the time difference between any two such firms and the larger the learning rate, the greater the performance benefits accruing to the first mover or incumbent. Knowledge dissipation or forgetting can be quantified also through learning curves, as another instance, with additional parameters used to represent a dissipation rate (Darr, Argote, & Epple, 1995). Production rate, technology introduction, workforce capability, and other factors can be integrated as well. Such factors have been studied extensively.

We use this to induce our ninth leadership mandate from the practical application section of this book. *Mandate 9. Knowledge can be lost and found.*

Another rule of thumb pertains to organizational culture, trust, and incentives. Such latter factors reflect considerable need for further study. Where people in an organization share knowledge freely with one another, one would generally expect learning curves to be steeper (learning rates to be higher). Knowledge sharing as such can have multiple effects. It can increase an individual's learning rate, as other, perhaps more experienced people provide guidance, assistance, and support to augment the trial and error of OJT. Individuals sharing knowledge about process flaws and opportunities can similarly improve a group's learning rate, as better methods and tools are developed for multiple workers to employ. The same phenomenon can apply at the organization level also. Conversely, where the organization culture does not exhibit knowledge sharing, one would generally expect slower learning. Hence, organizational culture represents an important determinant of success for a KM project.

In terms of trust, this relates directly to knowledge sharing. Knowledge is power, and sharing knowledge requires time and energy. Knowledge sharing also takes time and energy away from the task at hand (e.g., workflows). For someone — or some group or some organization — to share knowledge willingly, he or she should feel confident that such sharing will not be detrimental to his or her success. This is a matter of interpersonal trust. Inter-group and inter-organizational trust follows similar logic. For people in or in charge of a group to share knowledge willingly, they should likewise feel that the time and energy required to do so will be worth the corresponding monetary and opportunity cost. This is partly a matter of motivation and goals and partly a matter of incentives. This applies well to groups and organizations as well as individuals. Where trust between individuals, groups, and organizations is relatively high, one would generally expect faster learning. Hence, trust also represents an important determinant of success for a KM project.

In terms of incentives, these become important to ameliorate the negative impacts of organizational cultures and conditions of trust that inhibit knowledge sharing. In most cases, the knowledge manager cannot control the organizational culture that he or she inherits from an ongoing organization. Likewise, in most cases, the knowledge manager cannot control the trust that exists within an organization. Given that organizational culture and trust are important in terms of knowledge flows, the knowledge manager should seek to address any problems that may manifest along these lines. Incentives represent an approach to trying to shift organizational culture and/or promote trust. Where one finds a culture that does not involve knowledge sharing, for instance, individuals, groups, and organizations can be incentivized to share. The use of incentives is discussed thoroughly through a large literature on economics. Such use has both pros and cons, and a combination of pecuniary and intrinsic rewards can be employed for incentivization. Where one finds an organization in which people exhibit low levels of trust, as another instance, incentives may represent an approach to promoting trust. However, trust cannot be bought, so the use of incentives is challenging in this regard. In many respects, it should be clear how organizational culture and trust are closely related. For instance, a culture of knowledge sharing can promote trust, and trust can promote a culture of knowledge sharing. Incentives can be employed to promote both, but such employment of incentives entails risks as well as opportunities.

We use this to induce our tenth leadership mandate from the practical application section of this book. *Mandate 10. Trust cannot be bought.*

Practical Illustration

In terms of assessing knowledge-flow performance, learning curves can be used both predictively and descriptively. In the former sense, one can project the learning expected to occur by parameterizing a learning curve. For instance, where one had insight or information to expect an 85% learning rate would obtain for a particular group of tasks, curves such as those plotted previously could be projected for such tasks. Many major corporations (e.g., in the aerospace industry) do this routinely in the pricing of aircraft years or sometimes even decades before they have been built. The key is to predict accurately at what rate of improvement the organization will progress. Beyond heuristic rules of thumb (e.g., 80% for manual labor, 95% for automated processes), one must rely intensively upon empirical data to estimate improvement rates.

In this latter, empirical sense, one can measure the learning that occurs by fitting a learning curve to performance data. For instance, where one tracks the unit time required to complete a group of tasks (e.g., by unit or through time), the associated data can be plotted graphically and fitted via regression or like statistical technique to assess the learning rate. The same major corporations that use learning curves to project product prices also track process improvement rates to assess how well the organizational learning progresses relative to plan. For instance, consider the data presented in Table 6.

The data in this table reflect performance across 32 repetitions of some task, with performance measured in terms of the time required for each repetition. For instance, the first time the task was performed (Repetition = 1), it required 95 hours to complete (Time = 95 hours). The next time it required 85 hours (Repetition = 2, Time = 85); the third attempt took 65 hours, and so forth. When these performance data are analyzed via linear regression (e.g., taking the logarithm of both the Repetition and Time values transforms these into linear series), a curve is fit with properties very close to those of the predicted 80% learning curve. Specifically, the estimated slope is 80.2%. Clearly, an 80% improvement rate represents a good estimate in this case. The plot comparing the data and regression is presented in Figure 2 for illustration.

There is little reason why this kind of projection and measurement cannot be accomplished in every organization that engages in repetitive tasks. The problem of course is that some tasks are more repeatable than others (cf. R&D vs. assembly-line work). And without some kind of benchmark for comparison, it can be difficult to distinguish between "good" and "bad" improvement rates in practice. For instance, 90% improvement for numeric controlled

Table 6. Improvement data

Repetition	Time
1	95
2	85
3	65
4	64
5	62
6	58
7	52
8	53
9	48
10	45
11	47
12	43
13	45
14	41
15	43
16	39
17	41
18	38
19	38
20	37
21	36
22	38
23	37
24	34
25	36
26	34
27	36
28	33
29	35
30	33
31	34
32	35

machining is good, whereas 85% improvement for manual assembly work is bad, even though the former rate of improvement is less than the latter. Nonetheless, nearly every task has some repetitive component, and the learning curve can provide a useful tool for assessing the learning corresponding to its performance.

Even in software development, for instance, every implementation is heralded as unique and involves cumulative learning. It is common to have some software developers working at up to 30 times the productivity of others (STSC, 2000), for example. Hence, learning via performance improvement is clearly present in the software domain. The question becomes: what is the appropriate unit of

Figure 2. Performance data and regression fit lines

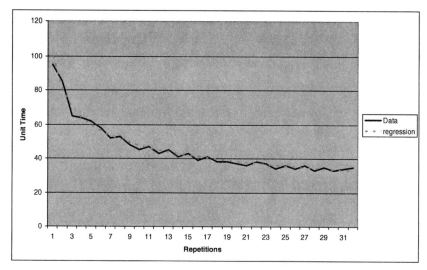

repetition for measuring such learning? Clearly, the software project or implementation represents an unsuitable unit, for each one is unique in some respects. Rather, finer-grained activities such as *determining system requirements*, *designing software architectures*, *using specific development tools*, *coding certain algorithms*, and the like involve considerable repetition. Ask a proficient software developer to adopt a new procedure, tool or environment, for example, and one should expect an immediate productivity drop.

Knowledge-Flow
Computational Modeling

Computational modeling represents an extension of simulation, which we discuss in the knowledge technology chapter. Computational models are used extensively in the physical sciences to represent the dynamics of phenomena such as fluid flows, heat transfers, and resilience of structures, for instance. Comparable models are also used in the social sciences to represent the dynamics of money flows, economic transfers, and communication structures, for instance. Models from the former sciences provide a basis for designing physical artifacts (e.g., airplanes, bridges, computers) by representing such artifacts via models and simulating their dynamic behaviors under various conditions. Models from the latter sciences provide a basis for making decisions about social systems (e.g., finance, trade, broadcasting) by representing such systems via models and simulating their dynamic behaviors under various conditions. In both cases, most of the design and analysis can be accomplished via computer, through iterative conceptualization, scrutiny, and refinement of virtual prototypes. A great many alternate, virtual prototypes can be designed and analyzed — via computational models — in relatively short periods of time without incurring the expenses and potential risks associated with using physical prototypes. For instance, nearly all modern aircraft are designed and tested virtually before a single piece of metal, plastic, or other structural element is made and long before any person is asked to risk his or her life in an untested airplane. Even before well-accepted wind-tunnel testing of scale models, the virtual equivalents of full-scale designs are conceived, analyzed, and refined iteratively via computer.

The key is to develop computational models that reflect well the structures and behaviors of the artifacts and systems they represent. With high-fidelity representations and simulations, the designer can attain considerable confidence that the behaviors obtained via simulation in a virtual world will mirror those of a physical or social system implemented in the real world. In the case of aircraft, to continue this instance, sophisticated computational models represent dynamic flows of fluids (esp. air at high speeds) in three spatial dimensions. The behaviors of such represented fluid flows match exceedingly closely the behaviors of physical fluid flows in comparable conditions (e.g., along a wing section or through an engine nozzle). When designers have conceptualized, analyzed, and refined an aircraft via computational analysis to the point at which it satisfies their requirements, they can begin the development and testing of a physical prototype. The same approach holds too for the design of bridges, buildings, computers, and many other physical artifacts.

This approach is used as well for designing some social systems, but the models generally lack the same level of sophistication and precision as exhibited by those representing physical artifacts. Micro-theory and analysis tools for designing physical artifacts rest on well-understood principles of physics (e.g., involving continuous numerical variables, describing materials whose properties are relatively easy to measure and calibrate). And analysis of such physical systems easily yields to differential equations and precise numerical computing. In contrast, theories describing the behavior of organizations are characterized by nominal and ordinal variables, with poor measurement reproducibility, and verbal descriptions reflecting significant ambiguity. Unlike the mathematically representable and analyzable micro-behaviors of physical systems, the dynamics of organizations are influenced by a variety of social, technical, and cultural factors; difficult to verify experimentally; and not amenable to numerical representation, mathematical analysis, or precise measurement. Moreover, quite distinct from physical systems, people and social interactions — not molecules and physical forces — drive the behavior of organizations. Hence, such behaviors are fundamentally non-deterministic and difficult to predict at the individual level. Thus, people, organizations, and business processes are qualitatively different than bridges, semiconductors, and airplanes. It is irrational to expect the former to ever be as understandable, analyzable, or predictable as the latter. This represents a fundamental limitation of the approach.

Within the constraints of this limitation, however, we can still take great strides beyond relying upon informal and ambiguous, natural language textual description of organizational knowledge flows (e.g., the bulk of extant theory). For instance, the domain of organization theory is imbued with a rich, time-tested collection of micro-theories that lend themselves to qualitative representation and analysis. Examples include Galbraith's (1977) information processing abstraction, March and Simon's (1958) bounded rationality assumption, and Thompson's (1967) task interdependence contingencies. Drawing from this theory base, symbolic (non-numeric) representation and reasoning techniques from established AI research are employed—in addition to time-proven methods of discrete-event simulation (e.g., approximating aggregate behaviors via statistical distributions, Monte Carlo techniques) — to develop computational models of dynamic organizational knowing phenomena. Once formalized through a computational model, the symbolic representation is "executable," meaning it can emulate the dynamics of organizational behaviors.

We use this to induce our eleventh leadership mandate from the practical application section of this book. *Mandate 11. Using computational models, organizations can be designed and tested virtually, in a manner similar to the design of airplanes, bridges, and computers.*

Virtual Design Team

In terms of computational modeling of knowledge flows, probably the most advanced application is associated with the Virtual Design Team (VDT). Over two decades, VDT research has focused on computational modeling of project work with the goal of designing project organizations in a manner analogous to that described previously for physical artifacts (see Nissen & Levitt, 2004). Using an agent-based representation (Cohen, 1992; Kunz et al., 1998), micro-level organizational behaviors have been researched and formalized to reflect well-accepted organization theory (Levitt et al., 1999). The VDT modeling environment has been developed directly from Galbraith's information processing view of organizations. This information processing view has two key implications (Jin & Levitt, 1996). The first is ontological: knowledge work is modeled through interactions of *tasks* to be performed, *actors* communicating with one another and performing tasks, and an *organization structure* that defines actors' roles and constrains their behaviors. In essence, this amounts to overlaying the task structure on the organization structure and developing computational agents with various capabilities to emulate the behaviors of organizational actors performing work.

The VDT modeling environment benefits from extensive fieldwork in many diverse enterprise domains; for example, power plant construction and off-shore drilling (see Christiansen, 1993), aerospace (see Thomsen, 1998), software development (see Nogueira, 2000), and healthcare (see Cheng & Levitt, 2001); and others. Through the process of "backcasting" — predicting known organizational outcomes using only information that was available at the beginning of a project — VDT models of operational enterprises in practice have demonstrated dozens of times that emulated organizational behaviors and results correspond qualitatively and quantitatively to their operational counter-parts in the field (Kunz et al., 1998). The VDT modeling environment has been validated repeatedly and longitudinally as representative of both organization theory and enterprises in practice. This affords considerable confidence in the simulation results.

Moreover, VDT is designed specifically to model the kinds of knowledge work and information processing tasks that comprise the bulk of KM processes. In particular, building upon knowledge-flow theory (e.g., as articulated in Part I of this book), VDT methods and tools have been extended to reproduce increasingly fine-grained behaviors of knowledge in action and motion. This includes knowledge-flow processes and tools such as direct experience, formal training, transactive memory, mentoring, and simulation, in addition to commonplace KM approaches such as Web portals, knowledge maps, and communities of practice.

Practical Illustration

As an example of assessing knowledge flows through computational modeling, here we employ the VDT modeling environment to represent work processes associated with a high-level technology development project. This illustration is described by Nissen and Levitt (2005). The key KM question of interest here is: To what extent should the organization focus on developing specialist knowledge within its two functional areas of design and manufacturing vs. promoting generalist knowledge across functional areas? Notice a hint of the tension between exploitation vs. exploration in this question. Where people develop deep specialist knowledge, it limits the variety of problems that can be addressed, but such knowledge is highly detailed, hence, powerful within its narrow domain. Where people develop broad generalist knowledge, in contrast, it enables them to address a wide array of diverse problems, but such knowledge is neither particularly detailed nor powerful within any given domain. Further, given limited time, energy, and like resources for learning and doing, an investment in learning specialist knowledge restricts one's ability to become a generalist, and vice versa.

Many economists view decisions such as this in terms of whether two alternatives represent complements or substitutes. Where two alternatives are complements, one's productivity from using one is limited without also using the other. The complementation between one's left and right shoes represents a classic example. Where two alternatives are substitutes, one's productivity from using one is unchanged when switching to another. The substitution between a single dollar bill and four quarters represents a clear example. Classical microeconomic theory (see Pindyck & Rubinfeld, 1998; Samuelson, 1974) imposes a number of relationships over the manner in which complements and substitutes affect one another as well as the marginal productivity associated with their use. In terms of complementation or substitution of specialist and generalist knowledge, such relationships are described in part by Postrel (2002).

Figure 3 presents a screenshot delineating two primary tasks (design and manufacturing), each performed by a corresponding organizational unit (design actor and manufacturing actor). The two milestone markers shown in the figure ("Start" and "Finish") are used in VDT to denote progress, but such markers neither represent tasks nor entail effort. The tree structure shown at the top left of the figure displays several of the different ontological elements of the VDT model (e.g., tasks, positions, milestones). The table shown at the bottom left displays numerous program-level parameters (e.g., team experience, central-

Figure 3. VDT baseline product development model

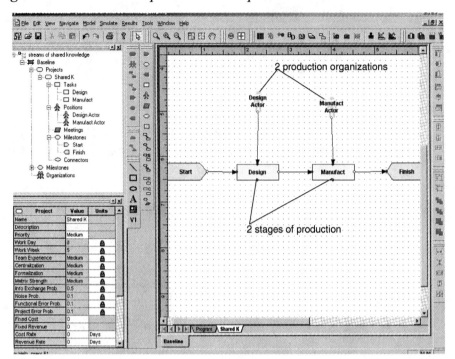

ization, formalization), which are all set to empirically determined "normal" values for product development work. Values for such parameters are held constant (controlled) across simulations of alternate cases and scenarios.

To analyze this computational model, it is parameterized to reflect "medium" specialist knowledge and "medium" generalist knowledge. We are interested in learning how varying the relative levels of specialist and generalist knowledge will impact organizational performance on the project. To develop insight into the dynamic behavior of this project organization, we examine a multitude of different conditions. Indeed, we conduct a full-factorial computational experiment, with knowledge representing "low," "medium," and "high" levels for all combinations of specialist and generalist settings. Examining each case individually provides us with precise control over which factors can vary, hence, excellent insight into causality. Examining exhaustively all combinations of specialist and generalist knowledge levels provides us with insight into the entire design space associated with these KM variables of interest. Using consistently the output measure *project duration* enables us to employ a common metric to assess relative performance. These benefits all accrue from analyzing

Table 7. Computational model results (project duration in work days)

Parameter	Low S	Medium S	High S
High G	226	178	141
Medium G	264	**216**	178
Low G	310	264	226

computationally a virtual prototype of the project organization. Moreover, using empirically determined and validated "normal" settings to depict the behavior of a representative technology project provides us with confidence that results of our simulations bear resemblance to those of operational organizational projects in the field. This benefit accrues from employing the general and validated modeling environment VDT.

Computational results for the product development model are summarized in Table 7. The values listed in the table reflect simulated project duration and are expressed in workdays. For instance, notice the result in the table's center (highlighted in bold font for emphasis): a project staffed with actors possessing medium levels of specialist manufacturing knowledge (S) and medium levels of generalist knowledge (G) is projected by the model to require 216 workdays to complete. This reflects a nominal 200 days of work specified (work volume), along with 16 days of additional problem solving (e.g., internal communication, delay and exception handling associated with noise, uncertainty and errors). The additional 16 days' problem solving time reflects empirically determined relationships between model parameters (e.g., levels of S and G) and organizational performance.

Table 7 reports full-factorial results of nine simulation runs, with both the S (specialist knowledge) and G (generalist) parameters varying across three levels: low, medium, and high. Notice the simulation results vary in understandable ways across the three levels of both specialist and generalist knowledge. For instance, holding the parameter G constant at the medium level of generalist knowledge, performance in terms of project duration ranges from 264 days when specialist knowledge is low to 178 days when specialist knowledge is high. The greater the level of specialist knowledge (holding the level of generalist knowledge constant), the better the organizational performance in terms of project duration, and vice versa.

This indicates the marginal product of such knowledge is positive (consistent with classical microeconomic theory). This same monotonic relationship is evident at the other levels of generalist knowledge (low G, high G) as well.

Likewise, holding the parameter S constant at the medium level of specialist knowledge, performance in terms of project duration ranges symmetrically from 264 days when generalist knowledge is low to 178 days when generalist knowledge is high. The greater the level of generalist knowledge (holding the level of specialist knowledge constant), the better the organizational performance in terms of project duration, and vice versa. This is also consistent with classical microeconomic theory and is evident too at the other levels of specialist knowledge (low S, high S).

The symmetry reflected in the results of Table 7 corresponds to the microeconomic case of *perfect substitution*: specialist and generalist knowledge can be substituted — unit for unit — to maintain performance at some arbitrary level (e.g., along an isoquant). For instance from the table, where specialist knowledge (S) is low, but generalist knowledge (G) is medium, performance (264 workdays) is the same as where specialist knowledge (S) is medium (one unit higher), but generalist knowledge (G) is low (one unit lower). Other instances of such substitutability can be identified readily through different combinations of knowledge types S and G (e.g., low S, high G <—> high S, low G [226 days], high S, medium G <—> medium S, high G [178 days]).

With this, the computational model indicates specialist and generalist knowledge represent substitutes for one another. It is important to note here that this result reflecting perfect substitution reflects an *emergent property* of the computational model, not an explicit behavior; that is, nowhere in the development of the VDT environment or this computational project model do we specify behaviors of perfect substitution. Rather, the nature of interactions between VDT actors, tasks, organizations, and environmental settings lead dynamically to this result. In a sense, this provides some additional validation of VDT behaviors (from classical microeconomics).

We use this to induce our twelfth leadership mandate from the practical application section of this book. *Mandate 12. Specialist and generalist knowledge represent (imperfect) economic substitutes for one another.*

Clearly, this relatively simple computational model excludes several factors and aspects of the world that would complicate the analysis and alter the symmetry of results. Nonetheless, we are able to computationally model actions associated with knowing in an organizational context. We are able to observe the dynamic behaviors of actors possessing and using different kinds of knowledge at different inventory levels. We are able to compare the relative dynamic performance of the organization associated with each case. This provides considerable insight that is useful for assessing knowledge-flow performance.

Knowledge-Flow Assessment Principles

Five principles developed in this chapter help shed light on knowledge-flow assessment: (1) knowledge management involves organizational change; (2) knowledge inventory can be used to assess an organization's readiness to perform its work processes effectively; (3) when estimating the value of knowledge, it is often better to light a candle than to curse the darkness; (4) culture, trust, and incentives affect organizational learning, hence, performance as much as process, technology, and training do; and (5) computational modeling is useful for knowing and learning about organizational knowing and learning.

Principle 26. KM projects involve change. There is much to learn from the literature on change management (e.g., BPR) in this regard. For instance, the knowledge manager can assess an organization's preconditions for success as well as preconditions for failure. KM-specific factors such as *knowledge representation, attention to tacit knowledge,* and *focus on organizational memory* are important too and can be evaluated and addressed by the knowledge manager. We also find how perceptual measures such as *pessimism, affective commitment,* and *normative commitment* are important in KM projects. **Hence, the knowledge manager has much to learn from business process re-engineering and like change-management approaches**.

Principle 27. Knowledge inventory can be used to assess an organization's readiness to perform its work processes effectively. The knowledge audit represents an approach to discovering and documenting sources, uses, and sinks of knowledge in an organization. Generally executed via some kind of survey instrument, the knowledge audit is often performed by consultants and like professionals from outside the organization, but there is little reason why an organization should not be able to audit itself. In addition to explicitly articulating certain aspects of knowledge inventories and flows, conducting a knowledge audit can produce positive effects simply by inducing people within the organization to think about what knowledge is important, how it is used, and how it flows. Alternatively, knowledge audits consume precious time and energy. Perhaps the greatest potential in terms of a knowledge audit lies in the prospect of measuring *knowledge inventory*. This construct offers potential to assess an organization's readiness to perform its work processes effectively. **Hence, the manager needs to measure the knowledge inventory for every organization**.

Principle 28. Knowledge value can be estimated. The KVA approach provides a set of techniques for attributing knowledge to various organizational processes and in turn prioritizing them based on a return on knowledge. The approach amounts to an allocation with no claims of superiority over other allocation schemes, but it places a premium on tacit knowledge. And it provides a set of measurement techniques that stand out among the dearth of alternatives for valuing knowledge. Although we remain cautious about KVA's theoretical acceptance and practical implementation, it reflects metaphorically the concept *candle lighting*: When in an environment without light, it is often better to light a candle than to curse the darkness (ancient Chinese proverb). **Hence, KVA provides an approach to measuring the relative value of knowledge associated with various organizational processes**.

Principle 29. Culture, trust, and incentives affect organizational learning, hence, performance as much as process, technology, and training do. Learning rates can be measured and projected. Through the well accepted and established learning curve, the knowledge-flow component of experiential knowing (learning) can be measured and related mathematically with the workflow component (doing). Several general rules of thumb provide guidance for application of learning curves. These include the well-studied roles of automation, calendar time, production rate, technology introduction, and workforce capability, in addition to less-understood factors such as organizational culture, trust, and incentives. Such latter factors can affect organizational learning, hence, performance as much as the former ones do. Every organizational process involving repetition should experience performance improvement through learning at multiple levels of reach (e.g., individual, group, organization). Where such improvement may not obtain, this signals a problem with knowledge clumping and calls attention to the associated knowledge flows. **Hence, every organizational process should improve and measure its performance over time**.

Principle 30. Computational modeling can be used to learn about organizational knowing and learning. Computational models are used extensively in the physical sciences for the design of artifacts. And their use in the social sciences is increasing. Through advanced computational models that describe dynamic behaviors of knowledge flows in the organization, one can represent, simulate, and analyze — virtually — many different organizational designs to assess the relative strengths and weaknesses of alternate approaches to enhancing knowledge flows. By analyzing how knowledge flows in different organizational designs (e.g., alternate structures, workflows, personnel characteristics, technologies), one can gain insight into how different flows of knowledge affect organizational performance. One can also gain insight into how the knowing and learning that takes place within an organization react to different managerial interventions (e.g., OJT, training, mentoring, simulation). This represents a risk-mitigation strategy for addressing the change aspect of KM projects: before deciding upon a specific KM approach and implementing a particular set of organizational, work, personnel, and/or technological changes, one can assess computationally the relative efficacy and efficiency of each alternative. **Hence, computational models of knowledge flows provide an approach to mitigating the risk inherent in KM programs.**

Exercises

1.   Use the preconditions for success and failure from Tables 1 and 2 to analyze a major change that took place in an organization with which you are familiar. Can you identify any lessons to be learned through such analysis?

2.   Describe how you would conduct a knowledge audit of a college course that you have taken or are taking currently. How long would it take to conduct such an audit, and what benefits would you expect from it?

3.   Explain if or how your performance conducting a KVA analysis to assess multiple organizational processes would be expected to improve through repetition or over time. Understanding that every process is different and, hence, no two KVA analyses would represent exact repetitions, how would this affect your answer?

4.   How could the knowledge-flow analysis discussed in the practical illustration of computational modeling be extended to increase the realism and fidelity of the simulation? How would you go about representing and simulating such increased realism and fidelity in the model?

Chapter VII

Application Cases in Business

This chapter concentrates on knowledge-flow visualization and analysis in the for-profit business sector. We look first at an advanced-technology company involved with new-product development. The discussion turns then to examine an independent production company involved with a feature film. The third case involves a technology-transfer project between a university and a microelectronics company. In each case, we draw from secondary data sources for background. This should prove helpful to the reader who is interested in following up to consider more details than presented in this volume. We draw also from our own research and professional experience to fill in missing information, and we apply principles and techniques of this book to contribute new insights through examination of knowledge flows in the cases. Each application case concludes with exercises to stimulate critical thought, learning, and discussion.

Advanced-Technology Company and New-Product Development

We draw from Massey et al. (2002a, b) for the background of this case. We first summarize important events and issues for context. Visualization and analysis of key knowledge flows follows with interpretation of management interventions discussed subsequently. The section closes with exercises pertaining specifically to this application case.

Context

An advanced-technology company in the communications and networks industry faces intense competition. In its technology-intensive competitive arena, product innovation represents a key determinant of performance. Just keeping up with the rapid pace of technological advance is required to avoid falling too far behind competitors, and pulling ahead of competitors requires sustained introduction of innovative products that have market appeal and make business sense. Indeed, the company's strategy centers on innovation. Managers view winning and keeping new customers as the principal means of attaining and sustaining competitive advantage. This competitive backdrop is common across most advanced-technology companies today.

We learn further from the case that management is dissatisfied with the company's performance. The intensity of competition appears to be increasing, and rival firms are beating this company to market with successive new products. When looking for the next new product for the company to introduce, most of the concepts center on extensions and revisions to existing products, as opposed to new-product innovations. The inventory of new products appears to be plentiful, but the inventory of *innovations* appears to have reached zero. A. P. Massey (personal communication, August 2004) adds, "some malaise [is present] in product development" at the company. Management is justifiably concerned that the company has lost its ability to innovate. Loss of innovation prowess would sound the death knell for an advanced-technology company such as this.

Through in-depth analysis of the problem, management learns the dearth of innovation does not stem from the knowledge of its people. On the contrary, company personnel appear to possess abundant, relevant knowledge necessary for new-product development, and many ideas for new products can be identified. However, such ideas remain generally stagnant, as the process for developing new products is ineffective. The organization does not provide the kind of guidance and support through its routines that people as individuals and in groups need in order to leverage new-product ideas into new product innovations. In other words, the individuals' knowledge appears to be ad-

Figure 1. Advanced-technology company knowledge flows

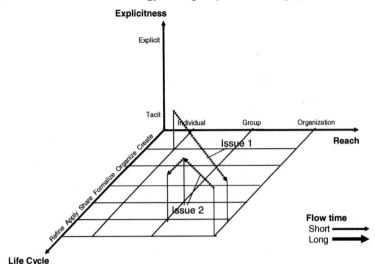

equate for the task environment, but knowledge embedded in the organization's routines does not. In particular, the problem centers on two issues: (1) new ideas do not flow well to become innovative products; and (2) concept-selection decisions do not reflect shared criteria learned through organizational experience.

Knowledge-Flow Analysis

Knowledge flows are critical to both issues. With the first issue, individual knowledge created in terms of new ideas does not move to organizational application through product innovation. We depict the knowledge flow associated with this first issue in Figure 1. The vector (labeled "Issue 1") represents our interpretation of problems with knowledge flows in the advanced-technology company; that is, we are not aware that either managers in the company case or researchers reporting the case originally visualized and analyzed knowledge flows in this manner. Rather, we illustrate through the case how knowledge-flow principles and analytic techniques can be applied to new-product development in an advanced-technology company such as this. The vector is represented as a dotted line to emphasize it *does not yet flow as delineated*; that is, the vector depicts the manner in which management would like the knowledge to flow. One can think of the vector in terms of a *knowledge-flow requirement* elucidated via analysis.

We use this to induce our thirteenth leadership mandate from the practical application section of this book. *Mandate 13. Knowledge-flow vectors can be used to represent dynamic knowledge requirements.*

This first issue pertains to knowledge clumping at the individual level. Specifically, the Issue 1 vector points from one knowledge-flow coordinate (tacit, individual, create) to another (tacit, organization, apply). Using our coordinate shorthand, this would be depicted as (TIC → TOA). Individual people are developing new ideas that offer potential for new-product innovation, but the knowledge associated with such ideas is not flowing to application at the organization level to manifest through innovative new products. Individual knowledge creation is arguably very tacit. Hence, this vector corresponding to Issue 1 is rooted as such (TIC). New-product innovation involves tacit knowledge as well. When such tacit knowledge is embedded within organizational routines, imitation becomes very difficult, and competitive advantage through appropriation can obtain. Hence, this vector corresponding to Issue 1 is headed as such (TOA). Notice the vector points toward the application stage along the life cycle dimension. Until such knowledge can be applied, its potential cannot manifest. This is part of the knowing-doing gap.

With the second issue, organizational knowledge about concept selection is not shared with groups of decision makers responsible for prioritizing new ideas. We depict the knowledge flow associated with this second issue in the same manner used for Issue 1 in Figure 1. Using our coordinate shorthand, this would be depicted as (TOR → TGS). This second issue pertains to knowledge clumping at the organizational level. The organization has considerable experience in this industry and has learned over time — through both success and failure — which product attributes (e.g., in terms of technology, marketing, business) are important. But the knowledge associated with such attributes is not explicit and does not flow to the group level to provide a consistent basis for evaluating alternate new-product concepts. Organizational learning refined over time is arguably very tacit. Hence, this vector corresponding to Issue 2 is rooted as such (TOR). Knowledge flowing as required for sharing would enable decision-making groups to know the important evaluation criteria. Hence, this vector corresponding to Issue 2 is headed as such (TGS). Notice this vector points toward the share stage along the life cycle dimension. It does not point toward knowledge application. As noted, until such knowledge can be applied, its potential cannot manifest. Hence, we include a second ray of this vector pointing to knowledge application at the group level (TGS → TGA). Also as noted, this vector is delineated using a dotted line to indicate that knowledge *does not yet flow* as such. One can think of the vector in terms of a *knowledge-flow requirement* elucidated via analysis. Notice each of these knowledge-flow vectors is delineated using relatively thin arrows. This depicts management's express requirements that such knowledge flows be accomplished quickly.

Management Interventions

To intervene in the situation and address the issues reported previously, management develops a conceptual model of its new-product development process. Recognizing the problem with idea-translation, it focuses in particular on the front end of this process. The goal is to analyze such conceptual model and use it to redesign the process in a manner that enhances the movement of ideas from the minds of individual employees to organizational routines that develop innovative new products reaching customers. Management thinks it important to ensure that whatever new process may emerge from the redesign will be consistent with (1) organizational resources that are available; (2) enterprise goals; and (3) organizational culture. The importance of fit with resources is clear in terms of not jeopardizing the enterprise's financial performance, but where new-product innovation represents the firm's core strategy, one may question the prudence of worrying about resources when survival appears to be at stake. The importance of fit with goals should be clear and self-explanatory. The importance of fit with culture may require some explanation. In many cases of process change, the organizational culture represents a major cause of problems and source of resistance to changing routines. In this case, the company appears to be trying to maintain its culture and fit an improved new-product development process within such culture. As with the point noted about resources, where organizational survival appears to be at stake here, one may question why the company does not address the culture too.

Management is also interested in establishing a set of processes that can quickly filter many new-product ideas and that could consistently apply evaluation criteria with marketing, technology, business, and human-factors perspectives. One proposal for changing the organizational routine for new-product development is to establish a relatively permanent team of experts (e.g., in marketing, technology, business, and human-factors) to screen new ideas and to facilitate their translation. However, management dismisses this proposal because of the high cost associated with maintaining such an expert group. Most of the other proposals center on requiring individual people who generate new ideas to evaluate and develop such ideas themselves. However, very few individuals who generate new ideas know all of the functions required to effectively accomplish such evaluation and development. Three alternatives are proposed to address this lack of knowledge: (1) train all employees in all functions and require them to formally evaluate their own ideas; (2) assign experts to screen ideas; and (3) capture and formalize expert knowledge via IT. The company selects the third alternative for implementation.

This "EPSS" IT (from the class electronic performance support systems) is described in the case:

EPSS technology could create an electronic version of a human subject-matter expert. ...It could provide efficiencies in process oversight and administration as well as electronic repositories of the intellectual property associated with idea generation. ...It may be considered an electronic infrastructure that captures, stores, and distributes individual and corporate knowledge to enable individuals to achieve desired levels of performance in the fastest possible time and with a minimum of support from others. ...The goal of the software environment is to provide access to integrated information, knowledge, learning experiences, advice, and guidance at the "moment of need." (p. 50)

This IT is further described in terms of "enabling performance in the context of work." Notice enabling work represents a fundamental element of knowledge, and this IT implementation is focused on enhancing knowledge flow to application. This is consistent with the Issue 1 vector delineated previously. The IT implementation in the case is called "Virtual Mentor" (p. 51) and said to automate "each phase of the intervention process" and support "the performance of those individuals who are working within the process." The company assigns a cross-functional team of experts to design and develop this system, which provides (performative) support to decision-makers as well as individual idea generators. This is consistent with the Issue 2 vector delineated previously.

In terms of knowledge flows, the company invests in expert systems style IT to make explicit and distribute formerly tacit knowledge about developing new-product ideas. Figure 2 includes vectors delineating the new knowledge flow associated with this IT approach. One vector is rooted in individual knowledge of the cross-functional experts who design and develop the system. This root

Figure 2. IT approach to management intervention

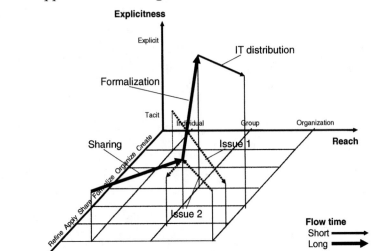

reflects tacit knowledge refined through years of individual experience (TIR). The first flow represented by this vector depicts the sharing of such individual knowledge among experts assembled into a group (TGS). The case is unclear on how long this process takes, but sharing tacit knowledge as such is expected to occur at a relatively slow pace. Hence, we use a relatively thick line to represent the corresponding vector. Shorthand for this first vector is thus (TIR → TGS). It is labeled "Sharing" in the figure. The second flow depicts the formalization of tacit shared knowledge (TGS) into explicit form suitable for capture in the EPSS (EGF). Comparable in many respects to knowledge formalization associated with expert systems development, this flow is expected to occur at a relatively slow pace also and is delineated accordingly using a relatively thick line for the corresponding vector. Notice this associated vector rises above the tacit plane, moving knowledge to an explicit coordinate (TGS → EGF). It is labeled "Formalization" in the figure.

The third flow depicts the organization-wide sharing of explicit knowledge embedded in the IT implementation (EGF → EOS). With knowledge formalized in explicit form and embedded in IT as such, the corresponding flow is expected to occur at a relatively fast pace. Hence, we use a relatively thin line to represent the corresponding vector. It is labeled "IT distribution" in the figure. Through development and implementation of this EPSS system, we understand from the case that the organizational routine changes to incorporate this new IT application and to support knowledge flows.

Notice at the organizational level that the knowledge associated with this routine is explicit and resident within the system. Hence, Figure 2 depicts only knowledge flows associated with developing and distributing the EPSS, but the figure does not yet depict how the EPSS *is used by people* to move knowledge created through idea generation (TIC) to product innovation (TOA). In other words, this knowledge flow does not depict how individual employees and groups would learn to use and interact subsequently with the IT application in the performance of their work processes. Recall, for instance, the dotted-line vectors used to represent knowledge-flow requirements depict *tacit* knowledge flows. Presumably, formal training courses, mentoring, and individual OJT would be required for this human-centered flow. Such latter, human-centered flows are not delineated in the figure, nor do we include the corresponding discussion here, leaving this question instead as a later exercise for the reader.

We use this to induce our fourteenth leadership mandate from the practical application section of this book. *Mandate 14. It is essential to plan how knowledge technologies will be used by people.*

This application case describes an advanced-technology company that faces problems with its knowledge flows and addresses them through performative IT. Discussion of the case enables us to visualize and analyze several of the key knowledge flows associated with this company, both in terms of requirements and interventions. Clearly, many additional details are pertinent to the case, which the interested reader can pursue through the source. The case highlights several of the principles developed in earlier parts of this book, and it provides generalizable insight into application of knowledge-flow principles to other cases. We leave such principles and application as exercises for the reader.

Exercises

1. Identify and describe three principles from earlier parts of the book that apply to this case. Can you induce additional principles from this application case that are not articulated in the earlier parts?

2. Delineate vectors to describe knowledge flows corresponding to how idea generators and decision makers in the Advanced-Technology Company would learn and use the IT application described in the case.

3.   Comment on other approaches the company could take to address its knowledge-flow problems. What relative advantages and disadvantages apply to your suggestions when compared with the approach described in the case?

4.   Describe how your learning from this case can be related to an organization with which you are familiar. Include a knowledge-flow diagram such as the one presented in Figure 1 or 2.

Independent Production Company and Feature Film Project

We draw from DeFillippi and Arthur (1998) for the background of this case. We first summarize important events and issues for context. Visualization and analysis of key knowledge flows follows, with interpretation of management implications discussed subsequently. The section closes with exercises pertaining specifically to this application case.

Context

An independent production company in the motion-picture industry is engaged in a feature film project. In its competitive arena, producing a film that appeals to audiences and generates box-office financial returns is important to principals in the filmmaking project (e.g., Producer, Director, Financiers). Such principals have an equity stake in the organization, but the company itself represents a "temporary enterprise" (p. 127), which forms solely for the production of a single film and is expected to dissolve after project completion. In contrast to such stakeholders, financial returns deriving from a particular film project are not particularly important to the many other people involved with the film (e.g., screen-writers, make-up artists, camera people), who are temporary employees paid for services rendered.

Many aspects of the motion-picture industry and its constituent companies are similar to those observable in advanced-technology industries and firms. For instance, both organizational contexts are project-based. In the advanced-technology company previously discussed, for example, each new-product innovation — which is developed and taken to market by a team of people —

represents a separate project. Likewise, in the independent production company of this case, each new film — which is produced and distributed by a team of people — represents a separate project.

As another instance, the work in both organizational contexts requires knowledge-based skills and experiences of diverse specialists to be integrated together. In the advanced-technology company discussed previously, for example, each new-product innovation requires scientists, engineers, marketers, manufacturers, accountants, and managers to work together to bring a . new-product idea — through innovation and development — to market. Likewise, in the independent production company of this case, each new film requires actors, directors, screenwriters, camera people, make-up artists, accountants, and producers to bring a new-film idea — through production and distribution — to the box office.

As a third instance, people in both organizational contexts must learn to work together in cross-functional teams, and the efficacy of workflows depends critically on such group learning. In the advanced-technology company, for example, cross-functional specialists are often assigned — as teams — to successive projects to exploit previous group learning. Likewise, in the independent production company of this case, specialists from diverse professions and guilds are often recruited — as teams — for successive films to exploit previous group learning.

Alternatively, many aspects of the motion-picture industry and its constituent companies are dissimilar to those observable in advanced-technology industries and firms. For instance, company longevity does not represent a consistent concern across the two organizational contexts. In the advanced-technology company, for example, one new-product innovation — which is expected to generate financial returns to the firm — is insufficient for the company to be successful. Rather, a stream of new-product innovations is required. By contrast with the independent production company of this case, each new film — which is expected to generate financial returns to the principals — is sufficient for the company to be successful. Any subsequent new films involving the firm's participants will be produced by a different independent company.

As another instance, people's learning is expected to have different contributors and beneficiaries across the two organizational contexts. In the advanced-technology company, for example, each new-product innovation provides an opportunity for participants on the project team to learn and acquire experience, and this same company expects (or at least hopes) to retain such participants, hence, benefit from their increased experience on the next project.

By contrast with the independent production company of this case, each new film provides an opportunity for participants on the project team to learn and acquire experience also, but this same company has little expectation (or even hope) of retaining such participants, hence, benefiting from their increased experience on the next project.

As a third instance, people's allegiance and sense of professional identity aligns to different kinds of organizations across the two contexts. In the advanced-technology company, for example, people identify largely with their employer and expect (or at least hope) to maintain their employment relationship across projects. People identify also with professional organizations (e.g., societies of accountants, engineers, managers), but such latter organizations can be viewed as subsidiary to employers. By contrast with the independent production company of this case, people identify only loosely with their employers and do not expect (but perhaps hope) to maintain their employment relationship across projects. Rather, people identify principally with professional organizations (e.g., guilds for screen actors, writers, camera people), and such latter organizations can be viewed as primary over employers.

Experience is paramount in the motion-picture industry. Generally, on film projects, budgets are very tight, and schedules are very demanding. People are hired based largely on their experience and are expected to perform well immediately when called to do so. There is negligible slack time or margin for learning through trial and error, but experienced people learn exactly through trial and error (e.g., this is the central process for gaining experience). A make-up artist with a dozen films' worth of experience is expected to outperform— and would be more desirable than— one working on his or her first production, but such experienced make-up artist worked on his or her first film at some point in time, and he or she was probably less desirable at the time than a more experienced person would have been. Because experience is valued so highly and film-production organizations have such short time horizons, entry into the industry is very difficult for most people. Even low-wage employment through a menial job can represent someone's "big break" in the film business.

Further, the role played by schools and colleges is minimal in this industry. Some skills and techniques can be learned and refined through formal education (e.g., acting schools, theater, film degrees), but the majority come through direct experience (OJT). Mentoring plays an important role also. Many junior people, who take on relatively menial and insignificant jobs (e.g., "runners" who deliver script changes to various sets and who fetch coffee for more senior people), do so principally for the opportunity to observe how professionals

Figure 3. Film company knowledge flows

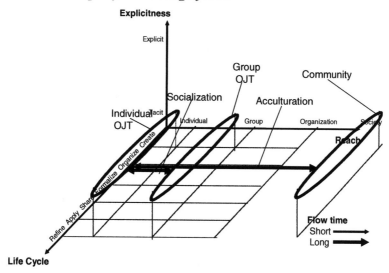

work and to get some tips from experienced practitioners during breaks and unplanned idle periods. Also, the tension between learning and doing is biased in an extreme manner toward the latter in the film business, which focuses heavily on exploitation over exploration. Yet success of the industry as a whole depends critically upon learning and exploration over time.

Knowledge-Flow Analysis

Knowledge flows are clearly important at the individual level. Individuals must acquire experience-based knowledge to gain employment. And their value to employers increases in rough proportion to their increases in knowledge. This importance of knowledge is similar to that experienced by individuals in most organizations (e.g., independent film companies, advanced-technology corpo-rations, government agencies, non-profit firms). A person seeks to learn through work experience and requires experience to work (hence learn). People are often willing to begin working at jobs that do not take full advantage of their potential, in part to acquire the experience necessary to qualify for jobs that do take such full advantage and in part to pay the bills while learning.

In Figure 3 we delineate individual learning through experience as a cycle of tacit knowledge moving iteratively between creation (learning), application (doing), and refinement (learning). This cycle vector is labeled "Individual OJT" in the figure. As a person works, he or she contributes in large part to workflows through individual knowledge application (TIA), but this person contributes to knowledge flows also through learning associated with refinement of individual knowledge (TIR). This is represented by the classic learning curve. Additionally, such person can learn through work variation and experimentation, which contributes to knowledge flows through individual knowledge creation (TIC). This often manifests through OJT or trial and error. The pattern continues then with subsequent flows through recurring application, refinement, and creation of knowledge.

We use this to induce our fifteenth leadership mandate from the practical application section of this book. *Mandate 15. The learning curve measures knowledge flows through OJT.*

The cyclic vector is represented using relatively thick arrows to depict correspondingly slow knowledge flows. This is consistent with evidence of experience-based learning at the individual level. Notice we could use a similar cyclic vector to depict individual knowledge flows in the advanced-technology case, for instance, to represent the learning and knowing of an engineer, marketer, accountant, or like individual in the technology organization. Likewise, we use this cyclic vector here to depict individual knowledge flows in the present case, for instance, to represent the learning and knowing of a screenwriter, camera person, accountant, or like individual in the film organization.

Knowledge flows are also clearly important at the group level. Individuals must acquire experience working with other people in groups, and such knowledge is requisite to gainful employment in the motion-picture industry. Moreover, in addition to learning how to work in groups generally, employers value individuals' experience working with specific people. In the case, we learn that collections of specific people are recruited — as teams — repeatedly to work on successive film projects. Here knowledge of how to work with specific people, in addition to knowledge of how to perform specialist work activities, is valued. And the value to employers increases in rough proportion to increases in both group (e.g., working with other people generally) and team (e.g., working with specific people) experience.

In the present case, the group represents a clear unit of analysis for knowledge flows. Each individual in every group would have knowledge flows that are described well by the cyclic pattern shown and discussed in Figure 3. But each collection of individuals (e.g., group, team) would have its own knowledge flows as well. Using the same logic as we used previously for representing individual-level knowledge flows that iterate between knowledge creation

(TIC), application (TIA), and refinement (TIR), we can depict group-level learning in comparable fashion. This latter vector is labeled "Group OJT" in the figure. As a group of people works together, they contribute in large part to workflows through collective knowledge application (TGA). But this group of people contributes to knowledge flows also through learning associated with refinement of collective knowledge (TGR). This is represented also by the classic learning curve. Additionally, such group of people can learn through work variation and experimentation, which contributes to knowledge flows through collective knowledge creation (TGC). OJT or trial and error apply at the group level as well as to individual knowing and learning. The pattern continues then with subsequent flows through recurring application, refinement, and creation of knowledge.

The cyclic vector is represented using relatively thick arrows to depict correspondingly slow knowledge flows. This is consistent with evidence of experience-based learning at the group level. Notice we could use a similar cyclic vector to depict group knowledge flows in the advanced-technology case, for instance, to represent the learning and knowing of a new-product team comprised of an engineer, marketer, accountant, and like individuals in the technology organization. Likewise, we use this cyclic vector here to depict group knowledge flows in the present case, for instance, to represent the learning and knowing of a film-production team comprised of a screen-writer, camera person, accountant, and like individuals in the film organization.

Further, we learn from the case about other knowledge-flow interactions between individuals and groups. For instance, some relatively ignorant individuals (e.g., inexperienced, junior people) join groups to work on film projects and to gain experience. Such individuals come to the organization with little knowledge to contribute to the group. The Runner represents one example made clear in the case, but the group may contribute substantial knowledge to the individual in terms of socialization. This is in addition to individuals sharing specialist knowledge (e.g., via mentoring). Here knowledge flows principally from group to individual, remaining in the tacit plane (e.g., TGS → TIS).

As another instance, some highly knowledgeable people join groups to lead film projects and to share experience. Such individuals come to the organization with substantial knowledge to contribute to the group. The Screenwriter and Producer represent two examples made clear in the case, but the group may contribute negligible knowledge to the individual through interaction. Here tacit knowledge flows principally from individual to group (e.g., TIS → TGS). These represent extreme instances in which knowledge flows are principally unidirectional. Alternatively, knowledge flows bidirectionally in the general case (e.g., when individuals and groups share knowledge and learn mutually). We depict such mutual sharing between individuals and groups using a two-headed arrow to represent the bidirectional knowledge-flow vectors. This is labeled "Socialization" in Figure 3, after the process characterized well by Nonaka (1994). The two-headed vector is represented using relatively thick arrows to depict correspondingly slow knowledge flows. This is consistent with evidence of sharing tacit knowledge through work activities.

Notice we do not include knowledge flows at the organizational level in Figure 3. Although knowledge is clearly being applied through organizational knowing that manifests via workflows on a film project, and the film-production organization clearly learns through its experience with a film, we understand from the case that such organization disbands at project completion. Hence, the organization does not represent a particularly insightful unit of analysis in terms of *dynamic knowledge flows*. In contrast, such organization represents a very insightful unit of analysis in terms of *pre-existing knowledge stocks* and workflows. Further, the organization-level knowledge flows taking place during the short time horizon of a film-production company do so relatively quickly (e.g., on the order of weeks and months) with respect to counterpart flows at the individual and group levels (e.g., on the order of years and decades). We know from the case, for instance, that an independent production enterprise can start, work, and dissolve well within one year, whereas people comprising some of the teams recruited to work on any particular feature film may have worked together for over a decade.

Alternatively, we do include knowledge flows at the trans-organizational level in Figure 3. Such flows pertain to the guilds and like professional societies. Knowledge flows associated with societies like these transcend film companies, production studios, and like economic organizations that employ workers. Such flows transcend also the group-level collectivities that perform project work on films. The knowledge flows associated with these societies involve professional interaction and knowledge exchange at a trans-organizational level. This phenomenon could be characterized well by the term *community of practice* that describes similar aspects of the process (see Brown & Duguid, 1991).

The case does not provide much insight into the innerworkings of guilds and like societies, but we interpret some recurring patters of knowledge flows at the trans-organizational level that are comparable to those described previously for individual- and group-level flows. Hence, we represent such patterns using the same kind of cyclic vector to depict recurring flows at other levels of reach. This is labeled "Community" in Figure 3. Likewise, the case does not provide much insight into exchanges between individuals and communities, but we interpret some mutual sharing patterns of knowledge flows between individuals and societies that are comparable to those described previously for socialization through individual-group sharing. Hence, we represent such patterns using the same kind of two-headed vector to depict bidirectional flows between these two levels of reach. This is labeled "Acculturation" in Figure 3. Other knowledge flows could be delineated for this film-production case as well (e.g., leveraging a new idea for a film into the film production), but we leave these for the reader as exercises below.

We use this to induce our sixteenth leadership mandate from the practical application section of this book. *Mandate 16. Socialization and acculturation represent viable approaches to enhancing tacit knowledge flows.*

Management Implications

Many business firms organize at least some aspects of their work along project lines. Such organizations include aerospace companies, computer firms, software development enterprises, and others. As such, the kinds of knowledge flows discussed and delineated in connection with this case generalize well to corresponding project work beyond the focal firm of the case. Management implications include, for instance, the importance of group-level experience and learning—in addition to individual-level experience and learning—on project performance. Indeed, the group represents the critical unit of analysis in project work. Implications include also, as another instance, the provision of some idle time and/or slack resources for learning (e.g., through experimentation, trial and error). Learning by observation and mentoring are noted too as important contributors to knowledge flows in the case, but many project organizations focus exclusively on exploitation of existing knowledge to drive workflows at the expense of exploration to gain new knowledge through learning. Where the company-level organization endures and organizes its work through successive projects, firm-specific, longitudinal learning across time can be as or more important to competitive advantage as knowing within any single project.

Additionally, some business firms organize all of their work along projects lines. In the extreme case exemplified by the independent film-production case, the organization exists solely for the performance of a single project. Similar organizations include architecture-engineering-construction consortia, military task forces, and political campaign offices. Such organizations have little concern for cross-project learning. Any learning from the organization's current project accrues to some other organization that comes into being after the focal enterprise has dissolved. Hence, a manager's relative emphasis on learning vs. doing should depend necessarily on the time horizon of the organization with respect to that of any particular project. Where the two time horizons converge, an emphasis on recruiting experienced people and on exploiting extant knowledge to enable workflows is in order. Alternatively, where the two time horizons diverge, an emphasis on developing firm-specific expertise in people and on exploring new knowledge for appropriation may be more in order.

Finally, the importance of guilds, unions, professional societies, and like trans-organizational collectives can vary considerably in terms of knowledge flows. We learn from the case, for instance, that such collectives play a central role in the professional identity, allegiance, and career-long learning of individuals. To the extent that such trans-organizational collectives are important to employees of an organization, such communities may have greater influence over employee knowledge, culture, and performance than leadership and management do. In other instances, collectives are non-existent or play a lesser role (e.g., social interaction). Membership in professional engineering societies represents an example in which management is likely to have greater influence over employees than trans-organizational collectivities do. In either case, trans-organizational collectivities can play an important role in terms of knowledge flows, a role that has managerial implications.

We use this to induce our seventeenth leadership mandate from the practical application section of this book. *Mandate 17. Trans-organizational collectivities (e.g., communities) may have greater influence over employee knowledge, culture, and performance than leadership and management do.*

This application case describes a film-production company that organizes around a single project and that dissolves following project completion. Discussion of the case enables us to visualize and analyze several of the key knowledge flows associated with this company, both in terms of individual and collective phenomena. Clearly, many additional details are pertinent to the case, which the interested reader can pursue through the source. The case highlights several of the principles developed in earlier parts of this book, and it provides generalizable insight into application of knowledge-flow principles to other cases. We leave such principles and application as exercises for the reader.

Exercises

5.   Identify and describe three principles from earlier parts of the book that apply to this case. Can you induce additional principles from this application case that are not articulated in the earlier parts?

6.   Delineate vectors to describe knowledge flows corresponding to how an individual with a new idea for a film in the Independent Production Company would know and learn to leverage such idea into a motion-picture production.

7.   Comment on other knowledge flows that are likely to be important to the company. What potential clumps and approaches to enhancing knowledge flows can you envision and suggest, respectively?

8.   Describe how your learning from this case can be related to an organization with which you are familiar. Include a knowledge-flow diagram such as the one presented in Figure 3.

Multinational Electronics Manufacturer and Technology Transfer Project

We draw from Daghfous (2004) for the background of this case. We first summarize important events and issues for context. Visualization and analysis of key knowledge flows follows, with interpretation of management implications discussed subsequently. The section closes with exercises pertaining specifically to this application case.

Context

A multinational microelectronics manufacturing company is engaged in a technology transfer project. Customers include telecommunication firms that use these products in global-positioning systems, signal-modulation equipment, and cellular-communication devices. This company is effective at present in its competitive arena. Superior knowledge embedded in the company's electronic products enables it to compete well. However, some of its core technologies remain somewhat dated with respect to the state of the art. In particular, the company identifies several internal problems centered on automated testing equipment for one of its principal products.

This testing equipment was designed nearly 25 years earlier by engineers who have long since left the company. The equipment — although perhaps state of the art in its day — performs at a level that is noticeably deficient. Its yield is comparatively low with respect to testing equipment that employed more current technologies. The system is somewhat unreliable, breaking down and requiring maintenance more frequently than expected. The equipment software and algorithms are documented poorly. The original engineers took the associated design with them in terms of tacit knowledge when they left the company. As a result, current engineers must often resort to a process of trial and error, along with deliberate experimentation, to learn about the equipment's myriad idiosyncrasies. The computer code used to automate the testing process via this equipment is written in an archaic and arcane software language that is known by only a couple of the company's employees. Several key parts of the automated test equipment have only a single vendor, leaving the company exposed to the risks of critical reliance upon a single source.

The company maintains a relationship with a university nearby. Through periodic interaction, company engineers and officers become aware of advancing software and testing technologies that offer potential to improve the dated, automated test equipment described. A small project forms around the objective of transferring the associated technology from the university to the company. This project begins with university researchers visiting the company frequently and interacting with engineers and operators to learn about the production process and existing automated test equipment. The university researchers report company personnel as very knowledgeable about the current process and equipment. This high knowledge level is seen to enhance researchers' ability to learn about the company processes in the early stages of the project (p. 79). But this same knowledge level is seen also to inhibit company engineers' ability to learn about the university's technology during these early stages.

The university team develops new technology for automated testing, but they do not start with a clean slate. Most of the existing software algorithms are used in the new technology. However, they are rewritten in a more-contemporary computer language. This modern language is one taught in universities and trade schools and is expected to be both easier to learn and known by a broader cross section of people. The university team also solicits input from current operators of the existing test equipment, input that is used to tailor the design of the new equipment to help satisfy operator wants and needs. After demonstration in the laboratory, the university team works with company personnel to implement the new technology in the production process. At first, the new technology operates in parallel with the old. This phased-implementation approach is a technique commonly used to reduce the risk of changing from one technology to another.

The new technology demonstrates some aspects of superior performance (e.g., increased yield), but its implementation proceeds more slowly than expected, and it evidences numerous problems. Considerable learning through trial and error is required of company engineers to integrate the new technology into the production process. Problems with new technology — particularly technology incorporating software — are to be expected generally in a project such as this. The new technology also produces some organizational changes. Several skills of operators are needed no longer to use the new technology, so such employees find their corresponding knowledge becoming obsolete. Other skills necessary to operate the new technology are absent from the company staff, so employees find themselves with a requirement for new learning. A combination of experienced and inexperienced (with respect to the old equipment) people is assigned to work on both the old and new equipment. As the production process transitions from parallel use of both systems toward sole reliance upon the new technology, the company fires some employees with obsolete skills and hires some new people to fill knowledge gaps remaining in the workforce.

Company personnel experience other difficulties associated with adoption of the new technology. In addition to the technical and process-integration problems noted previously, the heavy workload of employees constrains their ability to master the new system. Production quotas and efficiency norms are enforced by company supervisors, and negligible time is made available for employees to learn. This also limits the amount of experience-based feedback provided to the university project team. In this output-oriented environment, the day-to-day demands of the production job take clear priority over the technology-transition tasks required to implement, learn about, and refine the new automated test equipment. Indeed, we learn from the case that "experimentation was viewed by the project coordinator as non-value added unless it directly contributed to the bottom-line" (p. 76). We also learn that most knowledge sharing within the company is accomplished through informal discussion. A newsletter is circulated among employees to highlight and comment on lessons learned of interest, but no systematic process exists to collect, store, and disseminate such lessons (p. 77). The company is ISO-9000 certified, which indicates it has and employs considerable process documentation, but we learn from the case that such certification has not been extended to incorporate the processes associated with the automated test equipment.

Knowledge-Flow Analysis

Knowledge flows at several levels in this case, and we learn of factors that both enhance and inhibit various flows. Knowledge flows clearly at the individual level, both in operation of the old test equipment and in implementing the new. Operators of the old equipment, for instance, clearly apply knowledge to use the technology to support production workflows. To the extant that such technology is documented poorly, this suggests such knowledge is tacit and developed principally through processes of OJT and trial and error. This pattern of individual tacit knowledge flowing through creation (e.g., learning to use the system), application (e.g., knowing to use the system), and refinement (e.g., learning improved uses of the system) is similar to the "Individual OJT" cyclic vector described in the case of film production. We include and label accordingly this same cyclic vector in Figure 4 to represent the knowledge-flow pattern associated with operating the old automated test equipment. A similar pattern would apply well also to the company engineers who learn about, troubleshoot, and improve the new technology over time and while on the job.

The case makes clear that knowledge flows at the organization level within the company, too. The company's production process, for instance, has depended upon the old test equipment for 25 years, and it continues to function even long after the designers of this technology have left the company and even though such technology was not documented well. Hence, the organization's knowledge of how to produce and test its microelectronic products transcends and subsumes the knowledge of its individual employees. This is the nature of organizational routines, which are characterized best as tacit knowledge flowing at the organization level. Such routines are considered widely to involve learning over time, as new knowledge is acquired, put to use, and refined through an iterative cycle. Hence, the same kind of cyclic knowledge-flow

Figure 4. Technology transfer knowledge flows

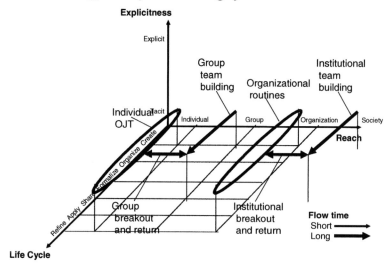

vector applies well to these organizational routines, too. One such vector is labeled "Organizational routines" accordingly and included in Figure 4.

One pattern of interest pertains to the shifting skills required for operators. At one point in time (e.g., before introduction of the new test equipment), operators required knowledge about the existing automated test equipment, and the company valued such knowledge. At a later point in time, however, some such knowledge had been made obsolete by the new technology, and the company no longer valued the obsolete knowledge. In terms of knowledge at the individual level, some employees were compelled to develop new knowledge pertaining to the new test equipment. Such new knowledge was applied and refined in the kind of cycle delineated in Figure 4 for individual OJT.

However, other employees apparently did not acquire new knowledge and were forced to leave the company. Such new knowledge had to be acquired by other (e.g., current or replacement) employees. For the individuals, their personal knowledge inventories would either reflect the new knowledge or not. For the organization, however, refinement of knowledge could be reflected by a partial substitution of new knowledge for old. For some period of time, both elements of knowledge would exist concurrently. But after implementation of the new test equipment, much of the old knowledge would flow out of the organization along with the people leaving the company. Still, some of the old knowledge would remain within the company, as tacit knowledge possessed by employees who had been reskilled (learned to use the new equipment). Hence we learn that some knowledge (e.g., pertaining to the new equipment) is valued more highly than other knowledge (e.g., pertaining to the old equipment) is. And we learn that such valuation is dynamic, shifting from one kind of knowledge to another over time.

One can identify vectors delineating similar patterns in the university. Individual researchers in the university lab, for instance, develop, apply and refine knowledge through iterative learning and knowing during technology design and development. This kind of knowledge flow would be represented well by the cyclic vector labeled "Individual OJT," even though it pertains to "research" accomplished in the laboratory environment and an educational context. The university has organizational routines of its own, as another instance, pertaining to admitting, educating, graduating and placing research students. This kind of knowledge flow would be represented well by the cyclic vector "Organizational routines," even though considerable variation is likely in terms of how any individual student progresses through the educational process. Knowledge and skills in the university can also ebb and flow in terms of novelty, obsolescence and value.

Some interesting knowledge flows pertain to inter-organizational patterns in the case. In addition to the business-as-usual flows within the company, and counterpart standard-practice flows within the university, an unusual set of knowledge flows pertain to the technology-transfer project. For instance, we understand from the case how individual engineers from the company and individual researchers from the university would meet in groups and interact periodically, essentially forming a project team. Notice this is the same kind of project team described in the advanced-technology and film-production cases. As such, the group represents the focal unit of analysis for project work.

The corresponding group-level knowledge flows could be represented using patterns similar to those delineated in the advanced-technology and film-production cases. But instead of process-level descriptions (e.g., how groups of actors, screen-writers and camera people work together over time) as in the film case, here we learn about how individual researchers, engineers and others on a team learn from one another and work together to implement new technology in the company *as a one-shot occurrence*. In other words, this technology-transfer case can be viewed as a single occurrence, not a process. Hence in Figure 4 we illustrate a series of knowledge-flow vectors.

The first group-level vector delineated in the figure is rooted in tacit knowledge creation at the group level (TGC). This depicts people from the company and university learning how to work together in a group. This first vector is headed to tacit knowledge sharing at the group level (TGS). This depicts engineers and operators in the company sharing with university researchers their undocumented, experiential knowledge pertaining to the existing test equipment and production process. It reflects also researchers from the university sharing with company participants their knowledge pertaining to automated test equipment in general along with that pertaining to the new-technology implementation. This first vector is labeled "Group team building" in the figure and delineated as such (i.e., TGC $\rightarrow$ TGS). It should be clear that no single best way of representing knowledge flows is likely to exist, and different people are bound to represent the same knowledge-flow phenomenon in different ways. This is true of all representational tasks (e.g., in IS design, free-body dynamics, architectural sketches) and does not detract from the technique. Indeed, it is known well that comparing different views of the same phenomena can lead to rich knowledge flows!

Once the project team members learn to work as a group and begin sharing knowledge with one another, the case describes an iterative series of flows between individuals performing their separate knowledge-based activities and group activities that both build upon and guide past and future such activities, respectively. For instance, group work and knowledge sharing in the early stages of the project led to independent laboratory research at the university. We can depict this with a vector from group sharing to individual application in the tacit plane (i.e., TGS $\rightarrow$ TIA). A comparable vector could depict knowledge flowing later in the project, as engineers and operators in the company follow group interaction with individual activities to learn about the new test equipment. Once the individual (e.g., researcher, engineer) returns to individual work, he or she is essentially back on the cyclic pattern of OJT (e.g., recurring knowledge creation, application and refinement). Of course knowledge flows from individuals back to the group as well. University researchers return from the lab to share results and ideas with company teammates, and company engineers and operators return from the production line to share results and ideas with research teammates. Hence the knowledge flows between the group and individuals would be represented best as bidirectional. They are labeled "Group breakout and return" in Figure 4 and depicted using a two-headed arrow (i.e., TGS $\leftrightarrow$ TIA) between the group sharing and individual cyclic patterns.

As with the project work represented in the cases noted previously, the group also applies knowledge to accomplish work (i.e., TGA). By iterative problem solving, the group refines its understanding of problems (TGR), and it develops new knowledge about how the test equipment technology affects the production process (TGC). Hence it cycles through a pattern of knowledge creation, application and refinement. To avoid clutter in the diagram, we omit a group-level, cyclic vector to depict this iterative knowledge flow. We omit also interactions between the group-level knowledge flows and ongoing organizational routines in both the company and university. Clearly the introduction of new technology in the company affects its organizational routines associated with production testing, for instance. And clearly the research project is part of the university educational routine. This case is relatively rich in terms of including a diversity of knowledge flows. The point is not to see how many different knowledge flows can be represented on a single diagram. Rather, we use the diagram to highlight the most-interesting ones in our present context of application to business firms.

One of the more-interesting knowledge flows pertains to inter-organizational knowledge exchanges. Such flows take place between the university and the company and differ from the kinds of trans-organizational flows discussed previously in the context of guilds, professional societies and communities of practice. The flows in our focal case here manifest themselves deliberately between two distinct organizations, whereas the ones noted previously occur amorphously between a web of companies, societies and other organizational forms. In other words, the inter-organizational technology transfer represents the point of the focal case and takes place between two organizations. The trans-organizational flows, by contrast, are more informative in terms of interaction between individuals and (trans-organizational) communities. In essence we have an organizational dyad here, which represents the organizational counterpart of group interaction at the individual level. By symmetry and analogy with the individual-group interaction described and delineated in this focal case, we use an equivalent set of single- and two-headed vectors to depict inter-organization knowledge flows. These vectors are labeled "Institutional team building" and "Institutional breakout and return," respectively, in the figure.

Management Implications

This application case illustrates a variety of knowledge flows, at several levels of reach, within and between multiple organizations. For instance, we find individual knowledge flows within the microelectronics company and within the university. We find also group-level knowledge flows within the project team, in addition to flows between the project group and individual team members in both the company and university. As another instance, we find organizational knowledge flows within the microelectronics company and within the university. We find also inter-organizational knowledge flows between the company and university, in addition to flows between the technology-transfer dyad and separate organizational participants (the company and the university). The knowledge manager would have a rich variety of flows to evaluate in a case such as this, and enhancing knowledge flows to overcome the clumping evident in the case could be very fruitful, particularly for the company striving to learn and apply the university's knowledge about the advanced test equipment.

This application case also illustrates how all of the important flows pertaining to a work process of interest involve tacit knowledge. Negligible knowledge is articulated in terms of documentation. The key knowledge is possessed by individual people and is embedded in organizational routines. Looking first at the company, for instance, the key workflows clearly center on producing and testing the company's microelectronic products. Knowledge flows critical to enabling such workflows center on tacit knowledge (e.g., individual OJT, organizational routines) that is created, applied, and refined over time within the company. Looking next at the university, as another instance, the key workflows clearly center on developing new test equipment technology. Knowledge flows critical to enabling such workflows center on tacit knowledge (e.g., individual OJT, organizational routines) that is created, applied, and refined over time within the university.

We use this to induce our eighteenth leadership mandate from the practical application section of this book. *Mandate 18. Knowledge flows critical to enabling critical workflows center on tacit knowledge.*

The technology-transfer project represents another important focus of workflows. Clearly, such workflows are enabled by knowledge flows associated with creating, sharing, and applying new knowledge about advanced test equipment. Hence, this case also illustrates how knowledge flows enable workflows and indeed lie on their critical paths. Without knowledge of producing and testing the company's microelectronic products, the workflows would not get accomplished or would not get accomplished well. Without knowledge of developing new test equipment technology in the university, the workflows similarly would not get accomplished (well).

The case further illustrates some important dynamics of knowledge flows. One dynamic pertains to individual knowledge that is created, applied, and refined through a recurring pattern over time. A similar dynamic applies at the organizational level. This pattern is noted in the other cases we discussed and instantiates the learning curve, as the performance of individuals as well as organizations improves over time and through repetition. Hence, the knowledge manager should *always expect performance improvement over time.* Where such improvement does not obtain, knowledge clumping is likely to manifest.

We use this to induce our nineteenth leadership mandate from the practical application section of this book. *Mandate 19. An organizational process without consistent improvement over time suffers from knowledge clumping.*

Another dynamic pattern pertains to the group interaction of project participants. Upon group formation, members must learn to work with one another before knowing how to work together on the project. This takes time and energy, and the associated phenomenon is documented well in the literatures on teams as well as projects. The knowledge manager should allow for and encourage such group-level knowledge flows before expecting group-level workflows that are dependent upon such learning.

We use this to induce our twentieth leadership mandate from the practical application section of this book. *Mandate 20. Members of a team must learn to work with one another before knowing how to work together on a project.*

A third dynamic pertains to the creation, application, refinement, and eventual obsolescence of knowledge. Knowledge associated with the dated test equipment, for instance, completed the whole cycle, but it did not disappear from the company. Much of the tacit knowledge possessed by individual workers flowed out of the company when such workers were fired, but much of such knowledge also remained within the company, possessed by workers who were not fired as well as embedded within organizational routines. Nonetheless, the value of such knowledge decreased appreciably over time, in particular, following introduction of the new test equipment. The knowledge manager should *expect the value of all knowledge to vary over time* and should seek out techniques for its valuation.

A fourth dynamic pertains to inter-organizational knowledge flows between participants in the technology-transfer dyad. Some knowledge flows were sustained even before the technology-transfer project began, as the university and company enjoyed an ongoing relationship. When the project began, knowledge flows of a more focused and specific nature commenced. Although the case does not elaborate, one can envision knowledge flows returning to their original state following completion of the project, and through continued interaction between the university and the company, perhaps another project would start one day. The key point is that the original knowledge flows between the company and the university were relatively modest in magnitude and importance. Yet they led to a substantial technology-transfer project that benefited both organizations. Hence, even small, seemingly inconsequential knowledge flows can serve to catalyze large, critical ones through a dynamic described best at present via metaphor (e.g., priming the pump). The knowledge manager should recognize inter-organizational — also inter-group and inter-individual — knowledge flows for their potential in terms of a dynamic priming effect.

Exercises

9. Identify and describe three principles from earlier parts of the book that apply to this case. Can you induce additional principles from this application case that are not articulated in the earlier parts?

10. Delineate vectors to describe knowledge flows corresponding to how some knowledge became obsolete, decreased in value, and flowed out of the company as described in the case.

11. Comment on other approaches the company could take to address its knowledge-flow problems. What relative advantages and disadvantages apply to your suggestions when compared with the approach described in the case?

12. Describe how your learning from this case can be related to an organization with which you are familiar. Include a knowledge-flow diagram such as the one presented in Figure 4.

Chapter VIII

Application Cases in Government

This chapter concentrates on knowledge-flow visualization and analysis in the public sector. We look first at a military organization involved with maritime warfare. The discussion turns then to examine a federal government agency involved with a knowledge management program. The third case examines a public service organization involved with large-scale IT integration. In each case, we draw from secondary data sources for background. This should prove helpful to the reader who is interested in following up to consider more details than presented in this volume. We also draw from our own research and professional experience to fill in missing information, and we apply principles and techniques of this book to contribute new insights through examination of knowledge flows in the cases. Each application case concludes with exercises to stimulate critical thought, learning, and discussion.

Military Organization and Maritime Warfare

We draw from Nissen (2002b) for the background of this case. We first summarize important events and issues for context. Visualization and analysis of key knowledge flows follows, with interpretation of management implications discussed subsequently. The section closes with exercises pertaining specifically to this application case.

Context

The military of a large industrialized nation is comprised of several services (e.g., Army, Navy, Air Force). It conducts many military endeavors using a composite organization called the Joint Task Force (JTF). The JTF integrates units from multiple services under a common commander to accomplish a substantial undertaking (e.g., requiring months or years to accomplish). Many joint operations also include coalitions of military forces from allied nations. In many respects, the JTF reflects a project organization. Work tasks and people are organized around a specific product of the organization; in this case, the "product" pertains to accomplishing objectives of warfare (e.g., defending territory, countering threat, projecting power). Such project organization is similar to the business case involving new-product development. In other respects, the organization of a JTF is virtual. Diverse people and units come together to compose a temporary organization focused on achieving limited objectives. After the mission is accomplished or abandoned, the organization disbands. Such temporary organization is similar to the business case involving feature-film production. In still other respects, the JTF reflects a matrix organization. While diverse units are organized under a JTF Commander, they continue an enduring affiliation with their home organizations. Such matrix organization is similar to the business case involving technology transfer. Unlike the matrix from organization theory, however, people in the military have only one boss at a time.

The organization of a task force is relatively large (e.g., 10,000 people or more) and hierarchical in nature. The JTF is organized functionally for division of labor; relies upon standardized procedures for coordination; employs large technical and support staff organizations; utilizes centralized decision making; and maintains a unified chain of command. In these respects, it represents a classic machine bureaucracy (Mintzberg, 1980), but this military organization also depends heavily upon professionalism for quality and reliability of its work processes. It is steeped in tradition, with very strong cultural norming forces at every level. Attention to detail by senior-level managers — many refer to this as "micromanagement" — abounds. "Because lives are at stake," one senior officer in the case says, "commanders and officers at every level immerse themselves in the details of plans and operations." Direct supervision, through many hierarchical levels of management, also abounds as a mechanism for coordination.

Military culture is unique in many ways. For one, the organization has few avenues for lateral entry. People at all of its 20-plus ranks come into the organization at its lowest levels. Managers, executives, and other leaders are developed exclusively from within. The same applies to supervisors, professionals, and skilled laborers. As a result, negligible mixing of backgrounds and experiences beyond the military organization takes place. Within the uniformed services, all people in leadership positions have worked within the military throughout their entire careers. In the case of top leaders (e.g., Admirals and Generals), such military careers can span 30 years in duration. All military personnel are expected to serve for 20 years before retirement. This exerts considerable and homogeneous norming forces on personnel. The culture is also bifurcated along status lines. Officers and enlisted represent separate and distinct cadres of personnel with little informal interaction between them. Throughout military history, officers have represented broadly the white-collar work force, with enlisted representing blue-collar workers. The role of technology in warfare is shifting more enlisted jobs to white-collar status, however. A great many weapons and systems of war are computer-based now and linked via network. The military also rotates all personnel regularly (e.g., nearly one-third of the Navy changes jobs each year). This precludes long-term group working relationships from forming naturally, and it promotes the kind of culture associated often with itinerant workers.

The JTF organization is technologically sophisticated. This is evidenced in part by its ability to plan, coordinate, and execute continuous, sustained, geographically distributed work activities around the clock and around the world. JTF network and communication technologies enable it to transfer information very rapidly across great distances. For instance, reconnaissance images obtained by satellite and unmanned vehicles are sent to operational planners and decision makers in near real time half way around the world. Today, new technologies are being developed to enable control of missiles in flight to pass automatically from one organization and location to another, as the cycle of target acquisition, tracking, attack, and monitoring collapses to a matter of minutes or even seconds. The JTF is also risk averse. It relies upon considerable redundancy and can fall back upon manual operations for nearly every work task.

In many respects, the military represents a *total institution*: "place[s] of residence and work where a large number of like-situated individuals, cut from the wider society for an appreciable period of time, together lead an enclosed, formally administered round of life" (Goffman, 1961, p. xiii). In particular, when units are deployed overseas for months or even years at a time, people spend all day, every day, working, living and socializing with fellow employees (e.g., shipmates). Military commanders organize people's entire day, specifying (albeit in general terms) when they awaken; what they eat; what work they do; what clothes they wear; how their hair is cut; what kinds of fashion accessories they are permitted to wear; with whom they can socialize and eat meals; where they work, eat, and sleep; if, when, and for how long they may be allowed to leave the physical confines of the unit (e.g., base, ship, encampment); and when they are to sleep. To people outside this kind of environment, military life appears widely as constrained and limiting, but many people within such environment relish the structure and praise the organization.

The JTF environment is hazardous. Military units are designed and trained to go into harm's way. Injuries and deaths are anticipated in every JTF operation, even during routine peace-time training exercises, but not all military jobs entail mortal or physical hazard, at least not all of the time. Indeed, many jobs reflect the kinds of professional office work found in most business and government organizations. Examples include staff meetings, planning sessions, report writing, e-mail communications, Web site development, and inventory management, along with myriad leadership, management, and supervisory activities. Numerous other jobs involve the kinds of skilled and manual labor observable in service and manufacturing industries. Examples include engine maintenance, machine shop work, painting, building repair, electronic diagnostics, equipment service, janitorial, and cooking tasks, along with myriad other professional and manual jobs. Alternatively, a great many military jobs are perilous by design. Examples include flying in supersonic aircraft that are catapulted off of — and have to land on — the decks of ships at sea; parachuting into hostile territory; servicing operational nuclear reactors; exchanging artillery fire; defusing explosive ordnance; and myriad other hazardous jobs rarely found outside the military environment.

The JTF environment is also time-critical. The speed of some weaponry reduces decision and reaction cycles to minutes and sometimes even just seconds. Yet such time-critical cycles are set against a backdrop of long days (e.g., 14-hour shifts are common), weeks (e.g., seven-day workweeks prevail at sea), and months (e.g., JTF deployments can extend to a year or more). Hours, days, weeks, and even months may pass without significant events in some units, but any one event (e.g., attack by missile, aircraft, or submarine) can have mortal consequences. Geographical dispersion depicts another key aspect of the JTF environment. Military units on land and at sea can cover thousands of square miles and operate halfway around the world from their home bases and ports. Yet such units are very interdependent and required to coordinate their plans and actions across great distances in both space and time. They even use a common time zone (termed *Zulu Time*) worldwide to facilitate such coordination. Communication in the field, at sea, and in the air is clearly wireless, and requirements for security are strict. Radio represents the time-proven method of choice for distributed, synchronous communications. Sophisticated frequency-hopping and encryption technologies enable widespread wireless communication to be secure. E-mail, chat, video teleconferencing, and other electronic communication technologies are employed as well.

The military task environment further tends to be quite Spartan. Units in the field may move daily and set up tent camps in the evenings. Soldiers in the field may have to dig holes in the dirt in which to sleep. Showers are a luxury in many areas, and many days in the field may pass without a hot-cooked meal. Naval warships have an industrial look and feel to them, providing a stark contrast to life onboard a cruise ship. Many aircraft have strict size and weight restrictions for crewmembers and passengers due to cramped space. Above all, the work of a JTF is mortally serious. Mistakes cause losses to life and materiel. Successes cause losses to life and materiel, too. The only difference is whether such losses are to an adversary's forces or to one's own units.

The focal JTF of this case includes two large naval formations: (1) a carrier battlegroup and (2) an amphibious ready group. The battle group includes a full-size aircraft carrier, which is large enough to launch and recover fixed-wing jet aircraft (e.g., fighter, attack, surveillance) and a host of support vessels (e.g., cruisers, destroyers, submarines) to make up an ensemble for conducting offensive and defensive maritime and air operations. The ready group includes a smaller carrier, which is used to launch and recover rotary-wing aircraft (e.g., attack, anti-submarine, transport) and amphibious-landing craft, along with its own complement of support vessels. The primary mission of the battle group is power projection and to establish military superiority (especially air and maritime). It is designed and trained for strike, intercept, anti-submarine, and maritime-interdiction missions. The ready group is employed principally for invasion purposes. It is designed and trained to get Marines ashore for expeditionary warfare. The joint operations of this task force also include several Air Force squadrons and a number of Army units, along with a coalition of military forces from multiple allied nations.

The task force conducts an operation called DELTA WATCH (a pseudonym) in international waters, with operating areas extending hundreds of miles from East to West and nearly a thousand miles from North to South. Adjoining international waters are territories of several different countries — allied, neutral, and (potentially) hostile. Each country represents a sovereign nation. Each has its own air, land, and naval forces in the area. In all, the operating area may have several hundred *contacts* (e.g., aircraft, ships, submarines) — identified on tactical and operational displays as "friendly," "hostile," and "unidentified" — at any one time. Contacts include civilian and commercial planes and ships, in addition to their military counterparts. Identifying, interrogating, keeping track of, and responding to such a large number of contacts exceeds the bounded rationality of any single individual. Hence, people work in teams to monitor and make sense of the JTF environment.

Knowledge-Flow Analysis

Tacit knowledge gained through cumulative military experience is prized in the Joint Task Force. People are assigned to specific jobs based on the experiences they have accumulated over their military careers. Leaders value experience over education, training, intelligence, and like performance-relevant attributes. Personnel rotation and experience on the job (OJT) represent the central processes behind JTF knowledge flows. Tacit knowledge moves along with each person who is assigned to a new job every two or three years. And each person acquires new knowledge through experience associated with his or her job assignments. Formal training in specialized military schools is also quite prevalent. Nearly every military employee goes through one or more formal schools (e.g., Officer Candidate School, Basic Training) before the first job assignment. Many people are sent to specialized schools (e.g., electronics, warfare, leadership) in between job assignments as well. And some military specializations (e.g., aviation, nuclear power, SEAL) require extensive training.

We learn from the case that Table 1 summarizes the knowledge deemed to be most critical by JTF organization participants. The table identifies also how JTF participants obtain such knowledge. For instance, *situational awareness* (see Column 2 of the table) is noted as essential to performing effectively in the Battle Watch Unit (listed in Column 1 of the table). The Battle Watch Unit is in charge of the Joint Operations Center — the "nerve center," from which the entire task force operation is directed and monitored. This center is equipped with

Table 1. Critical task force knowledge

Organization	Critical Knowledge	How Knowledge Is Obtained
Battle Watch	Situational awareness	OJT, training, IS use, information synthesis, teamwork, mentoring
Operations	Warfighting	OJT, Training, intelligence operations
Training	Warfighting	OJT, Training, mentoring
Intelligence	Warfighting	OJT, Training, assignment
Planning	Task force planning	Evaluation, mentoring
Chief of Staff	Task force planning	OJT, command
JTF Commander	Task force planning	OJT, Training

numerous computers and displays connected to networks of various kinds, along with other communication and work artifacts such as telephones, radios, video teleconferencing equipment, maps, charts, and white boards. Situational awareness involves developing deep understanding of the external task force environment.

Seven knowledge-flow processes are included in the table as the source of knowledge that enables situational awareness: (1) OJT (tactical military experience); (2) formal training (e.g., in specialized military schools); (3) IS use (e.g., understanding how to use information systems, the kinds of information available through each, limitations such as inaccuracy and latency associated with such information); (4) information synthesis (synthesizing numerous different sources of knowledge and information into a coherent understanding of the operational environment); (5) teamwork (e.g., developing a shared understanding of the operational environment among the team of six to 10 people assigned to a particular Battle Watch); and (6) mentoring (e.g., when a senior officer with Battle Watch experience works with a junior officer to help him or her learn while working).

The other areas of critical knowledge listed in the table include *warfighting*, which pertains to executing tactical combat processes, and *task force planning*, which pertains to planning future combat engagements. Knowledge in these areas of warfighting and task force planning is developed through several

Figure 1. Knowledge flow visualization

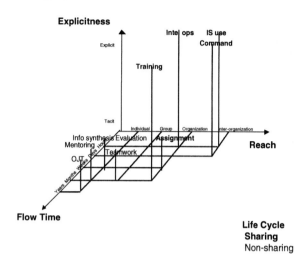

of the same flow processes listed in Table 1 for situational awareness. In particular, OJT and training are prominent in both areas. We also note four additional processes: (7) intelligence operations (e.g., formal reports and briefings developed by the Intelligence organization); (8) assignment (transferring knowledge along with people from one organizational unit to another); (9) evaluation (e.g., understanding alternate battle plans and courses of action by evaluating their relative advantages and disadvantages); and (10) command (e.g., the Commander articulating explicitly and distributing widely his primary battle goals, key intelligence needs, and time tables). Including OJT, training, and the other processes noted previously in connection with situational awareness, we identify a total of ten unique flow processes associated with critical JTF knowledge.

We use this to induce our twenty-first leadership mandate from the practical application section of this book. *Mandate 21. Ten unique knowledge-flow processes are required for military task force efficacy.*

The case presents some figures to support visualization of knowledge flows. Figure 1 delineates the ten knowledge-flow processes in terms of four dimensions from our previous theoretical discussion: *explicitness, reach, life cycle,* and *flow time.* Here the life cycle dimension is reflected only to highlight knowledge sharing (in bold print) vs. non-sharing (normal print) activities. For instance, from the table and using our coordinate shorthand, OJT (TICY) is plotted at the Tacit level of *explicitness*, Individual level of *reach,* Create level of *life cycle*, and Years level of *flow time*. As another instance, formal training (EOSM) is plotted at the Explicit level of *explicitness*, Organization level of *reach*, Share level of *life cycle*, and Months level of *flow time*. The fourth coordinate parameter represents *flow time* as one of six discrete orders of magnitude: H (hours), D (days), W (weeks), M (months), Y (years), and C (decades). The other eight table entries are plotted in similar fashion.

The figure provides a visual representation and reveals two distinct clusters among the 10 JTF knowledge flows. For instance, as an overall pattern discernable in the graph, one can observe some correspondence between flow time and the other dimensions. The knowledge-flow processes plot roughly along a diagonal from the bottom-left-front corner (highly tacit, narrow organizational reach, long flow time) to the top-right-rear corner (highly explicit, broad organizational reach, short flow time). From this rough pattern in the figure, relatively fast knowledge flows (e.g., with flow times on the order of hours and days) correspond principally to explicit knowledge, broad reach, and knowledge sharing activities (e.g., associated with processes such as IS use, intelligence operations, and command) in the JTF organization. IT plays a central, performative role (e.g., organizing, storing, and disseminating knowledge) in — and in many cases enables — such fluid (fast) knowledge flows. Alternatively, the relatively slow knowledge flows (e.g., with flow times on the order of months and years) correspond mainly to tacit knowledge restricted to individuals and small groups (e.g., associated with processes such as OJT, mentoring, and teamwork). IT plays a minor, supportive role (e.g., providing information, facilitating remote conversations, summarizing work tasks and results) in such sticky (slow) knowledge flows.

Figure 2 delineates an alternate view of JTF knowledge flows. We include the same axes as earlier for *explicitness* and *reach*, but use *life cycle* here instead as the third axis; relatively long vs. short flow times are differentiated by the thickness of arrows depicting knowledge flows. This is comparable to the knowledge flows delineated in the figures for the business application cases. Here we focus in detail on the dynamics of two knowledge flows noted as predominate in the case: OJT and formal training. We also graphically depict dynamic interactions between the OJT and training flows.

Specifically, the OJT process is delineated as a cycle of two knowledge-flow modes in the tacit plane of the figure. The cycle connects points C (TICY) and A (TIAD) corresponding to knowledge creation and application, respectively. Notice the flow represented by this cycle reflects tacit, individual knowledge

Figure 2. Knowledge flow trajectories

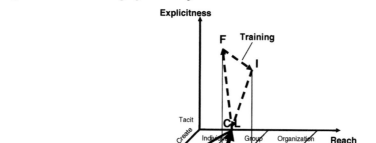

flowing at two different speeds (requiring years vs. days) along the life cycle axis. Drawing from our previous discussion, we depict the flow corresponding to knowledge creation at point C using a relatively thick line (slow flow) and the flow corresponding to knowledge application at point A using a relatively thin line (fast flow). The formal training process is delineated by its own cycle that intersects with OJT but rises up out of the tacit plane in the figure. Beginning at point C (TICY), which reflects the accumulation of knowledge through experience (the OJT process cycle), working knowledge is formalized, by a group of experienced military people, through course development into an explicit state at point F (EGFM). We depict classroom instruction in military schools as a subsequent flow to point I (EOSM), through which explicit training material is shared organization-wide. Learning by individual students is denoted by point L, which we depict as an individual process of knowledge creation. Here the training cycle then intersects with OJT again. This depicts students as they would leave military schools and return to apply knowledge on the job. The interrelated cycles continue interacting over time, as many former students return — generally years later — to military schools and serve as instructors.

We use this to induce our twenty-second leadership mandate from the practical application section of this book. *Mandate 22. OJT involves knowledge flowing at two different speeds: Knowledge application through doing is fast; knowledge creation through learning is slow.*

Management Implications

This application case illustrates a variety of knowledge flows at several levels of reach within and between multiple organizations. For instance, the case identifies several flows of knowledge that have to be completed before the Battle Watch work process can begin productively. All Battle Watch officers, for example, require substantial tactical warfare experience before being assigned to a Battle Watch job. Knowledge flows pertaining to naval indoctrination, training on combat tactics and equipment, and leadership experience likewise have to be completed before an officer can work productively in the Battle Watch. Given the time-critical nature of warfare, all of this knowledge must already be in place when the officer first reports for duty. This instantiates a set of important timing constraints between knowledge flows and their corresponding workflows. The leader or manager who is concerned about flows of work in the JTF should be concerned vitally about the enabling flows of knowledge that are prerequisite.

We use this to induce our twenty-third leadership mandate from the practical application section of this book. *Mandate 23. Given the time-critical nature of warfare, most tacit knowledge must already be in place when the officer first reports for duty.*

This application case also illustrates how some knowledge-flow processes are preferred — tacitly if not explicitly — over others. For instance, in terms of interactions between OJT and formal training, people in the case are asked why more JTF personnel are not sent to military schools (e.g., to learn to work together in teams to perform Battle Watch work processes). The common response from the case is simply, they are needed to work. When someone is sent ashore for training, the organization gets little or no work out of him or her until he or she returns. This instantiates a general preference in the JTF organization for the knowing activity of doing over that of learning. Even though the knowledge-flow component associated with OJT is small, this represents the method of choice in terms of JTF knowledge flows. Here training, despite its relatively large knowledge-flow component, is used sparingly because it makes so small a workflow contribution.

The case illustrates further how a wide variety of knowledge flows can be classified and visualized to identify patterns through similarities, differences, and interrelationships. For instance, we noted previously how relatively fluid knowledge corresponds principally to explicit movements across broad organizational reach, generally in the Class-I part of the life cycle (e.g., knowledge organization, formalization, sharing). Sticky knowledge, in contrast, corresponds more to tacit movements with narrow organizational reach but enabling action in the Class-II part of the life cycle (e.g., knowledge application, refinement, creation). Where the leader or manager is interested in rapid knowledge flows across broad organizational reach, this visual pattern suggests that such knowledge should be articulated first in explicit form. Likewise, where the leader or manager is interested in tacit knowledge flows, this visual pattern suggests that such knowledge will flow slowly and narrowly through the organization. Other knowledge-flow patterns may be visualized and interpreted through similar analysis.

Exercises

1. Identify and describe three principles from earlier parts of the book that apply to this case. Can you induce additional principles from this application case that are not articulated in the earlier parts?

2. Delineate vectors to describe knowledge flows corresponding to how a team of people performing the Battle Watch would work together to learn and do situational-awareness activities as described in the case.

3. Comment on other approaches the JTF could take to address its knowledge-flow problems. What relative advantages and disadvantages apply to your suggestions when compared with the approach described in the case?

4. Describe how your learning from this case can be related to an organization with which you are familiar. Include a knowledge-flow diagram such as the one presented in Figure 2.

Federal Government Agency and Knowledge Management Program

We draw from Liebowitz (2004b) for the background of this case and augment such background with information gleaned from various agency reports (e.g., Bran, 2002) and Web sites (e.g., NASA, 2004). We first summarize important events and issues for context. Visualization and analysis of key knowledge flows follows, with interpretation of management implications discussed subsequently. The section closes with exercises pertaining specifically to this application case.

Context

A medium-sized agency of the federal government enjoys considerable prestige and undertakes bold, unprecedented scientific missions. It relies critically upon the technical expertise of its workforce. Employees are expected to exhibit unselfish teamwork through participation in interdisciplinary and cross-functional task forces and groups. Experience is prized in this agency, but technical expertise is essential. Most people in the organization have educational and professional backgrounds in science and engineering, including many advanced degrees (e.g., MS, PhD). Technical proficiency represents a necessary factor, but it is not sufficient. Experience is seen as making the difference between mission success and failure. This is the case, in particular, because each mission is unprecedented and involves novel combinations of technical challenges. Hence, the technical work is non-routine in nature and inherently risky.

With experience prized as such, the agency requires a sizeable cadre of relatively senior employees to manage projects, lead interdisciplinary activities, and organize technical specialists. Over a period of several decades, the agency has developed a well-balanced organization comprised of senior, mid-grade, and junior personnel. However, the balance is shifting rapidly, today. Senior personnel are retiring in greater numbers. Mid-grade personnel do not demonstrate many of the desirable work behaviors that have been important in the past. Junior personnel represent a continually decreasing proportion of the agency workforce. In short, the level of experience and expertise is decreasing in the agency, and imminent retirements portend to exacerbate this effect.

To address such effect, the agency has undertaken a major initiative to address problems stemming from its "graying workforce" (p. 254). This initiative includes some technical emphasis imparted from government superiors: "The Administration will adopt information technology systems to capture some of the knowledge and skills of retiring employees" (p. 254). However, the agency's strategy now emphasizes human capital to an extent greater than any time in recent history. Indeed, we learn from the case that agency KM representatives assert, "80 to 90% of knowledge management is people, process, and culture versus technology" (p. 255).

A KM task force organizes and develops a set of organizational goals (e.g., improved productivity through embedding KM processes into daily work; capture, share, and generate knowledge; increase sense of community; increase collaboration) and knowledge-sharing tenets (e.g., integrate knowledge sharing into everyone's job; share the message that with creativity comes failure; educate people about what types of knowledge are valuable; enhance the recognition and reward system to promote learning and knowledge-sharing behaviors).

In terms of organizational changes, several knowledge-specific positions are created and staffed. For instance, a Knowledge Management Officer is appointed to spearhead the KM project. A number of Knowledge Stewards are matrixed into the KM project from their home units and assigned a variety of duties (e.g., leading and coordinating KM activities within their home units; conducting knowledge-capture sessions; enlisting and coordinating case studies about unsuccessful as well as successful projects). Knowledge Retention Managers are responsible for a related but different set of duties (e.g., facilitating sessions to elicit and capture lessons learned, documenting and posting lessons learned via an online repository system, developing documents to describe "good practices" in the organization).

Several techniques employed for capturing and sharing knowledge involve technology. For instance, the agency maintains an intranet, which includes information such as lessons-learned documents and summaries of good practices. It also maintains a library, which catalogs and makes available multimedia resources such as videos of project managers recalling lessons learned. An expertise locator (knowledge map) is maintained and distributed also. People are actively encouraged to use and update this system, which summarizes employees' areas of expertise and experience. This represents an important enabler of the organization's *transactive memory* (who knows what) (see Weick & Roberts, 1993). The organization further encourages people to participate in online communities of practice.

Several techniques employed for capturing and sharing knowledge involve people and processes. For instance, the organization strives to incorporate factors such as *continued learning* and *knowledge sharing* into its formal reward system. It also strives to recruit retirees as part-time consultants and mentors (e.g., working one day weekly). Despite some drain on productivity, the organization formally encourages mentoring and shadowing. Mentoring involves a relatively experienced person providing guidance to a less-experienced counterpart. Shadowing involves one person with a particular job or area of expertise spending a week or so with someone who performs a different job or who possesses expertise in a different area (e.g., to learn what they do and to observe how they do it). Additionally, knowledge-sharing fora are set up, and formal storytelling workshops are facilitated. Further, audits are conducted to identify "knowledge gaps" (p. 258). Focused mini-courses are developed to address such gaps deemed critical and at risk of imminent loss.

Knowledge-Flow Analysis

This application case is informative in comparison with several of those discussed previously. For instance, the government agency engages in project-oriented work. Most of the previous cases involve project work as well. Knowledge is critical to this agency, particularly experience-based tacit knowledge. Tacit knowledge plays a critical role in most of the cases noted previously as well. The agency recognizes some knowledge-flow problems and establishes management initiatives to identify and dissolve the knowledge clumps. We discuss management initiatives for each previous case also. Alternatively, the focal case here is engaged in a major KM project. This constitutes a project within a project: a project-based organization, while undertaking a portfolio of mission projects, simultaneously endeavors to pursue a KM project. Hence, this case directly focuses on knowledge management.

We learn from the case how the agency pursues a combination of organizational, personnel, process, and technological initiatives. This conforms to one of our previous principles. One can also perceive how the agency has satisfied several preconditions for success (e.g., senior management commitment, appropriate people participating full-time, sufficient budget) and has attempted to avoid many preconditions for failure (e.g., wrong sponsor, reliance upon external expertise, narrow technical focus). However, the informed reader must wonder about other preconditions for success (e.g., realistic expectations, strategic context of growth and expansion, shared vision) that may have been overlooked or that may simply not apply in this case. Likewise, the informed reader must question other preconditions for failure (e.g., consensus management, unsound financial condition, too many improvement projects under way) that appear to be present in the case. Although all such preconditions (developed in the evaluation chapter) derive from expertise acquired through re-engineering projects and the associated radical change, the kind of

Figure 3. Lessons-learned knowledge flows

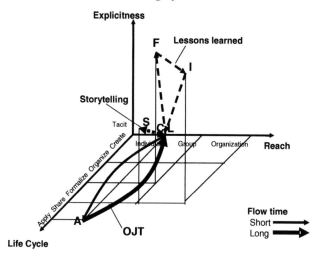

KM project undertaken at this government agency reflects in many ways large-scale change. Hence, one can argue that much of this re-engineering expertise would apply well to the case.

One noteworthy knowledge-sharing approach described in the case involves knowledge capture via lessons learned. Recall a Knowledge Retention Manager is responsible in part for facilitating sessions with experienced people to elicit and capture lessons learned from recent technical projects. Such role is one of an intermediary, as it bridges a chasm between an expert's tacit knowledge and an online repository. By interviewing an expert, the Retention Manager is performing a role very similar to that of a Knowledge Engineer, described earlier in the section on expert systems. Through its use for retention, organization, and distribution, the repository is performing a role somewhat similar to that of an expert system. However, a key difference lies in the respective supportive vs. performative natures of repository and expert systems. Whereas the repository system is employed to *support* people who want to learn lessons from past projects, an expert system is used to *perform* key tasks in lieu of people.

We delineate some key knowledge flows pertaining to the lessons-learned approach in Figure 3. Notice this figure is very similar to the one previously in the JTF application case. In particular, the figure includes a two-part OJT vector (points A to C: TIC ↔ TIA) depicting the experience-based, tacit knowledge flows associated with the development of individual expertise. This vector delineates the gradual accumulation of expertise via experience that is required before someone can be considered an expert. The other, three-part lessons-learned vector is quite analogous to the kind of formal training process involved with JTF knowledge flows. The first ray of this vector (points C to F: TIC → EGF) rises up from the tacit-knowledge plane through a process of formalization. This represents the interviewing, storytelling, writing, and documentation activities associated with articulating lessons learned. It is depicted as a group activity, for an intermediary works with the expert to accomplish such activity. Once formalized and organized in an online repository, the lessons-learned document and related media (e.g., video) can be disseminated organization-wide. This is represented by the second ray of the vector (points F to I: EGF → EOS) associated with knowledge sharing at an organizational level of reach. The third vector (points I to L: EOS → TIC) represents individual learning accomplished by a person reading the lessons learned. As with formal training, such person is acquiring new knowledge (new to him or her), which must be learned, internalized, and made tacit for application to a project endeavor. Hence, the lessons-learned approach shares much in common with formal training. One key difference, of course, pertains to individual, instructorless learning of the former approach as opposed to classroom participation of the latter. Another key difference stems from the likely volume and labeling of lessons-learned documents. Particularly when compared with formal training courses, a great many lessons-learned documents are likely to exist and require a search to find. Also, it may be relatively more difficult to tell whether any particular lessons-learned document is relevant to a specific task at hand.

Nonetheless, a lessons-learned document can make explicit many events, considerations, actions, inactions, decisions, and factors that an expert considers to be relevant to a project's relative successes and failures. When read by another person who lacks the experience of the expert, such person may learn from past successes and failures, hence, improve his or her performance on the basis of the knowledge associated. Of course, lessons-learned documents entail several drawbacks as well. For instance, such a document can reflect only a tiny fraction of the experience-based tacit knowledge possessed by the expert. Although creating and reading someone's lessons learned may help fill a knowledge gap and in turn improve performance, the gap does not get filled completely. For example, one would still expect the expert to perform the task better than the novice does, even after the novice has read — perhaps repeatedly — the lessons-learned document. As another instance, reading about how to perform some knowledge-based activity is only a partial substitute for performing the activity. This reflects the previous distinction between knowledge and knowing. For example, recall the previous discussion pertaining to reading a book about riding bicycles vs. physically experiencing the activity of riding bicycles. As a third instance, even if the best possible lessons-learned document can be developed (e.g., it may include multimedia, immersive simulation technology, expert systems tutorials, and like components in addition to static, textual documents), it may be difficult to find the specific lesson or set of lessons most applicable to one's particular circumstances. Consider if everyone in the agency recorded every lesson learned throughout his or her career. Depending upon the indexing and search schemes employed by the repository system, the metaphorical needle in a haystack may apply well here.

Storytelling represents another noteworthy knowledge-sharing approach described in the case. This is similar in many respects to capturing lessons learned. For instance, someone recognized as an expert is selected to share knowledge about a particular project; the kind of knowledge of interest is tacit and experience-based in nature; people with less expertise are intended to benefit through some gap-filling and improve their performance. A key difference lies in the sharing activities. With lessons learned — as with formal training and expert systems — a central task involves moving tacit knowledge to an explicit form and then making such formalized knowledge available organization-wide (e.g., via intranet). Through storytelling, on the other hand, the formalization step is omitted. Conversation represents the key activity associated with knowledge sharing, and instead of an expert trying in advance to articulate through lessons learned all the knowledge someone else might be expected to need one day, in a storytelling forum, the expert interacts with people in the audience, the latter of whom can ask focused questions and influence which "lessons" get articulated and at what level of detail.

The level of explicitness also differs in part between lessons learned and storytelling. The knowledge captured via lessons-learned documents is clearly explicit. One can argue that storytelling involves making knowledge explicit as well, for the expert articulates through conversation the key contexts, events, and decisions associated with a project, along with what he or she learned through the experience. Also, the storytelling session can be preserved via video and distributed for viewing by others at different times, but a key difference lies in the interactive nature of the storytelling session. Arguably, with different people participating in a session and asking the questions they feel are most relevant personally and professionally, no two sessions would be the same. This reflects much more of a mentoring context of (tacit) knowledge sharing than formal training or other explicit-knowledge focus. Interpersonal bonding can also ensue from storytelling fora, and relatively inexperienced people can establish some trust and personal relationships with storytellers in a face-to-face setting. Some of these same benefits may accrue, as well, through the recording and reading of lessons-learned documents, but such documents detach the lessons from the storytellers, and the documents become the media of learning, not the experts directly. Hence, storytelling involves some aspects of apprenticeship for (tacit) knowledge-sharing. These differences are subtler than those pertaining to many of the diverse knowledge flows described and delineated previously in this book.

The flows associated with storytelling are not completely tacit but neither are they completely explicit. In Figure 3, we represent storytelling knowledge flows as a two-headed vector (points C to S: TIC $\leftrightarrow$ T'GS). This vector stems from the same Point C as earlier that reflects an expert's accumulated, experience-based tacit knowledge (TIC). It depicts also a flow to the group level through sharing. Notice this vector rises up from the tacit plane a bit: not as much as the lessons-learned vector, yet reflecting some explicitness in the knowledge sharing. Point S represents such group-level sharing of what we can refer to only as *semi-tacit knowledge*. We use an apostrophe in our coordinate shorthand (T'GS) to indicate the semi-tacit nature of such sharing. Although knowledge sharing via lessons learned has many similarities to that via storytelling, the corresponding knowledge-flow vectors delineate considerably different processes underneath.

We use this to induce our twenty-fourth leadership mandate from the practical application section of this book. *Mandate 24. Systematic storytelling can increase the reach of this time-honored and effective approach to sharing tacit knowledge.*

Management Implications

This application case illustrates how knowledge management can be approached in a project environment, complete with a project manager and staff matrixed from home units within an organization. The tone of the application case is positive, suggesting successful progress toward enhancing knowledge flows in the focal organization. However, one must question whether the project environment is matched well with the organization's stated goals such as "embedding KM processes into daily work." The use of a change agent such as the KM Task Force (Knowledge Management Officer, dedicated staff and budget) represents a time-proven approach to planning and effecting organizational change. By its very nature, the project represents a temporary undertaking, demarcated by a distinct project organization. Alternatively, daily work and organizational routines are perennial processes undertaken by ongoing line and staff organizations. The results remain to be seen. The informed reader has good reason to question how well a KM project such as this can institutionalize enhanced knowledge flows over time.

The case also illustrates how KM-program evaluation factors such as preconditions for success and failure can be employed to assess KM projects in practice. The focal organization described in the case is reported in terms of a success story, but we observe how some preconditions for success appear to be missing and how some preconditions for failure appear to be present. Again, the results remain to be seen. The informed reader has reason to question the likelihood and extent of success the focal organization will enjoy as its KM project continues to unfold and play out. Clearly, other KM-program evaluation factors from the previous chapter can be applied as well to practical projects such as this. But details presented in the case do not permit the same depth of evaluation that would be possible through analysis by experienced people onsite and interacting directly with organizational personnel.

The case further illustrates how the KM project involves more than just a narrow technological focus. Indeed, we describe organizational, personnel, and process initiatives, in addition to technological support. This is consistent with our previous principles and can be considered as such to represent "good practice." Moreover, the various organizational, personnel, process, and technological initiatives complement one another. Organizational initiatives such as appointing Knowledge Retention Managers combine with personnel and process initiatives such as encouraging and facilitating the development of cases and lessons learned. Technological initiatives such as maintaining an intranet and equipping a multimedia library enable the organization and sharing of such cases and lessons beyond the limits of interpersonal conversations and even paper documents. Hence, the organization appears to be effectively leveraging its KM efforts through coordinated, complementary initiatives.

We describe in some detail from case two noteworthy knowledge flows: (1) lessons learned and (2) storytelling. These two flows share several similarities as well as differences. In particular, we highlight how the former involves movement of knowledge from tacit to explicit form to a greater extent than the latter does. Such greater explicitness supports broader reach and faster sharing through the organization than the more tacit approach does, but some major part of the underlying experience-based tacit knowledge of the experts is lost through formalization into explicit knowledge. Through storytelling, the associated semi-tacit knowledge cannot be shared as broadly or as quickly through the organization as its explicit counterpart can. Alternatively, it can likely be shared more broadly and quickly than can tacit knowledge that remains embedded within an individual's professional expertise.

Other knowledge flows such as OJT are clearly prominent in this application case. Hence, several alternate approaches to enhancing knowledge flows are available to the leader or manager. Each alternate approach has some common and some unique properties with respect to the others. An informed leader or manager can consider such common and unique properties when trying to determine which approaches will match relatively better or worse than others in terms of addressing any particular knowledge flow and/or clump. The kinds of knowledge-flow diagrams delineated here can help managers visualize and understand the phenomena of knowledge flows. Hopefully, such visualization and understanding can improve KM decision making and implementation.

Exercises

5. Identify and describe three principles from earlier parts of the book that apply to this case. Can you induce additional principles from this application case that are not articulated in the earlier parts?

6. Delineate vectors to describe knowledge flows corresponding to how the tacit knowledge possessed by a retired expert in the organization could be shared through part-time mentoring as described in the case.

7. Comment on other approaches the agency could take to address its knowledge-flow problems. What relative advantages and disadvantages apply to your suggestions when compared with the approach described in the case?

8. Describe briefly how your learning from this case can be related to an organization with which you are familiar. Include a knowledge-flow diagram such as the one presented in Figure 3.

Public Service Organization and IT-Integration Project

We draw from Mueller and Dyerson (1999) for the background of this case. We first summarize important events and issues for context. Visualization and analysis of key knowledge flows follows, with interpretation of management implications discussed subsequently. The section closes with exercises pertaining specifically to this application case.

Context

A medium-sized government service agency is involved with a large-scale IT development and implementation project. This agency performs several financial services for the government and has hundreds of branch offices distributed throughout the country. IT innovation has been sweeping for many years through the commercial finance sector of the host nation, but counterpart organizations in the public sector have been slow to adopt such innovation. This is attributed in part to conservatism inherent in government organizations and in part to the absence of competition to motivate service innovation.

Nonetheless, the time has come for large-scale automation in this agency, principally to address concerns about efficiency and service in a public organization. The organization plans for new-system development and implementation across its nationwide branch network of 600 local offices. Automation is targeted to redesign a host of largely manual processes. Examples include financial collection, recording, and processing activities. These processes are also being redesigned to transition from locally controlled, branch-based activities to centrally administered, automated processes.

The project involves IT development and implementation, which takes place over an extended period of more than five years. Although the IT implementation represents a one-shot project in many respects, the extended period of time devoted to the project also reflects an ongoing operation and continuous process. Indeed, the organization creates a new and separate division to develop, operate, and maintain the new IT, as well as to perform the centralized process activities. Here we find the organization taking a long-term view of the process, both its IT development/implementation and its ongoing process operations. Hence, the case illustrates aspects of a project-oriented organization along with those of an ongoing operational concern.

Employees in the new division are drawn from various branch offices and transferred to the centralized unit. Such employees reflect a mix of business analysts and technologists who work together on cross-functional teams. The business analysts are intended to restrain the technological zeal of computer programmers and systems analysts and to focus on business issues instead of just new technology. The technologists are intended to provide expertise necessary for effective system development. Teamwork is promoted broadly and formally in the organization. Not only does teamwork permeate the organizational culture, but the formal reward system (e.g., involving promotions and raises) emphasizes teamwork as well. For instance, many employees are compensated in large part based on *organizational performance*, not just individual efforts and accomplishments.

The organization's employee base is very stable. Turnover is noted as comparatively low (less than 5% annually). Promotion from within company ranks is predominant. Organization-specific expertise is considerable. For instance, most managers employed currently have been with the organization for multiple decades and have risen from the lowest-level professional and technical positions (e.g., business analysts, programmers). We also learn from the case that the organization has culture and processes centered on committee-based decision making. Such factors suggest the organization possesses considerable, experience-based tacit knowledge and is able to retain such knowledge, not only in its employees, but in its organizational routines also.

However, we learn further from the case that despite such considerable, organization-specific knowledge base, the employees possess collectively relatively little experience in terms of large-scale IT development and implementation (p. 246). As a result, the organization decides to engage external consultants to help with the integration. Yet the organization is concerned about the appropriability of knowledge by the consultants. It is common in public organizations, for instance, to have a great part of their expertise possessed and retained by consultants over time. One comment in the case suggests that consultants to some government agencies stay with such organizations for longer periods of time than employees do (p. 248).

To address such potential appropriability problems, organization leaders decide to integrate the consultants directly into their line-management processes. For instance, consultants report individually to line managers, according to their function. This represents a vivid contrast to many consulting engagements, in which consultants report collectively (e.g., through a partner in the consulting firm) at a relatively high level in the organization (e.g., Vice

President, Director). Further, consultants are integrated expressly into cross-functional work teams with organization employees. Organization employees are further encouraged to shadow the consultants in their work areas, to observe what they do and how they do it. This too represents a vivid contrast to many consulting engagements, in which consultants work independently, accomplish their project objectives (or not), get paid handsomely, and then leave the organization. Many times, critical knowledge — both brought to the organization and learned from organizational work by consultants — leaves the organization at the end of the consulting contract.

Knowledge-Flow Analysis

As in most of the cases discussed previously, tacit knowledge flows are important in this application case. For instance, we learn about the organization's stable employee base and history of promotion from within. Organization-specific knowledge flows are notably sticky and require considerable time where tacit, experience-based knowledge is concerned. A stable employee base allows substantial time (e.g., years, decades) for workers to acquire organization-specific knowledge. Such substantial time also allows for workers to share, apply, and refine their knowledge. Hence, a stable employee base facilitates successive flows of knowledge through the life cycle, and successive flows through the life cycle are not limited to individual-level knowledge. Rather, groups also enjoy substantial time to work together on a variety of tasks and projects, and organizational routines likewise enjoy substantial time for creation, application, and refinement.

We represent these stable and successive tacit knowledge flows in Figure 4 by using three interconnected cyclic vectors. The first cyclic vector is labeled "Individual OJT," reflects tacit knowledge, and cycles from creation through refinement along the life cycle. A parallel cyclic vector is labeled "Employee teamwork" and cycles tacit knowledge similarly along the life cycle. A third parallel cycle (labeled "Org routines") is delineated at the organization level of reach. Each cyclic vector is connected to another through two-headed knowledge-sharing vectors. These are labeled "Socialization" and "Acculturation," which depict individual-group and group-organization knowledge sharing, respectively. All of the vectors in this figure reflect thick arrows to depict the relatively slow flows associated with sticky, tacit knowledge. Knowledge flows appear to circulate well in this organization. Hence, we label the diagram "Healthy" in Figure 4.

Figure 4. Healthy knowledge-flow circulation

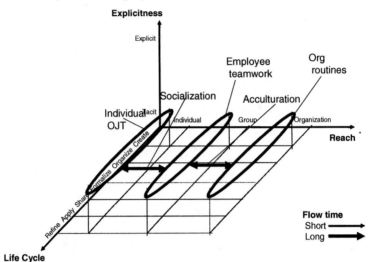

We use this to induce our twenty-fifth leadership mandate from the practical application section of this book. *Mandate 25. Socialization, teamwork, and acculturation must interconnect to enable healthy knowledge-flow circulation.*

With a less-stable employee base, several alternate flow patterns could be envisioned. For instance, perhaps the socialization and acculturation flows would not form as well (e.g., only single-headed vectors) or may not form at all. Group teamwork and organizational routines similarly may not have ample time to form complete cycles, and with sufficient instability in the workforce, even individual OJT cycles may fail to form (e.g., knowledge may be created but never applied; knowledge may be applied but never refined). Hence, the stable employee base enhances tacit knowledge flows at all levels of reach and across the complete life cycle.

The knowledge flows associated with the external consultants are particularly noteworthy in this application case. Figure 5 depicts two, separate cyclic tacit knowledge-flow vectors at the group level. One vector is labeled "Employee teamwork" and represents the cross-functional teams comprised of organizational employees. This is the same group-level cyclic vector delineated in Figure 4. We repeat it here for reference, but we omit the individual- and organization-level cyclic vectors from before to reduce clutter in the diagram. The other vector in Figure 5 is labeled "Consultant teamwork" and represents the teams of external consultants. This vector cycles similarly at the group level. Because

Figure 5. Unhealthy knowledge clumping

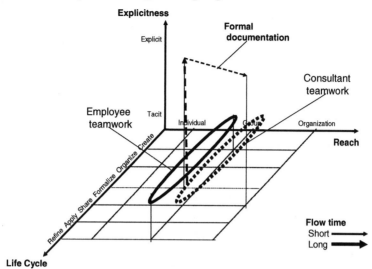

external consultants tend to stay for extended periods (e.g., years) with large-scale IT-integration clients such as our focal organization. We use thick arrows here also to represent the relatively slow flows associated with sticky knowledge. For contrast, the consultant cyclic vector is delineated using a dotted line instead of the solid one representing employee teamwork.

Notice the two cyclic vectors are separate and have no single- or two-headed knowledge-sharing vectors connecting them. This represents the common approach *not taken in the case*, in which a consulting team is brought in and works independently. Such approach offers negligible opportunity for knowledge sharing between consultants and employees. When the consultants leave at the end of an engagement, the knowledge represented by the dotted cyclic vector in the figure leaves with them. Hence, this diagram depicts a problem in terms of knowledge flows: tacit knowledge clumps in the consultants' flows and fails to move into the client organization. Were we to overlay the individual- and organization-level cyclic flows from the previous figure, we would also include the two-headed knowledge-sharing vectors. But such sharing vectors *would not connect with* the tacit flows represented by the *cyclic consultant teamwork* vector. The dotted-line representation is thus appropriate to depict the temporary nature of the consultant knowledge flows. In contrast with the tacit organizational knowledge flows represented in Figure 4, consultants' tacit knowledge appears to clump badly in this latter representation of organizational flows. Hence, we label the diagram "Unhealthy" in Figure 5.

However, even with such an approach (again, not taken in the case), some knowledge would clearly move from the consultant group to the organization. For instance, assuming the consulting group is successful in implementing the large-scale IT system, knowledge embedded in the IT artifact would remain within the organization even after the consulting engagement terminated. Unfortunately, such embedded knowledge may not be accessible to the organization's employees (e.g., necessary to modify or maintain the system). As a related instance, the consulting organization would likely develop documentation and procedures for the IT system. Articulating their tacit knowledge in explicit form as such would ameliorate some of the knowledge gap created when the consultants complete their engagement with the organization. However, such explicit documentation clearly represents only a portion of the tacit knowledge possessed by the consultants, and it may or may not be sufficient for the organization's purposes (e.g., system modification or maintenance). We represent such explicit documentation in Figure 5 by using a vector rising up from the tacit plane. This two-ray vector is rooted in tacit knowledge application at the group level of the consultant cyclic vector (TGA). The first ray is headed to explicit knowledge formalization at the group level (EGF). This reflects the articulation of tacit knowledge via explicit documentation. The second ray is headed to explicit knowledge sharing at the organization level (EOS). This reflects the documentation acquired by the focal organization. Notice these two rays are represented using relatively thin arrows to depict faster knowledge flows associated with explicit knowledge. Other knowledge flows between external consultants and organizational employees are likely as well (e.g., conversations with management), but these are comparatively minor flows, which we omit from the diagram.

Alternatively, *the approach taken in the case differs* from the knowledge-flow representation depicted in Figure 5. Because of the manner in which external consultants are integrated in the case (e.g., at the line-management level, into cross-functional employee work teams), the disjoint cyclic vectors depicted in Figure 5 would not obtain. Rather, the same kinds of vectors delineated in Figure 4 would continue to apply instead. Integration of the consultants enables knowledge sharing over an extended period of time. Even though all individual consultants may retain higher levels of expertise than even the best organizational employees do, the group-level knowledge flows are more likely to resemble composite vectors delineated in Figure 4 than counterpart, disjoint flows represented in Figure 5. From a knowledge-flow perspective, the approach taken in the case appears to be superior. It ameliorates the problem with knowledge clumping in the consulting organization. Of course, other lenses (e.g., in terms of project cost or completion time) may reveal the opposite in terms of superiority; that is, enabling superior knowledge flows through a project may cost more and take longer to achieve than completing a project with less knowledge flow. This question reflects our previous tension between learning and doing. The "best" approach depends fundamentally upon the organizational leaders' and managers' preferences for exploration vs. exploitation in the context of this project. We discuss this further below in terms of management implications.

Management Implications

Knowledge appropriability is a serious concern, even for organizations in the public sector. Such organizations are not as concerned as their for-profit counterparts are with using knowledge for competitive advantage. But knowledge is key to performance, and serving constituents well represents a stated objective of most public-sector organizations. Further, dependence upon external consultants can be expensive, particularly where a mission-critical IT system is involved. Consultants enjoy knowledge asymmetries over clients, and they face powerful economic incentives to maintain such asymmetries. Unless a client organization can get important knowledge to flow from consultants, it risks the expensive proposition of becoming dependent. Additionally, the kinds of explicit reports, documents, and procedures that are developed by consultants as work products fail to substitute for the rich tacit knowledge possessed. This is the case with most attempts to articulate tacit knowledge via explicit documents. Client organizations may develop a false sense of security when purchasing such explicit documentation.

This application case illustrates, through two figures, a contrast between comparatively healthy and unhealthy knowledge flows. The former flows are represented previously in terms of complete, tacit flow cycles at all levels of reach. Such cyclic knowledge movements are interconnected richly with bidirectional sharing and acculturation flows. The pattern delineated in this former figure can be used by managers to illustrate at least one instantiation of healthy knowledge flows. Here the circulation of knowledge appears to be flowing smoothly. In contrast, the latter flows are represented previously in terms of disjoint, tacit flow cycles at the group level of reach. The cyclic knowledge movements associated with the consulting group are separate and isolated from those associated with employee knowledge flows. Negligible knowledge sharing takes place within the tacit plane. Although a single vector rises up from the tacit plane and flows to the organization in terms of explicit documentation, this represents a very poor substitute for tacit knowledge sharing. The pattern delineated in this latter figure can be used by managers to illustrate at least one instantiation of unhealthy knowledge flows. Here the circulation of knowledge appears to be constricted by a noticeable clump in the consultants' flows.

We close this section by addressing the question of cost. We noted how the approach taken in the case appears to be effective in terms of enhancing knowledge flows and ameliorating problems with knowledge clumping and appropriation by consultants. As a result of cross-functional, consultant-employee work teams, substantial technical knowledge is shared between consultants and employees. Many organizational processes improve their performance and retain collective knowledge through routines. From a knowledge-flow perspective, this case reads like a success story. We can use knowledge-flow diagrams such as the one presented in Figure 4 as a pattern reflecting healthy circulation.

But the informed reader must ask about the cost of such success. Engaging consultants represents a relatively expensive approach to obtaining expertise. We do not know how expensive it would be to hire and train a technically proficient cadre of employees. In particular, given the long time period associated with the project, it may be less expensive to hire and develop expertise from within the organization than to depend upon an external organization over a period of multiple years. Additionally, assigning consultants and employees to work together on teams has its costs as well. Working with relative novices (employees) is likely to slow down the consultants, as they are in effect mentoring and teaching — or at least spending time explaining — as well as working. Likewise, encouraging employees to shadow consultants decreases the amount of time and energy they have for contributions to the organization's workflows. In particular, again, given the long time period associated with the project, a less-expensive approach may be to hire and develop expertise from within the organization. The case does not provide sufficient information for us to assess this tradeoff, but the informed leader or manager would want to consider it. A model to help leaders and managers to balance such factors would be very helpful in circumstances like these — circumstances that confront nearly every knowledge-based organization. Unfortunately, at present, such models are confined to ongoing research and not yet ready for practical application.

Exercises

9. Identify and describe three principles from earlier parts of the book that apply to this case. Can you induce additional principles from this application case that are not articulated in the earlier parts?

10. Delineate vectors to describe knowledge flows corresponding to how the tacit knowledge possessed by individual consultants could be shared with individual employees as described in the case.

11. Comment on other approaches the agency could take to address its knowledge-flow problems. What relative advantages and disadvantages apply to your suggestions when compared with the approach described in the case?

12. Describe how your learning from this case can be related to an organization with which you are familiar. Include a knowledge-flow diagram such as the one presented in Figure 4 or 5.

Chapter IX

Application Cases in Non-Profits

This chapter concentrates on knowledge-flow diagnosis and intervention in the private, not-for-profit sector. We look first at a national youth soccer organization. The discussion turns then to examine a local tennis club. The final case examines a nondenominational community church. In each case, we draw in part from secondary data sources for the background. This should prove helpful to the reader who is interested in following up to consider more details than presented in this volume. Here we also draw considerably from our own research and personal experience to fill in missing information, and we apply principles and techniques of this book to contribute new insights through examination of knowledge flows in the cases. Each application case concludes with exercises to stimulate critical thought, learning, and discussion.

National Youth Soccer Organization

We draw from AYSO (2004) and Nissen (2004b) for the background of this case. We first summarize important events and issues for context. Discussion and analysis of key knowledge flows follows, with interpretation of management implications discussed subsequently. The section closes with exercises pertaining specifically to this application case.

Context

Founded in 1964, a national organization provides a number of organized youth soccer programs. It is a non-profit organization, established to promote soccer for children between the ages of five and 18. The organization can be characterized well via multi-tier structure. A small national headquarters with a board of directors governs the overall organization. The national organization is divided geographically into multiple sections, which range in area from collections of populous cities to the inclusion of multiple smaller states. Sectional organizations are further divided geographically into multiple areas, which are comprised in turn of multiple regions. The region represents the atomic, community-level organizational unit.

This organization competes in a loose sense with other soccer enterprises, most of which are non-profits also. However, the competition is not based on profit, capital stock enhancement, market share, or like financial measure. Rather, the competition is based on philosophy — which differs appreciably across the various other soccer organizations — measured by the number of players and volunteers participating and adhering to the philosophy. At the time of this writing, the focal organization lists roughly 50,000 teams with 650,000 youth players nationwide.

Volunteerism represents an important philosophical element of the organization. Indeed, the organization is practically all volunteer. Only 50 paid employees on the headquarters staff are compensated for their time and effort. Another 250,000 parents, grandparents, siblings, business and community leaders, and other people serve as volunteers to organize, oversee, and promote youth soccer throughout the sections, areas, and regions. Indeed, volunteers are responsible for every aspect of the soccer organization below the headquarters level. Primary staff roles include positions on sectional, area, and regional Boards of Directors (e.g., Commissioner, Treasurer, Coach Administrator), but the operating core of the organization is comprised of volunteer coaches, referees, team parents, snack-shack operators, field maintainers, and like jobs. Local community businesses and like organizations also donate time and money to the soccer organization. Enlisting such volunteer family and community involvement enmeshes youth players in a culture of encouragement, participation, and sharing. Additionally, many such volunteers are highly paid professionals (e.g., doctors, lawyers, business people). At current rates (e.g., $100,000 including indirect and overhead costs), volunteers' time invested in this organization makes it comparable roughly to a billion-dollar enterprise!

Many competing soccer organizations perform the same operational aspects of providing soccer opportunities for kids. However, several noteworthy differences with our focal organization pertain. For one, most such competing organizations do not rely upon volunteers to an extent anywhere near that of the focal organization. For instance, all people participating as coaches, referees, and like official positions are compensated financially for their time and expertise in the competitive organizations. For another, these competing organizations tend to promote highly competitive soccer teams, players, and games. For instance, children of all ages must try out for teams. Many lesser-skilled players are turned away. Those who make the teams must play the positions determined by coaches. Many kids play the same positions on the same teams with the same coaches, year after year. Children with the best skills are allowed to play the most in games. Less-advanced teammates are often confined to watch from the bench. Winning and the development of superior soccer skills is stressed in the competitive leagues. Teamwork represents the means toward an end of winning games. Unevenly matched teams and lopsided games represent a common occurrence in this soccer environment. Also, in great part because of its competitive environment, many of the teams and players in such soccer organizations exhibit greater skill levels than counterparts in the volunteer focal organization. A great many children who progress to play collegiate and professional soccer emerge from these competitive organizations. Nonetheless, such primary emphasis on competition does not mesh well with the philosophy of the focal organization.

The focal soccer organization has a strong and unique philosophy that permeates its myriad community leagues and is embedded (albeit somewhat tenuously) within the culture. Organizing an environment in which children can play competitive soccer games is certainly part of the mission. The organization shares such mission with other soccer federations and enterprises, but competitive soccer represents only a minor part of the mission. Instead, the organization notes "dedication toward the development of responsible individuals" as its central mission focus (AYSO, 2004). Soccer represents the focal activity of the organization, but such activity is used as a vehicle to enhance the whole-life development of its youth players.

Five philosophical pillars support this central tenet. Organization-wide policies operationalize them. The first is that *everyone plays*. The program's goal is for all of its participating kids to play soccer, not just to be accepted onto a team and watch from the bench. The headquarters organization mandates that every player on every team must play at least half of every game, and teams are sized to enable most youth participants to play three quarters of every game, regardless of skill level. The second is *balanced teams*. Program founders believe children develop best and have the most fun when teams of equal ability play against one another. The national organization mandates that new teams form each year to ensure they are balanced as evenly as possible in terms of skill levels. The third is *open registration*. The focal organization does not condone discrimination on any basis, not even soccer-playing ability. The youth soccer program is open to all children of age (five to 18) who want to register and play soccer. Interest and enthusiasm are the only criteria for playing, and players at any skill level, including beginners, are welcome at any age. The fourth is *positive coaching*. The program founders believe encouragement provides for greater enjoyment by the players and ultimately leads to better-skilled and better-motivated players. More importantly, positive coaching is viewed as enhancing children's sense of self-worth and confidence. The fifth is *good sportsmanship*. The organization strives to create a positive environment based on mutual respect rather than a win-at-all-costs attitude. The soccer program is designed to instill good sportsmanship in every facet of the organization.

Knowledge-Flow Analysis

Knowledge is important for the performance of the youth soccer organization. In every region, one finds a mix of experienced and novice volunteers. One also finds a mix in terms of willingness to serve as a volunteer. Volunteers must know how to recruit and register players; organize leagues, teams, and games; enlist people to serve as coaches, referees, board members, and other roles; set up and maintain playing fields; purchase soccer uniforms and equipment; and organize players' parents and like affiliated people to help accomplish the myriad operational activities required to be performed each season. Although numerous informative written procedures have been written to articulate how each of these activities should be performed, it is unclear how many volunteers read them or even know they exist. Yet volunteers in thousands of community regions come together each weekend of every season to perform such operational activities.

Knowledge that enables such operational activities is possessed in great part through organizational routines. The knowing associated with such activities also emerges to a large extent. For instance, with negligible formal organization, in each of a thousand regions across the country, a cadre of people seems to show up for registration. A few people in each regional cadre may have some prior experience with registration, but most of the volunteers do not. The former gravitate to the critical activities, but few if any can articulate all of the registration tasks or perform all of the requisite activities. The latter help out where they can, but many do not understand the significance of the actions they perform or where their efforts fit into the overall process. By the end of the day, however, an inexperienced collection of volunteers emerges into a coherent team that whisks players and parents through the registration process with considerable efficiency. The enabling knowledge flows are principally experience-based, reflecting rich tacit knowledge held only in part by individuals. Through processes such as group interaction, observation, and individual practice — along with trial and error — the knowing appears to emerge within each group of volunteers across a thousand regional soccer communities. Yet it reflects and affects—nationwide and to various extents—the overarching philosophical principles of the focal organization as a whole.

In terms of knowledge-flow processes, creation, sharing, and application appear to predominate the dynamics of soccer-program operations (e.g., tasks noted previously such as registration, forming teams, organizing coaches, and referees). Creation takes place within each volunteer group—at the individual and group level alike — as inexperienced people learn how to perform unfamiliar tasks, and groups of people with negligible prior common experience learn how to work effectively together as a team. As suggested previously, trial and error accounts for a major portion of such knowledge flows. By learning through trial and error, individuals and groups can improve their performance gradually. Knowledge sharing plays a part also. The few people in each regional group with prior experience as volunteers in the organization generally set the agenda and organize the work tasks, sharing ideas for how each task may be accomplished in some orderly manner. Such volunteer groups are generally relatively small, and there appears always to be much more work required than resources available. Hence, the amount of knowledge sharing within each community group (region) is relatively limited.

Some additional knowledge sharing takes place along hierarchical lines. Area volunteers, for instance, are generally quite experienced at all aspects of regional operations. Such volunteers are also generally quite willing to help regional volunteers to understand what needs to be accomplished. The same applies in terms of sectional volunteers assisting their area counterparts, and so forth, up to the national headquarters. Regions are dispersed geographically. The number of area volunteers is small and so is the volume of knowledge that flows in this manner. Another hierarchical vehicle for knowledge sharing is more formal in nature. Several training courses are offered at every level of the focal organization. However, few of the volunteers appear to take such courses. Hence, the volume of knowledge that flows in this manner is small also. Although hierarchical knowledge flows may appear fluid and dynamic on paper, knowledge of soccer-program operations appears to be sticky and static in practice. Instead, slow but steady OJT via trial and error predominates at the individual as well as the group level. In a departure from the application cases described previously, here we omit graphical representations of these knowledge flows. Many representative depictions of OJT knowledge flows are included in the preceding chapters.

Considerable individual knowledge is necessary for coaches and referees to perform their activities well. Here we discover a much more fluid collection of knowledge flows than those noted previously pertaining to soccer-program operations. People who volunteer to perform in coach and referee roles tend to self-select to a great extent. For instance, many volunteer coaches and referees played youth soccer themselves, with a relatively small number having advanced to play at collegiate and even professional levels. Such experienced volunteers enter the season with an *a priori* understanding of the game and how to coach players and/or officiate games. This represents a contrast with the comparatively inexperienced volunteers described earlier, who self-select for soccer-program operations.

The knowledge flows associated with formal training of coaches and referees also appear to be more fluid and dynamic than those enabling soccer-program operations. Several levels (e.g., Beginner, Intermediate, Advanced) of coaching and refereeing courses are offered each season, and coaches as well as referees must be generally certified at the appropriate level before they can perform the corresponding duties. For instance, as one's children advance in age from one league to another (e.g., from leagues of eight- or nine-year olds to 10- or 11-year olds), the volunteer coaches must complete higher-level coaching courses (e.g., the Intermediate course). The same applies to advanced-level courses for older children (e.g., coaches of 14- to 18-year olds take the Advanced course). Alternatively, only the beginner-level courses are required to coach the younger children. As a similar instance, the referees who officiate increasingly advanced games (e.g., played by 12- or 13-year olds or 14- to 16-year olds) must take more advanced refereeing courses than their counterparts refereeing younger kids' (e.g., six- or seven-year olds or eight- or nine-year olds) games. Mentoring plays a role here too. Many coaches with relatively more experience appear very willing to share tips with their less-experienced counterparts. Observation plays a role as well. Many teams share the same field on practice days, so coaches of different teams can observe how their counterparts work with the kids and conduct their drills. We omit graphical representations of these knowledge flows. Many representative depictions of formal training and mentoring knowledge flows are included in the preceding chapters.

Perhaps the most noteworthy and challenging knowledge flows pertain to the organizational culture and philosophy. With only 50 paid employees to oversee a quarter million volunteers, clearly, direct supervision would not represent an effective approach to acculturating organizational participants and instilling the organization's philosophy. Instead, the organization employs several other techniques in attempt to effect knowledge flows pertaining to culture and philosophy. For one, the concept *Kids' Zone* outlines the kinds of positive, supportive good-sportsmanship behaviors expected of parents when they participate in games, practices, and other official organizational soccer events. Every parent is asked to read and required to sign a Kids' Zone Pledge, which outlines such expectations. Kids' Zone buttons and signs abound on people and fences, respectively, around soccer fields, but this approach appears to be limited. Many people can be observed signing pledges without reading them. Many parents wear buttons without being able to articulate what the Kids' Zone is. Many participants at soccer practices and games (within Kids' Zones) exhibit behaviors (e.g., criticizing referees, commenting negatively about coaches, encouraging unsportsmanlike play) that are inconsistent with the organizational philosophy. In this respect, knowledge flows associated with philosophical acculturation clump largely at the higher levels of the focal organization.

Alternatively, a number of people do appear to exhibit the kinds of behaviors formally encouraged by the focal organization. In great part, such people tend to be the same few experienced volunteers described previously, who know how registration and other soccer-program operations should be conducted. They tend to be the more experienced coaches and referees. They tend to volunteer to serve on Boards of Directors for their local community regions. They tend to be a minority group.

The formal training courses can account for some acculturation knowledge flows within this minority group. For instance, every training course—whether for coaching, refereeing, administration, or other volunteer activity—includes a section on the organization's philosophy. One can expect to take a test with questions pertaining to the five philosophical tenets in every course. Repetition of these philosophical tenets appears to have some effect — over considerable time — in terms of sharing the rich, tacit knowledge underlying the philosophy. The experienced volunteers appear to incorporate the philosophy into many decisions and actions pertaining to soccer practices, games, and operations. When asked to explain why (e.g., why Johnny cannot play forward all of the time; why Suzie must sit out one quarter each game even though she is a better player than Amy; why abusive parent spectators are asked by referees to leave games; why hyper-competitive coaches are not allowed to supervise youth players; and other similar questions), coaches, referees, board members, and like people often provide explanations that reflect the focal organization's philosophy. By repeating the same explanations, again and again, to parent after parent, such coaches, referees, board members, and like people appear — over considerable time — to influence the parents, spectators, and others. In essence, these evangelical people are leading by example. They repeat the philosophical tenets to others and apply them to their own decisions and actions. Knowledge flows — albeit very slowly — through tacit movements via a blend of conversational repetition, mentoring, observation, and more subtle processes (e.g., evangelism) that defy explanation from the details available in this case.

We omit graphical representations of these knowledge flows. Many representative depictions of such knowledge flows are included in the preceding chapters. In many respects, we appear to be saturating our list of knowledge-flow processes and corresponding vector diagrams. That is to say, the same set of processes and vectors appears to account well for a diversity of knowledge flows, across a variety of business, government, and non-profit organizations. Little contribution is expected here from repeating the same diagrams again and again.

Management Implications

The environment of a non-profit organization shares both similarities and differences with that of business and government counterparts. Similarities include an organization of people that attempts to accomplish more than the disorganized collection of individuals could; a mission and set of workflow processes that define the organization's focus and activities; and a combination of formal and informal structures, communication channels, and routines. Differences center on the organizations' profit motives and compensation schemes. Non-profit organizations generally require revenues to cover expenses and function effectively, but they do not generally seek to return earnings to stakeholders. Government organizations (without profit motive) are more like non-profits than businesses in this regard. Many non-profit organizations compensate their employees at lower (e.g., below-market) wage rates — the extreme of this depends upon (zero-wage) volunteers — than either business or government organizations do. Particularly in the kind of all-volunteer organization described in this case, participants who are responsible for accomplishing the organizational work are not interested in careers or even paid jobs with the organization. The kinds of processes that leaders and managers can employ successfully vary accordingly.

Nonetheless, knowledge enables action, and action produces performance. This applies to the non-profit organization as well as to other forms in the private and public sectors alike. People need to know what to do and how to do it before they can effectively accomplish the organizational activities that are important. Hence, knowledge needs to flow in non-profit organizations just as well as it does in their business and government counterparts. Many of the same kinds of knowledge-flow processes described previously pertain to non-profit organizations as well. Indeed, we find familiar processes such as OJT, formal training, and mentoring in the focal case.

We also find some less familiar — or at least less-emphasized — knowledge-flow processes in the focal organization. The role of conversational repetition, for instance, stands out. This process appears to be key in terms of acculturation, which involves very slow flows of rich, tacit knowledge. Conversational repetition is likely to exist as well in the other kinds of organizations described previously, but we do not find it emphasized to the same extent as it is in the focal organization. Leading by example and evangelism are similar. They clearly pertain to other kinds of organizations as well as to non-profits, but they are not emphasized as much as they are in the focal organization.

We use this to induce our twenty-sixth leadership mandate from the practical application section of this book. *Mandate 26. Leading by example and evangelism represent viable approaches to enhancing acculturation knowledge flows.*

The point about saturation is noteworthy. A relatively small number of knowledge-flow processes (e.g., OJT, formal training, mentoring) appears to account for a relatively large variety of knowledge flows, across a diversity of different organizations. The number of *combinations* of such processes is practically uncountable, so the specific vectors and sequences that pertain to any particular organization are likely to be unique. However, the underlying *components* used to form such combinations derive from a relatively small set. Hence, once one understands this set of knowledge-flow components, he or she can likely describe, visualize, and analyze any knowledge flows — healthy or pathologic — in any organization. As noted in the beginning of the book, this represents an important factor in harnessing knowledge dynamics.

We use this to induce our twenty-seventh leadership mandate from the practical application section of this book. *Mandate 27. Once one understands a relatively small set of key knowledge-flow processes, he or she can analyze any knowledge flows — healthy or pathologic — in any organization.*

Exercises

1.   Identify and describe three principles from earlier parts of the book that apply to this case. Can you induce additional principles from this application case that are not articulated in the earlier parts?

2.   Delineate vectors to describe knowledge flows corresponding to how the tacit knowledge associated with good sportsmanship flows to youth players as described in the case.

3.   Comment on other approaches the organization could take to address its knowledge-flow problems. What relative advantages and disadvantages apply to your suggestions when compared with the approach described in the case?

4.   Describe how your learning from this case can be related to an organization with which you are familiar. Include a knowledge-flow diagram such as the ones presented throughout this book.

Local Tennis Club

We draw from USTA (2004) and Nissen (2004c) for the background of this case. We first summarize important events and issues for context. Discussion and analysis of key knowledge flows follows, with interpretation of management implications discussed subsequently. The section closes with exercises pertaining specifically to this application case.

Context

Founded in 1974, a small private club provides tennis, swimming, and other recreational facilities for use by its members. Like most private clubs, only members and their guests are allowed to use the facilities. Members pay both initiation fees and monthly dues to participate in the club. Unlike most private clubs, however, the focal organization is wholly owned by its 110 members, with each holding one share of voting stock. The club is notably non-profit. Its owner-members are interested in playing tennis, swimming, exercising, and socializing through the club, not earning a profit. Yet as with the non-profit soccer organization described in the previous case, the tennis club must earn revenues to cover expenses that are necessary to operate and provide services to its members.

The club has a Board of Directors, which meets monthly. The Board consists of members elected for three-year terms. Board members serve on a volunteer basis. Their only compensation comes in the form of waived guest fees. All other members must pay guest fees whenever non-members are brought into the club. Together, Board members meet to establish policy, oversee the club from a high level, and address novel or particularly challenging issues that arise from time to time. The Board also hires a Manager who is responsible for day-to-day operations of the club. The Manager represents one of the few paid positions in the club. The Manager, who is supported by a small cadre of part-time assistants, schedules tennis courts, organizes tournaments and social events, oversees club maintenance activities, and takes care of the modicum of paperwork associated with any non-profit organization. The other paid position is that of Pro (Tennis Professional). The Pro is paid a small stipend and allowed to use select courts for tennis instruction, from which he or she derives primary income. People of all ages come and pay for such instruction. The Pro also offers periodic clinics (e.g., for doubles partners to work together) on a fee basis. Unlike many tennis clubs, the focal organization has decided not to collect a portion of the Pro's earnings in return for use of club facilities for instruction.

In contrast with the small group of people from earlier with official positions in the club, the majority of club participants are members, who have no official duties, and who use the club facilities for exercise and entertainment. A majority of club members use the tennis courts, but a sizeable fraction of members use only the swimming pool and training room. On any given hot afternoon or weekend, the pool may be filled with swimming kids, while the tennis courts are nearly empty. The opposite may hold for any given cool day. At least one person is using the training room at nearly all times.

The tennis players have several avenues for arranging matches. The most common is person-to-person. Everyone in the club receives a list of members and telephone numbers, but tennis is a game that requires considerable time to develop skill, and players vary widely in their relative abilities. The club encourages members to have their skill levels rated (e.g., the United States Tennis Association has a standardized seven-point scale that is commonly used nationwide). Unlike golf and like activities in which a person plays largely against himself or herself, tennis is competitive, and matches between people with even marginally different skill levels can be very lopsided. Hence, it is important for members to find others at roughly the same skill level. This takes time, as people watch one another play, ask about others who play at various levels, and play matches on a trial-and-error basis. Tennis is a social game to a large extent. People who are matched evenly in skill may be matched unevenly in disposition, and vice versa. Particularly with doubles (two people on each team) and mixed doubles (one man and one woman on each team), many tennis matches represent more of a social occasion than a competitive sporting event. In either case, once club members discover with whom they are matched evenly and enjoy playing, they call one another to set up play dates and/or establish regular patterns of play (e.g., the Ladies' Tuesday/Thursday Morning Group).

Another avenue for arranging matches involves league play. Most tennis clubs organize teams by skill level to play against teams fielded by other local clubs. Each individual match (e.g., singles, doubles, mixed doubles) is played competitively against members of other clubs. Clubs will field a team (e.g., two singles players, six doubles players) to compete against one another in a series of matches. Unlike the more social approach to arranging matches, members on a team have no input into whom they play against on other teams, and they have negligible input into whom they play with on their own team. Matches are also scheduled well in advance, on the home courts and away, so people on teams have little to say about when they play. Competitive matches are followed generally by social time, during which players from both teams interact over snacks. Signing up for and playing on a team represents a well-practiced approach to meeting other players at a member's skill level. Many person-to-person matches arranged during the off-seasons are between members who have met through team play.

The third avenue for arranging matches is through club tournaments and social events. Roughly every two months, the club will organize some kind of tennis event that is open to all of its members. Examples include the club singles and doubles tournaments — men and women compete in separate flights — mixed doubles and youth tournaments, and holiday occasions such as Valentine's Day, Independence Day, Thanksgiving, and the like. The tournaments and social events provide another common approach to meeting other players at a member's skill level. Many person-to-person matches arranged during the off-seasons are between members who have met through such events. A great many social activities that take place outside the club have their roots in people who have met through such events. People in the club share a number of common interests, and many establish friendships that carry through off the court as well as on it.

Knowledge-Flow Analysis

Knowledge plays a central role in the tennis club. The most obvious knowledge flows pertain to tennis playing. We noted previously how tennis requires considerable time to develop skill. Unlike many games that can be fun even for beginners and novices, tennis is not very enjoyable to most people until they develop a basic level of proficiency. Such basic level can take a year or more of lessons and/or routine practice to establish. Many intermediate and advanced players have devoted decades to developing and refining their games. Hence, knowledge required for playing tennis — that is, knowing tennis — flows relatively slowly, on the order of years and decades. Like bicycle riding, such knowledge is largely tacit. Many books have been written that describe, in great detail, how to play tennis, but reading such books is insufficient for knowing tennis.

Tennis lessons represent a very common approach taken by beginners (especially youth players). Such lessons can be individual, group, or class in nature. Generally, a single individual such as the Pro is providing instruction. Such instruction includes demonstrating techniques, observing, and critiquing how students perform them and offering guidelines for practice. Such instructional modes are limited in terms of the number of students who can be trained simultaneously. Indeed, most tennis instruction reflects more of a mentoring arrangement than formal training or classroom instruction.

Practice has a connotation of working on specific techniques to improve one's performance. Very few people practice tennis. The game requires considerable redundancy for one's muscle memory to develop. Many people describe such redundant activity as boring and prefer to play. Practice can involve play as well. The key is whether one is looking to learn from points that are played or seeking instead simply to play the points. Hence, the same activity — playing tennis — can take on different roles depending upon whether a person is focusing on the knowing activities of learning vs. doing while playing points. Sometimes, tennis coaches (e.g., from league play) and professionals (e.g., from lessons) will observe and comment on one's playing during matches. Some people find such critiques beneficial, and some find them annoying. Again, this appears to depend upon one's knowing focus.

Of course, playing contributes also to developing tennis skill. This is essentially OJT. A learning component is involved with every game played, but as with OJT in other knowledge domains, the contribution of OJT to learning is relatively small with respect to doing. Hence, people who play but do not take lessons or practice tend to improve comparatively slowly. A great many such people are able to progress only so far before reaching a skill plateau. Such plateaus are similar in many respects to the kinds of competency traps discussed previously in terms of organizational routines. People become somewhat proficient at a particular style of play, which is effective in common situations (e.g., against people at the same skill level), but such style of play is often ineffective against better players, who to continue the metaphor, have reached a higher plateau.

In addition to developing one's tennis-playing ability — whether in individual, dyadic, or team matches — another knowledge flow is very important in the tennis club: socialization. We noted how enjoyment and social interaction represent important activities that members seek from their affiliation with the club. This local tennis club is not a professional tennis academy with a mission of developing professional players nor is it a collegiate or professional sports organization that exists exclusively for high-level competition. Rather, tennis represents both a physical and social activity that people enjoy. One need not be a particularly skilled tennis player in order to derive enjoyment through socialization in a club. Indeed, players at both extremes in terms of playing ability (beginning and advanced) are often less skilled socially than are club members in the middle of the distribution.

Socialization is in great part about finding people with common interests. Tennis represents clearly one interest that most club members share, but conversations about tennis do not seem to be self-sustaining. Many conversations begin with comments pertaining to a recent tennis match but tend to drift quickly to other sports, activities, people, and events. Tennis is the *raison d'etre* for a club such as our focal organization, but it is not the only reason the club exists. From an individual perspective, socialization is a process with which every reader is likely to be intimately familiar. From an organization perspective, what models appear to apply? Perhaps the community of practice can describe well the knowledge flows associated with socialization. People who engage in a common activity are able to exchange stories and ideas pertaining to such activity. Through such process, people become acquainted with one another, establish trust, and develop personal relationships that transcend activities of their "home" organizations (e.g., employers). Socialization in the kinds of guilds and like trans-organizational groups discussed previously in connection with the film-production case offers similar insights. We examined earlier tacit knowledge flows associated with socialization and do not repeat such examination here, however.

Management Implications

The local tennis club is wholly owned by its members. This makes it somewhat unique with respect to the other organizations examined previously. The organization exists for the benefit of its members, who are its owners. A Board of Directors, Club Manager, and Pro are elected, hired, and commissioned, respectively, to oversee and effect the organizational activities required for the club to operate effectively. The majority part of the club's activities involve members playing tennis and socializing with one another. In this sense, the workflows correspond to playing tennis and interacting socially. It does not matter that members derive enjoyment from such "work." Indeed, this represents a valuable lesson for leaders and managers: people will self-organize when they share activities in common and enjoy what they do.

We use this to induce our twenty-eighth leadership mandate from the practical application section of this book. *Mandate 28. The key to self-organization is having people enjoy what they do together.*

An important activity of the tennis club involves arranging matches between members. People are able to accomplish this for themselves once they know one another. Discovering which players exhibit various skill levels and social dispositions takes considerable time. The club facilitates such discovery by publishing a list of members' telephone numbers. It also includes ratings for various players to signal approximate skills levels. The club also facilitates this discovery by organizing league matches and a combination of club competitions and tennis socials. In any organization, different people will exhibit a variety of skill levels and areas of interest. Rating employees' skill levels and publishing such ratings may represent an approach with potential beyond the tennis club. In any organization, different people will exhibit a variety in terms of interpersonal compatibility. The ability of different people to work together on teams is important in business, government, and non-profit organizations alike. The tennis club has established some organizational routines that facilitate self-organization based on compatibility as well as skill. Business and government may have something to learn here.

We use this to induce our twenty-ninth leadership mandate from the practical application section of this book. *Mandate 29. The ability of different people to work together on teams is just as important as the individual skills and experiences they bring individually.*

In developing skill levels, we learn from the case how mentoring, OJT, and practice contribute toward tennis knowledge flows. We have discussed mentoring and OJT repeatedly through the previous cases. Alternatively, the activity *practice* is unusual in the context of workflows and knowledge flows. Clearly, tennis is a game, whereas new-product development, technology transfer, film production, warfare, public service, and like activities are serious endeavors. Tennis involves considerable skill development, and practice represents a disciplined approach to such development. What would be the organizational equivalent to *practice*? For one, simulation provides a venue for people to practice workflow activities virtually. Through repeated and varied, simulated work sessions, a person, team, or organization can improve its skills. Pilots practice their flying skills regularly using flight simulators. Soccer and other sports teams practice their playing skills regularly using simulated game situations. Military units practice their warfare skills routinely through simulated battles. There may be a lesson here for organizations involved with new-product development, technology transfer, and the like. Notice by *simulation* we include but do not limit our discussion to computer-based approaches.

Exercises

5.   Identify and describe three principles from earlier parts of the book that apply to this case. Can you induce additional principles from this application case that are not articulated in the earlier parts?

6. Delineate vectors to describe knowledge flows corresponding to how the tacit knowledge associated with socialization flows as described in the case.

7. Comment on other approaches the organization could take to address its knowledge-flow problems. What relative advantages and disadvantages apply to your suggestions when compared with the approach described in the case?

8. Describe how your learning from this case can be related to an organization with which you are familiar. Include a knowledge-flow diagram such as the ones presented throughout this book.

Nondenominational Community Church

We draw from Grace (2004) and Nissen (2004d) for the background of this case. We first summarize important events and issues for context. Discussion and analysis of key knowledge flows follows, with interpretation of management implications discussed subsequently. The section closes with exercises pertaining specifically to this application case.

Context

Founded in 1956, a small community church provides worship, youth, mission, and other faith-based services to people in a semi-rural, semi-suburban area. It is a non-profit, religious organization. This local church has a leader, a Board of Directors, officers who serve in various capacities (e.g., youth ministry, teaching, missionary), and a congregation of members and non-members. The church is nondenominational. Although it is richly interconnected with other similar churches worldwide, it remains independent. This represents something of a contrast with many local churches that represent "branch offices" of major national or international denominations. As a relatively independent organization, this church sets its own operating and governance guidelines. As a richly interconnected organization, it conforms with others to a common set of theological principles and reference materials. The church includes *growth* among its mission elements. In further contrast with many major denominational counterparts, it does not seek to become a large church. Indeed, as membership grows to 250 or so, the church guidelines suggest it will split off to form a "daughter church" (Grace, 2004) somewhere nearby, the latter of which will have its own, separate leader, Board, officers, and congregation. The church Pastor prefers to term the church's primary mission element *health* (Pastor Bill, personal communication, October 2004).

From a congregational perspective, the church provides faith-based services. For instance, many adults and children participate in weekly educational programs on a weekend morning in addition to a worship service later the same morning. Times before, between, and after these official events are designated for social conversation. As another instance, a youth group meets later in the evenings, and different groups of people meet on a weekly basis outside of the weekend days. Other services such as counseling and support are provided by the organization as well, as are various larger-scale social events such as barbeques, trips, and like occasions for extended interaction between members. The church provides faith-based services. For instance, it seeks to help people develop spiritually and to provide guidance for living their secular and religious lives. As another instance, it seeks to increase church membership selectively, accepting as members only people with a prescribed set of beliefs. Other activities include staffing and organizing the services, various administrative tasks, and other endeavors required to pursue the church mission.

Knowledge-Flow Analysis

Knowledge is important in this church. As a religious organization, faith is stressed, and beliefs are made explicit. Reading and discussing common passages from reference materials represents a central knowledge-flow activity. Much of the knowledge associated with the church's belief system has been articulated and collected through a canon of historical documents, although such documents are subject to a variety of interpretations, and applying such knowledge through action requires tacit internalization of knowledge principles. Notice this represents the reverse movement of knowledge formalization. Through formalization, tacit knowledge is made explicit. Through internalization of principles, explicit knowledge is made tacit.

An enduring series of separate and combined conversations serve to help people exchange ideas about what the various principles mean. Conversation represents a central knowledge-flow process in this respect. Also, through the conduct of various faith-based services such as those noted previously, the church leader provides regular guidance to facilitate interpretation of written principles. Such plenary services tend to be one-on-many and resemble the university lecture in many ways (e.g., including assignments from a common "textbook"). Independent reading and contemplation is noted as a process for learning and interpretation. People are encouraged to regularly read passages from the reference materials. Formal "training" classes are offered as well to help people learn about and interpret the principles. Such classes are organized into smaller groups than those of the plenary sessions. Continuing with the university metaphor, such one-on-not-so-many classes resemble lab sessions and are led often by the equivalents of teaching assistants.

Applying the knowledge acquired and interpreted requires operationalization of principles. Instantiating the knowing-doing gap, simply knowing about the various principles is insufficient to know the principles through action. Such operationalization is accomplished by example in many respects. The reference materials are replete with examples of people who have performed in manners consistent with the principles. They are replete with heuristic rules for performing as such, but many of the examples and rules are dated, and numerous people experience difficulty when trying to apply the principles to contemporary decisions and events in their lives. This is addressed in part through the plenary and small-group conversations and interpretation activities, and it is addressed in part through individual reading and contemplation. A major share of the learning that enables principled application through the workflows of life entail knowledge flows of everyday experience. This is tantamount to OJT. Instead of learning by doing applied to some prescribed set of organizational work activities, however, the OJT in this sense consists of learning by doing applied to the everyday lives of church members. Considerable trial and error is involved, and discussing the various trials and errors with others represents another, conversation-based knowledge-flow process.

Management Implications

The local church shares aspects in common with other organizations described in previous application cases. For instance, knowledge flows are important; the organization has a structure, leader, governing body, and set of members; and the organization has a mission and executes processes to pursue organizational objectives. Further, as a non-profit organization, the church shares much in common with the two other application cases in this chapter. For instance, it relies heavily upon volunteers; it does not pursue profit and like pecuniary objectives; it exists in great part to provide services to its members. The local church is also quite small compared to several of the other application cases. It is somewhat larger than the independent film-production company and the private tennis club, but it is much, much smaller than any of the business or government organizations examined in this book.

The church provides a set of services based upon faith. This is distinct in many respects from the other organizations, but it resembles in part the soccer organization and tennis club, which provide services based upon athletic activities. Probably the most-defining difference of the church relative to the other organizations examined in this book condenses to a focus on members' beliefs. Leaders and managers of nearly every organization are interested clearly in members' beliefs to some extent. In business enterprises, for instance, employees' beliefs in the mission, organization, and culture represent important concerns of leaders and managers, but the importance of such beliefs tends to pale in comparison with the performance of useful workflows. The same can be said for government agencies, as another instance. In the soccer organization, philosophy plays a central role. Leaders and managers are concerned about acculturating participants. This has many parallels with religious beliefs associated with the church. But even in the soccer organization, the purpose of shaping participants' beliefs is to enhance the developmental experience of its youth players. Alternatively, in the church, the beliefs themselves represent the central concern of its leaders and managers. Leaders and managers with concerns about or problems with employees' beliefs can learn from the knowledge-flow processes and priorities of this church.

The local church has the benefit of an explicit set of principles that underlie its system of beliefs. Many business, government, and non-profit organizations have mission statements, codes of conduct, and like attempts to articulate their culture, but they seem to fall far short of those used by the local church. The church also has its workflow processes devoted to helping members learn about and interpret the key principles of its belief system. Indeed, this represents a principal mission of the church organization. In other organizations, if any time and energy are invested in like learning and interpretation, it is comparatively minor in magnitude, emphasis, and importance. To the extent that leaders and managers in other types of organizations seek to address and shape the beliefs of their employees, customers, members, or other stakeholders, much may be learned from the local church in terms of knowledge flows.

Of course, the local church does not have a product or service that it sells in the marketplace. As with the soccer organization and tennis club, church expenses are covered by fees collected from members, but members have an abundance of different churches from which to choose. Therefore, in a financial sense, the local church faces competition for "customers" (e.g., congregational members) in much the same way that other non-profit organizations do. In the process of shaping members' beliefs, the local church organization examined in this case provides a service to members that encourages them to belong to the organization and to contribute toward its goals through donation of time, talent, and money. Additionally, this is accomplished without employment contracts, without membership fees, indeed without anything other than member volition and generosity. Again, in terms of shaping knowledge flows, leaders and managers in many different kinds of organizations have something to learn from the local church.

We use this to induce our thirtieth leadership mandate from the practical application section of this book. *Mandate 30. Leaders who are concerned about acculturation knowledge flows must address participants' beliefs.*

Exercises

9.   Identify and describe three principles from earlier parts of the book that apply to this case. Can you induce additional principles from this application case that are not articulated in the earlier parts?

10. Delineate vectors to describe knowledge flows corresponding to how the explicit knowledge associated with religious principles is internalized and interpreted by individuals as described in the case.

11. Comment on other approaches the organization could take to address its knowledge-flow problems. What relative advantages and disadvantages apply to your suggestions when compared with the approach described in the case?

12. Describe how your learning from this case can be related to an organization with which you are familiar. Include a knowledge-flow diagram such as the ones presented throughout this book.

Chapter X

Forward!

This chapter includes guidance for learning from the book and for continuing to develop new knowledge about principled organizational knowing and learning. We first summarize the principles developed in Section I of the book. The discussion turns then to applying such principles to harness knowledge dynamics in your organization. We summarize in turn the leadership mandates induced in Section II of the book. The chapter concludes with our outline of the critical research agenda in the area of knowledge flows and principled organizational knowing and learning.

Summary of Knowledge-Flow Principles

Recall from earlier the 30 knowledge-flow principles developed in Section I of the book. We list these principles in subsequent paragraphs for reference and summarize briefly the key points pertaining to each. This section can serve as a primer for harnessing knowledge power (e.g., for those people who read the last chapter first). It can serve also as a pocket summary for the principled organizational knower and learner (e.g., for those people who read the last chapter last).

1. Knowledge is distinct from information in enabling competitive advantage. In Chapter 1, we note first that distinguishing knowledge from information is important. One effective operationalization is that knowledge enables direct action (e.g., correct decisions, appropriate behaviors, useful work), whereas information provides the meaning and context for such action (e.g., decision criteria, behavior norms, work specifications). As a Gedanken experiment, consider two people tasked to perform a knowledge-intensive activity. These could be captains on the bridge of a ship, surgeons at the operating table, managers at the negotiating table, professors in a classroom, attorneys in a courtroom, or many like situations requiring knowledge. Provide these two people with exactly the same information (e.g., books to read, charts and reports to reference, instruments to monitor, direct views and sounds, advisors to consult, others). Say that one person has 20 years of experience, whereas the other has much less experience (or possibly none). Most informed leaders, managers, and scholars would expect differential performance from these two people. Such differential performance can be attributed generally to differences in knowledge. **Hence, shuttling *information* around via computers, networks, reports, and communications does not address the flow of *knowledge*, at least not directly or on the same time scale**.

2. Knowledge is distributed unevenly, hence, must flow for organizational performance. In Chapter I, we note second that knowledge clumps in particular people, organizations, regions, and times of application. Power through competitive advantage requires knowledge to flow, but tacit knowledge, in particular, is sticky, difficult to imitate, and slow to move. This same property, which enables knowledge-based competitive advantage to be sustainable, inhibits simultaneously sharing and transfer within the organization. **Hence, knowledge clumps need to be identified, and knowledge flows need to be enabled through the organization.**

3. Tacit knowledge supports greater appropriability for competitive advantage than explicit knowledge does. In Chapter I, we note third that explicit knowledge that can be articulated is distinct in many ways from the kind of tacit knowledge that accumulates, often slowly, through experience. Neither is individual expertise quite the same as knowledge shared across members of a group, team, or other organization. Knowledge can also be quite situated, ephemeral, and local, meaning a person on the "front lines" cannot always communicate the richness of what he or she knows to

someone at headquarters. Yet people at headquarters tend to demand abundant information flows to support decision making that is often better made on location. Of course, the person on the scene with detailed and local knowledge often lacks the high-level integrative understanding of managers at headquarters, and the need for functional specialists to share specific knowledge for complex problem solving is well known. Central to the point of knowledge power is that tacit knowledge supports greater appropriability than explicit knowledge does. **Hence, knowledge managers may benefit from an emphasis on tacit knowledge flows.**

4. Knowledge flows must balance exploration through learning with exploitation through doing. In Chapter I, we note fourth that not all knowledge, not even tacit knowledge, is of equal value, and not all knowledge needs to be shared to effect performance. Indeed, there is a classic tension between exploration and exploitation. Because resources such as time, energy, and attention are limited, investing in exploration of new knowledge and opportunities necessarily limits the resources available to exploit the knowledge and opportunities that exist, and vice versa. Further, to the extent that an organization focuses solely on exploitation, for instance, it can quickly develop competency traps (Levitt & March, 1988) and suffer from debilitations associated with single-loop learning (Argyris & Schon, 1978); that is, an organization can learn to do the wrong thing very well and not realize that its competency is no longer suited well to the environment. Likewise, to the extent that an organization focuses solely on exploration, as another instance, it can quickly see its demise, as competitors capitalize upon current opportunities and take advantage of the organization's time away from task; that is, the organization can prepare itself well for a future environment but fail to survive until such future arrives. Similar tensions arise between learning and doing, sharing and hoarding knowledge, acquiring general vs. specialized expertise, and like knowledge-oriented tradeoffs. **Hence, understanding the kinds of knowledge that are important in an organization's particular environment is essential for promoting the most important knowledge flows.**

5. Enhancing knowledge flows requires simultaneous attention to personnel, work processes, organizations, and technologies. In Chapter I we note fifth that it is known well that organizational personnel, work processes, structures, and technologies are interconnected tightly and interact closely (Leavitt, 1965). When seeking to redesign and change organizations to

identify knowledge clumps and to enhance knowledge flows, it is important to focus simultaneously upon all of these interconnected and interacting elements. Most people can quickly identify a technological "innovation" that failed to produce favorable results when implemented in an organization, for instance. Bringing in people or teams with different backgrounds in terms of education, training, skills, and experience represents a similar instance (e.g., conjuring up memories of failed implementation), as does changing work processes or organizational reporting relationships and responsibilities without addressing personnel and technologies. **Understanding whether flows of data, information or knowledge are required in a particular situation depends upon what needs to be accomplished (e.g., resolving uncertainty, deriving meaning or enabling action, respectively).**

6. Knowledge enables action directly, whereas information provides meaning and context for such action. In Chapter II, we note first that distinguishing knowledge from information is important. One effective operationalization is that knowledge enables direct action (e.g., correct decisions, appropriate behaviors, useful work). Alternatively, information provides the context for such action (e.g., decision criteria, behavior norms, work specifications). Data reduce uncertainty or equivocality (e.g., supplying parameters to an equation, providing numbers for a formula, specifying states in a relationship). We also identify a fourth level for the knowledge hierarchy: *signals.* One can say with confidence, "only signals flow across time and space," not knowledge, information, or even data. Signals (e.g., light reflecting from objects in the world or computer-generated images; sound waves propagating through a room; electrical currents alternating in discrete and analog patterns) are perceived by people. Where they are interpretable, they can provide the basis for data; where uninterpretable, they constitute noise. Where data are provided in context, they can inform. Where information enables direct action, knowledge exists. **Hence, the four organizational elements of personnel, work processes, structure, and technology operate as a cohesive system and should be addressed as an integrated design problem.**

7. Data, information, and knowledge flows are interrelated dynamically yet are distinct *mental* processes. In Chapter II, we note second that data, information, and knowledge are interrelated closely, yet distinct from one another, as mental processes. A number of Gedanken experiments and practical examples can be used to distinguish between the interrelated

concepts, but all three involve mental, not physical processes. Whether interpreting data from signals, deriving information from data, or learning knowledge from information, such processes take place in the minds of people, not in computers, networks, and databases. **Hence, people play the critical role in flows of data, information, and knowledge**.

8. Flows of knowledge require supplementary flows of information, data, and signals. In Chapter II, we note third that knowledge flows require flows of information, data, and signals. Physically, only signals flow. Data, information, and knowledge flows via cognitive processes, but such cognitive processes of different people require communication. For knowledge to flow from a producer or sender, information is required to produce data, which are required to encode signals. In reverse sequence, for knowledge to flow to a consumer or receiver, signals must be interpreted into data, which must be placed into meaningful context to inform. Every conversion (e.g., interpreting data from signals; ascribing meaningful information from data; learning knowledge from information) involves some kind of knowledge (e.g., language, context, physiology). **Hence, every flow (data, information, and knowledge) from signal interpretation through knowledge creation requires some kind of knowledge**.

9. *Explicitness* represents a very discriminatory dimension for evaluating the uniqueness of knowledge. In Chapter II, we note fourth that *explicitness* characterizes an important dimension of knowledge uniqueness. In particular, tacit knowledge can be distinguished along such dimension from its explicit counterpart. One's ability to articulate his or her knowledge provides an operationalization for explicitness: explicit knowledge has been articulated; tacit knowledge has not. Further, some kinds of tacit knowledge can be articulated into explicit form more easily than others can. Some kinds cannot be articulated at all. Most knowledge made explicit loses power in at least two important ways: (1) knowledge made explicit often fails to enable the same levels of performance corresponding to actions enabled by the tacit knowledge from which it is formalized; and (2) explicit knowledge shares many properties with information, which is more difficult to appropriate than tacit knowledge. **Hence, moving knowledge through tacit vs. explicit flows represents a management decision in many cases, a decision which has implications in terms of power**.

10. Information technology principally supports flows of explicit knowledge. In Chapter II, we note fifth that IT support is limited principally to explicit knowledge flows — and information/data — but enable large amounts of such knowledge to be organized, aggregated, and disseminated broadly and quickly. Where knowledge is explicit — or can be formalized into explicit form — IT offers great power to enhance the corresponding flows. Where important knowledge is tacit — and cannot be formalized readily into explicit form — IT offers less potential to effect knowledge flows. **Hence, the nature of knowledge represents a critical factor for determining where IT can be expected to enhance knowledge flows**.

11. Knowledge exhibits some properties of inertia such as *tendency to remain at rest*. In Chapter III, we note first how knowledge at rest tends to stay at rest. If a leader or manager seeks to have knowledge flow, then something must be done to induce it to flow (e.g., formal training, OJT). Further, knowledge in motion tends to stay in motion in some cases (e.g., via employee defections). If a leader or manager seeks to cease or restrict knowledge flows in such cases, then something must be done to stem its flow. In contrast, if the leader or manager is content with such flows, then no action is required. In other cases, however, knowledge in motion (e.g., student learning through classroom interaction) appears to require additional action just to keep it in motion. If a leader or manager seeks to cease or restrict knowledge flows in such cases, then no action is required to stem its flow. In contrast, if the leader or manager wants such flows to propagate further, then something must be done to continue the flows. **Hence, knowledge-flow processes represent direct focuses of leadership and managerial action**.

12. Experiential processes contribute principally toward workflows (doing), whereas educational processes contribute principally toward knowledge flows (learning). In Chapter III, we note second that workflows and knowledge flows interact, and various processes contribute in different magnitudes toward doing vs. learning. If a leader or manager is interested in promoting knowledge flows in the organization, then it will be important for him or her to understand how the specific knowledge flows of concern interrelate with workflows of value to the organization. In some cases, workflows and knowledge flows are independent, so one can be changed without affecting the other. In other cases, however, workflows and knowledge flows are interrelated tightly, so altering one will affect the

other directly. **Hence, changes to workflows demand changes to knowledge flows, and vice versa**.

13. Knowledge flows always lie on the critical paths of workflows, hence, organizational performance. In Chapter III, we note third that the activities associated with organizational processes are responsible for the phenomenon of knowledge flows. Knowledge-flow processes represent the organizational analogs to physical forces. The nature of different kinds of knowledge represents the organizational analogs to physical masses. Together, the two determine the direction, rate, and extent of knowledge flows. If a leader or manager is interested in inducing, enhancing, restricting, or ceasing knowledge flows, then he or she should examine the associated organizational processes. Because processes are composed of activities, which have long been the focus of leadership and managerial attention, such a process focus should be quite natural. Also, there appears to be considerable opportunity for such a process focus to be supported by the same kinds of tools and techniques for the planning, organizing, monitoring, and control of work (e.g., Gantt Charts, PERT networks, work/knowledge specifications). Indeed, in every case of knowledge-based action, knowledge flows lie on the critical paths of workflows and the associated organizational performance. **Hence, knowledge flows should be planned and managed like workflows are**.

14. Time-critical workflows must wait for enabling knowledge flows to run their course. In Chapter III, we note fourth that knowledge flows and workflows vary in terms of timing. Some workflows require quick, precise, and thorough activities that can be performed by only knowledgeable people. In such cases, the enabling knowledge flows are prerequisite to their corresponding workflows. Other workflows afford greater tolerances in terms of performance, which can be performed by people who learn over time and by trial and error. In such cases, the enabling knowledge flows can be concurrent with their corresponding workflows. Indeed, in many cases such as OJT, the learning associated with knowledge flows takes place *through* the doing associated with workflows. Before deciding upon and implementing a particular approach to inducing, enhancing, restricting, or ceasing knowledge flows, the leader or manager needs to consider how the target flows interact temporally with corresponding workflows of importance. **Hence, most knowledge flows must complete their course before critical and dependent workflows can begin**.

15. *Knowledge* is a multifaceted, dynamic, and multidimensional concept. In Chapter III, we note fifth that *knowledge* is not a single, static, monolithic concept. Rather, it is multifaceted, dynamic, and multidimensional. Different kinds of knowledge behave in different ways, exhibit different properties, and manifest different dynamic patterns. Such differences present various obstacles and imply alternate approaches to overcoming them. The leader or manager interested in overcoming obstacles to knowledge flows in his or her organization should understand the nature of the knowledge associated with such flows and should use such understanding to identify the most appropriate managerial, organizational, and technological interventions. **Hence, managerial efficacy through intervention can be increased by learning the principles of dynamic knowledge**.

16. Information technology is helpful and necessary but not sufficient for knowledge management. In Chapter IV, we note first how IT plays an important role in supporting knowledge flows. In many cases, IT is even necessary for knowledge to flow, but there is more to flows of knowledge than processing and flowing information, which is the principal domain of IT. **Hence, the manager needs to employ non-technological interventions to enhance knowledge flows**.

17. People — not information technology — are central to tacit knowledge flows. In Chapter IV, we note second how problems abound in terms of KM programs that rely heavily upon IT. Many leaders and managers expect naively that IT will improve knowledge flows. Looking at the "I" in IT, however, and understanding the distinctions and relationships between knowledge and information, it should be apparent why such expectations can be considered naive. In particular, people — not information technology — are central to tacit knowledge flows. **Hence, one cannot manage tacit knowledge without managing people**.

18. Information technology plays supportive roles in organizational work routines, whereas people play the performative roles. In Chapter IV, we note third that the life cycle involves different kinds of knowledge activities, grouped broadly into classes to represent localized and expanded views of KM. We note how IT supports activities in these two classes differently. For the localized activities, IT plays a supportive role and does so well. For the expanded activities, however, a performative role is called for, but few extant IT applications are capable of — or used for — playing such role. **Hence, most IT plays a supportive role in the organization, whereas people play most of the performative roles**.

19. Expert systems, software agents, and like "intelligent" applications address and apply knowledge directly. In Chapter IV, we note fourth that expert systems, software agents, and like "intelligent" applications address knowledge directly, in addition to information and data. They also enable direct action and, hence, can play some of the performative roles called for previously. Specifically, once developed, an expert system can apply knowledge directly to perform knowledge work. Expert systems can also be distributed broadly through the organization and used in parallel, even by novices who can sometimes raise their performance to expert levels. **Hence, "intelligent" applications can play a performative role in the organization**.

20. Simulation technology can enhance knowledge flows in addition to workflows. In Chapter IV, we note fifth how simulation technology can be used to enhance knowledge flows in addition to workflows. By using simulation to learn about some systems or processes of interest in the real world, one can create new knowledge quickly and safely. Knowledge associated with a simulation model can be shared and applied, corresponding with multiple phases of the knowledge life cycle. **Hence, simulation represents a different class of IT, one that facilitates learning as well as doing through virtual practice**.

21. Knowing reflects knowledge in action. In Chapter V, we note first that knowing reflects knowledge in action. It is knowledge manifested through practice and involves doing (knowledge-based work). In most circumstances, it is insufficient to simply know something. Whether to convince someone else that you know, to accomplish some objective associated with knowledge, or to otherwise make knowledge useful, some kind of action is required. **Hence, knowledge must be put to use through action in order to be useful**.

22. Learning reflects knowledge in motion. In Chapter V, we note second that learning reflects knowledge in motion. It represents the action associated with acquiring "new" knowledge (e.g., through scientific discovery or knowledge moving from one coordinate to another). Learning requires knowledge and is action oriented, so it constitutes a form of knowing. But the focus on acquiring knowledge distinguishes learning quite generally from other knowing activities (e.g., doing). **Hence, learning both uses and increases knowledge**.

23. Knowing and learning beyond the individual offer the greatest potential for knowledge superiority. In Chapter V, we note third that knowing and

learning both take place at multiple levels of analysis. Individuals, groups, organizations, groups of organizations, and so forth can know and learn. Whereas individuals can know and learn without being affiliated with groups or organizations, groups and organizations require individuals for knowing as well as for learning. Individuals are indispensable to groups and organizations, but there is more to groups and organizations than the collection of associated individuals. The phrase, "the whole is greater than the sum of its parts," applies well here. Indeed, performance effects of knowledge flows can be amplified as they reach broadly through the organization. **Hence, the impact of KM increases in direct proportion to the reach of knowledge flows through an organization.**

24. Knowing and learning are dynamic, mutually reinforcing activities. In Chapter V, we note fourth that knowing and learning are interrelated. Knowing requires knowledge, which must be learned. Learning involves knowing focused on acquiring new knowledge. Knowing can also involve learning. Knowing contributes to learning, and learning contributes to knowing. Further, learning and doing involve tension and require decisions. Learning is associated with exploration and focuses on knowledge flows. Doing is associated with exploitation and focuses on knowledge stocks. Both serve important purposes, but constrained time and energy impose some degree of tradeoff between them. To the extent that an individual, group, or organization focuses on one, to some extent, the other must suffer. **Hence, promoting knowing promotes learning, and vice versa.**

25. Knowing and learning are path-dependent, enabling both competencies and rigidities. In Chapter V, we note fifth that knowing and learning involve action and potential. Knowing reflects knowledge put to use through action, which requires knowledge to be acquired before such use. Learning reflects knowledge acquisition, which increases the potential range of actions enabled. Learning from experience (from action) represents a primary contributor to new knowledge and stems directly from knowing, but knowing is inhibited by what has been learned previously, and learning is inhibited by what experiences have been known previously. **Hence, an organization's knowledge inventory both enables and inhibits what actions it can take.**

26. Knowledge management involves organizational change. In Chapter VI, we note first that KM projects involve change. There is much to learn from the literature on change management (e.g., BPR) in this regard. For

instance, the knowledge manager can assess an organization's preconditions for success as well as preconditions for failure. KM-specific factors such as knowledge representation, attention to tacit knowledge, and focus on organizational memory are important too and can be evaluated and addressed by the Knowledge Manager. We also find how perceptual measures such as *pessimism, affective commitment,* and *normative commitment* are important in KM projects. **Hence, the knowledge manager has much to learn from business process re-engineering and like change-management approaches.**

27. Knowledge inventory can be used to assess an organization's readiness to perform its work processes effectively. In Chapter VI, we note second that several aspects of knowledge can be audited. The knowledge audit represents an approach to discovering and documenting sources, uses, and sinks of knowledge in an organization. Generally executed via some kind of survey instrument, the knowledge audit is often performed by consultants and like professionals from outside the organization, but there is little reason why an organization should not be able to audit itself. In addition to articulating explicitly certain aspects of knowledge inventories and flows, conducting a knowledge audit can produce positive effects simply by inducing people within the organization to think about what knowledge is important, how it is used, and how it flows. Alternatively, knowledge audits consume precious time and energy. Perhaps the greatest potential in terms of a knowledge audit lies in the prospect of measuring *knowledge inventory*. This construct offers potential to assess an organization's readiness to perform its work processes effectively. **Hence, the manager needs to measure the knowledge inventory for every organization.**

28. When estimating the value of knowledge, it is often better to light a candle than to curse the darkness. In Chapter VI, we note third that knowledge value can be estimated. The knowledge value added (KVA) approach provides a set of techniques for attributing knowledge to various organizational processes and in turn prioritizing them based on a return on knowledge. The approach amounts to an allocation with no claims of superiority over other allocation schemes. However, it places a premium on tacit knowledge, and it provides a set of measurement techniques that stand out among the dearth of alternatives for valuing knowledge. Although we remain cautious about KVA's theoretical acceptance and practical implementation, it reflects metaphorically the concept *candle*

lighting: when in an environment without light, it is often better to light a candle than to curse the darkness (ancient Chinese proverb). **Hence, KVA provides an approach to measuring the relative value of knowledge associated with various organizational processes.**

29. Culture, trust, and incentives affect organizational learning, hence, performance as much as process, technology, and training do. In Chapter VI, we note fourth that learning rates can be measured and projected. Through the well-accepted and -established learning curve, the knowledge-flow component of experiential knowing (learning) can be measured and related mathematically with the workflow component (doing). Several general rules of thumb provide guidance for application of learning curves. These include the well-studied roles of automation, calendar time, production rate, technology introduction, and workforce capability, in addition to less-understood factors such as organizational culture, trust, and incentives. Such latter factors can affect organizational learning, hence, performance as much as the former ones do. Every organizational process involving repetition should experience performance improvement through learning at multiple levels of reach (e.g., individual, group, organization). Where such improvement may not obtain, this signals a problem with knowledge clumping and calls attention to the associated knowledge flows. **Hence, every organizational process should improve and measure its performance over time**.

30. Computational modeling is useful for knowing and learning about organizational knowing and learning. In Chapter VI, we note fifth that computational modeling can be used to learn about organizational knowing and learning. Computational models are used extensively in the physical sciences for the design of artifacts, and their use in the social sciences is increasing. Through advanced computational models that describe dynamic behaviors of knowledge flows in the organization, one can represent, simulate, and analyze—virtually—many different organizational designs to assess the relative strengths and weaknesses of alternate approaches to enhancing knowledge flows. By analyzing how knowledge flows in different organizational designs (e.g., alternate structures, workflows, personnel characteristics, technologies), one can gain insight into how different flows of knowledge affect organizational performance. One can also gain insight into how the knowing and learning that takes place within an organization react to different managerial interventions (e.g., OJT, training, mentoring, simulation). This represents a risk-mitigation strategy for addressing the

change aspect of KM projects: Before deciding upon a specific KM approach and implementing a particular set of organizational, work, personnel, and/or technological changes, one can assess computationally the relatively efficacy and efficiency of each alternative. **Hence, computational models of knowledge flows provide an approach to mitigating the risk inherent in KM programs**.

Harnessing Knowledge Dynamics in Your Organization

Not all of the knowledge-flow principles stated previously will apply to or be compelling in every organization. Hence, it is important for the leader and manager to understand the principles as a set and to assess the applicability of each to his or her organization. In this respect, the principles can be employed to guide a knowledge audit. For instance, using each of the 30 principles, one can assess the extent to which it applies, is relevant, and/or elucidates a problem area. Here we use the previously mentioned principles to organize suggestions for how leaders and managers may seek to accomplish such a principled audit. Notice in each case how this signals a need for leaders and managers to know and learn more about how their organizations know and learn.

1. Knowledge is distinct from information in enabling competitive advantage. Leaders and managers can look to better understand the basis of their organization's competition. Nearly every activity of modern work requires knowledge. Hence, nearly every organization has potential for knowledge-based competition. An organization's strategic focus may merit review and possibly change to emphasize competitive advantage based on knowing and learning.

2. Knowledge is distributed unevenly and, hence, must flow for organizational performance. Leaders and managers can look to better understand where knowledge clumps in their organizations. Knowledge clumps are present in nearly every organization. The first problem is identifying such clumps. The second problem is dissolving them. The kinds of knowledge-flow analysis and visualization techniques illustrated previously can provide insight into addressing both problems.

3.   Tacit knowledge supports greater appropriability for competitive advantage than explicit knowledge does. Leaders and managers can look to better understand where tacit knowledge resides and how it flows — indeed, if it flows — through their organizations. Flows of tacit knowledge are particularly relevant in terms of promoting sustainable competitive advantage. The kinds of knowledge-flow analysis and visualization techniques illustrated previously can help focus attention on flows of tacit knowledge at all levels of reach throughout the organization.

4.   Knowledge flows must balance exploration through learning with exploitation through doing. Leaders and managers can look to better understand how their styles and priorities emphasize one vs. the other. A great many people in operational organizations emphasize exploitation through doing over exploration through learning. Such emphasis is often short sighted. This is the case in particular where the organization seeks to compete on the basis of knowledge. Intervening to enhance knowledge flows can improve workflows, which can improve organizational performance. One must first make the investment in knowledge flows before expecting to reap any returns from workflows and performance.

5.   Enhancing knowledge flows requires simultaneous attention to personnel, work processes, organizations, and technologies. Leaders and managers can look to better understand how these four aspects of the enterprise interrelate. A great many organizations will find such aspects are at odds with one another. This can be the case in particular where changes are made in terms of inserting new information technology into unchanging people, organizations, and work processes. The leader or manager should consider designing all four aspects of the enterprise, together, as an integrated system.

6.   Knowledge enables action directly, whereas information provides meaning and context for such action. Leaders and managers can look to better understand the actions required for effective organizational performance. Such actions can point directly to the knowledge that enables their effective performance. Such knowledge can point directly in turn to the knowledge flows that may exhibit clumping or like circulation pathologies. Intervening to dissolve knowledge clumps and to remedy flow pathologies can improve organizational performance by improving the knowledge-based activities they enable.

7.   Data, information, and knowledge flows are interrelated dynamically yet distinct *mental* processes. Leaders and managers can look to better

understand how people come to know what they do in an organization. Whenever discussions turn to technologies in the context of knowledge flows, it is important to remember that flows of data, information, and knowledge involve cognition. Technologies address flows of signals. It makes little sense to discuss new technologies in such context without discussing people too. Yet this is all too common of an occurrence.

8. Flows of knowledge require supplementary flows of information, data, and signals. Leaders and managers can look to better understand which signals, data, information, and knowledge are most important in their organizations. One should not lose sight of the complementary roles played at different levels of the knowledge hierarchy. Nor should one forget that the hierarchy points both ways, depending on whether one is viewing knowledge flows—along with corresponding flows of information, data, and signals — from the perspective of producer/sender or consumer/receiver. Understanding the critical flows can inform important decisions in terms of people, work, organization, and technology.

9. *Explicitness* represents a very discriminatory dimension for evaluating the uniqueness of knowledge. Leaders and managers can look to better understand how explicit vs. tacit knowledge is viewed in an organization. Many organizations seem to prize explicit knowledge, particularly at the individual level, over tacit knowledge with broader organizational reach. Yet we note previously how tacit knowledge offers greater potential in terms of competitive advantage and how such potential can be amplified through broader reach throughout the organization. The kinds of knowledge-flow analysis and visualization techniques illustrated previously can provide insight into explicit vs. tacit knowledge flows.

10. Information technology principally supports flows of explicit knowledge. Leaders and managers can look to better understand how IT can be employed to support tacit knowledge flows. In such role, IT and people must necessarily work together, and the former should serve the latter, not vice versa. Interventions to enhance tacit knowledge flows will often involve non-technological approaches (e.g., pertaining to people, work processes, organizations), but buying a solution in a box represents a perennially easy way out for leaders and managers who are not well-informed about knowledge flows.

11. Knowledge exhibits some properties of inertia such as *tendency to remain at rest*. This accounts for much of the knowledge clumping one finds in most organizations. Where such clumping is discovered, some

kind of intervention is required. Where such clumping pertains to tacit knowledge, technology represents an approach that, alone, is unlikely to be effective. The key point is that some action is required to move knowledge. Otherwise, it remains static.

12. Experiential processes contribute principally toward workflows (doing), whereas educational processes contribute principally toward knowledge flows (learning). Leaders and managers can look to better understand how their alternate approaches to enhancing knowledge flows (e.g., OJT, formal training, mentoring) contribute toward learning vs. doing. Different approaches are likely to apply relatively better or worse to various kinds of knowledge and organizational contexts; that is, one size is unlikely to fit all. It is important for the leader or manager to consider different approaches and to learn which approaches are relatively more or less effective in the various contexts of interest.

13. Knowledge flows always lie on the critical paths of workflows, hence, organizational performance. Leaders and managers can look to better understand how important workflows are affected by knowledge flows. A great many leaders and managers plan and manage workflows meticulously yet ignore the knowledge flows that enable them. Extensions to popular management tools and techniques such as Gantt Charts, PERT networks, and computational models to address flows of knowledge (in addition to flows of work) offer considerable promise in this light.

14. Time-critical workflows must wait for enabling knowledge flows to run their course. This point about managing enabling knowledge flows is particularly pertinent in cases of time-critical workflows. All requisite flows of knowledge must complete their trajectories before such workflows can begin effectively. Because knowledge—particularly tacit knowledge—flows on time scales that are qualitatively different than those of the workflows they enable, substantial and advance attention to and planning of knowledge flows is warranted in time-critical contexts.

15. *Knowledge* is a multifaceted, dynamic, and multidimensional concept. Leaders and managers can look to better understand how knowledge moves through their organizations. Knowledge-flow processes account phenomenologically for such movement. Intervening to enhance knowledge flows points necessarily to such processes. Further, because knowledge-flow processes are dynamic, every intervention entails some period of stopping, changing, ramping up, and performing sets of knowledge-based activities. It is important for leaders and managers to consider

explicitly the dimension *time* and the corresponding motion of knowledge when planning, effecting, and assessing such interventions.

16. Information technology is helpful and necessary but not sufficient for knowledge management. Leaders and managers can look to better understand how IT can support KM and where it falls short generally. In particular and as noted previously, IT enables impressive performance in terms of transmitting signals (e.g., at great speeds, across great distances, to great numbers of people and machines), which are necessary for knowledge flows. IT enables people to manage data well. It supports pervasive, high-volume data flows. IT can help people to derive meaning from data and to appreciate the corresponding context, particularly at a distance. This is important for remote communication and information flows. IT can enable people to formalize and encode knowledge in explicit form and to share such knowledge quickly and broadly through an organization. This represents a powerful application of IT for KM. Alternatively, most IT at present offers little to people interested in creating, sharing, or applying tacit knowledge. The kinds of knowledge-flow analysis and visualization techniques illustrated previously can help differentiate tacit knowledge flows from counterpart flows of explicit knowledge, information, data, and signals. Leaders and managers can rely upon such differentiation to identify where IT is comparatively more or less likely to support KM effectively.

17. People — not information technology — are central to tacit knowledge flows. Leaders and managers can look to better understand how on-the-job experience, trial and error, direct observation, mentoring, shared interaction, reflective communication, contemplation, and like dynamic processes account for most tacit knowledge flows in the organization. Most IT offers little support for such processes. It is important for leaders and managers to know which knowledge-flow processes pertain to human-centric tacit knowledge and to appreciate how such flows center on people.

18. Information technology plays supportive roles in organizational work routines, whereas people play the performative roles. Leaders and managers can look to better understand how supportive and performative roles are played in their organizations and how IT contributes toward the corresponding knowledge-based activities. It is important for leaders and managers to know the central roles played by people and the support roles played by IT in flows of both tacit and explicit knowledge. The kinds of

knowledge-flow analysis and visualization techniques illustrated previously can help leaders and managers to identify which roles apply to the various organizational routines of interest and importance to enterprise performance.

19. Expert systems, software agents, and like "intelligent" applications address and apply knowledge directly. Leaders and managers can look to better understand how software applications in this class work directly with knowledge, in addition to information and data. Although such knowledge is necessarily explicit, it enables effective, performative actions (e.g., informed decision making, appropriate organizational behaviors, useful contributions to workflows) through machines. Leaders and managers may identify methods for integrating intelligent applications into the personnel systems, work processes, and organizational structures of interest. It is important for work to be allocated on the basis of relative capability. People are much better at some activities (e.g., understanding social norms) than even the most intelligent machines are; and even the least-intelligent machines can be much better at other activities (e.g., brute computation) than people are.

20. Simulation technology can enhance knowledge flows in addition to workflows. Leaders and managers can look to better understand how simulation enables virtual practice by people in groups and organizations as well as individually. Such virtual practice can support learning through trial and error without the risks and consequences of mistakes and failures in operational organizations. Alternatively, virtual practice through simulation contributes only rarely and minimally — if at all — to workflows. Hence, the focus is on knowledge flows through learning to a much greater extent than it is on workflows through doing. Through simulation, leaders and managers may find an effective balance between traditional knowledge-flow processes such as formal training and OJT.

21. Knowing reflects knowledge in action. Leaders and managers can look to better understand how knowing contributes to capitalizing on investments in knowledge and how putting knowledge into action can help obviate the knowing-doing gaps in organizations. The knowing activity *doing* is often associated with overcoming such gaps, but *formalizing, sharing, refining,* and other activities along the life cycle contribute toward knowledge in action as well. Leaders and managers may benefit by shifting their focus from knowledge (e.g., an emphasis on possession) to knowing (e.g., en emphasis on practice) in the organization.

22. Learning reflects knowledge in motion. Leaders and managers can look to better understand how knowledge flows depend upon learning in the organizational context and how knowing depends upon learning for the performance of knowledge-based activities. The knowing activity *learning* corresponds most closely with the creation stage of the knowledge life cycle. However, learning takes place also through other activities such as *formalizing* (e.g., machines can learn explicit knowledge), *sharing* (e.g., people can learn from one another), *application* (e.g., people can learn from experience). Leaders and managers need to appreciate the power of learning and may benefit by emphasizing learning activities to the same extent as — or possibly to an even greater extent than — their doing counterparts.

23. Knowing and learning beyond the individual offer the greatest potential for knowledge superiority. Leaders and managers can look to better understand how knowledge-based performance can be amplified as knowledge flows across increasingly broad reaches of organizations. Examples from music, sports, business, military, politics, and many other domains make clear how broad-reaching knowledge flows enable performance at levels superior to those enabled by narrow-flowing counterparts. In particular, where leaders and managers seek knowledge superiority as a means to competitive advantage, promoting broadly flowing knowledge is key. The kinds of knowledge-flow analysis and visualization techniques illustrated previously can help leaders and managers to assess the breadth of knowledge flows — explicit and tacit, fast and slow, around the whole knowledge life cycle — through their organizations.

24. Knowing and learning are dynamic, mutually reinforcing activities. Leaders and managers can look to better understand how learning is critical for acquiring the knowledge that enables knowing and how knowing in practice can contribute to learning. In particular, the more that is known in some domain, the faster learning is in that domain. This highlights the interaction between knowledge inventory and knowledge flows. The implications are strategic. Where one individual, group, or organization can obtain a lead over its competitors in terms of knowledge, such leader can expect to learn more quickly than its competitors can. By learning more quickly, the leader can expect in turn to acquire more knowledge than its competitors can. This enables even faster learning, even more knowledge, and so forth. It is important for leaders and managers to appreciate the dynamic nature of knowledge-based compe-

tition: especially how even a small lead can grow over time to an insurmountable edge.

25. Knowing and learning are path-dependent, enabling both competencies and rigidities. Leaders and managers can look to better understand how what has been learned to date, at any point in time, affects the ability to learn something new and how what is known, at any point in time, affects the ability to perform knowledge-based actions. The experiences of any organization contribute toward its knowledge inventory, and the associated learning can contribute toward its core competencies. However, the knowledge possessed by an organization also limits the relative ease and difficulty of learning something new in a particular domain. The associated knowledge can contribute instead toward core rigidities. It is important for leaders and managers to appreciate the path-dependent nature of knowledge flows. When abrupt shifts in knowledge flows (e.g., to learn in a new domain) become necessary, the organization may benefit in particular by "forgetting" collectively (e.g., via personnel actions, work-process changes, organizational restructurings) knowledge that constrains new organizational learning.

26. Knowledge management involves organizational change. Leaders and managers can look to better understand how managing knowledge can entail considerable deviation from the stable routines of many organizations. Managing change has been studied considerably and practiced extensively. Hence, substantial knowledge in terms of lessons learned, case experiences, heuristic principles, preconditions for success and failure, and other forms is available. It is important for leaders and managers to anticipate substantial change and to both prepare for and implement such change in an informed manner. Several of the techniques described in Section II of the book can help with such informed preparation and implementation.

27. Knowledge inventory can be used to assess an organization's readiness to perform its work processes effectively. Leaders and managers can look to better understand how various activities in terms of work experience, education, training, mentoring, social interaction, simulation, reflective contemplation, and other knowledge-flow processes contribute toward the knowledge stocks or inventories of individuals, groups, and organizations. Such inventories enable knowledge-based actions and facilitate within-domain learning. Where a set of critical knowledge-based actions can be identified in an organization, it may be possible to link such actions

with the kinds of knowledge — the corresponding knowledge-flow processes — required to enable them. Where a person, group, or organization possesses all of the requisite knowledge associated with a set of actions, one can infer a positive degree of readiness to perform such actions. In contrast, where all of the requisite knowledge is not possessed in current inventory, one can infer a negative degree of readiness and identify the knowledge-flow processes appropriate to fill the corresponding knowledge gaps. Leaders and managers may benefit by working to measure knowledge inventories at various levels of reach in their organizations.

28. When estimating the value of knowledge, it is often better to light a candle than to curse the darkness. Leaders and managers can look to better understand how knowledge contributes toward workflows, hence, performance in their organizations. Several aspects of knowledge management exhibit tension between competing focuses (e.g., learning vs. doing, exploration vs. exploitation) and require tradeoff decisions to be made (e.g., allocation of finite time and energy). Knowledge is inherently intangible and difficult to measure, particularly at broader reaches (e.g., teams, groups, departments, organizations), but its role is critical. Even crude measurements can be illuminating and informative. Several of the techniques discussed in Section II of the book can help leaders and managers to measure knowledge. Much research remains to be conducted in this area to improve knowledge-measurement techniques, but it is important for leaders and managers to measure knowledge in their organizations. Even crude measurements are often better than no measurements.

29. Culture, trust, and incentives affect organizational learning, hence, performance as much as process, technology, and training do. Leaders and managers can look to better understand how factors such as a culture of knowledge sharing, interpersonal trust, and incentivized knowledge hoarding can affect knowledge dynamics in the organizational context. In particular, where problems with tacit, human-centered knowledge flows are discovered, organizational culture and interpersonal trust often play key roles. Incentives provide a well-recognized approach to changing behaviors. It is important for leaders and managers to assess the knowledge-creating and -sharing nature of their organizations in terms of culture and trust and to devise incentives for enhancing knowledge flows. Such incentives should necessarily complement other management interventions in terms of personnel systems, work processes, technologies, and learning activities.

30.   Computational modeling is useful for knowing and learning about organizational knowing and learning. Leaders and managers can look to better understand how computational models of organizations provide relatively high-fidelity representations of operational organizations in practice. Many different kinds of organizational behaviors can be examined through such models, and the relative efficacy of numerous alternate management interventions can be assessed via simulated performance. By learning about how different organizational processes interact, leaders and managers can better know how to diagnose knowledge-flow pathologies and how to intervene more effectively to enhance knowledge flows. In turn, by knowing their organizations better, leaders and managers can develop and refine higher-fidelity computational models and can derive greater insight from them. Computational models of knowledge dynamics are still emerging from the research lab, but they offer considerable promise in terms of organizational knowing and learning. It is important for leaders and managers to know the capability and potential of computational models.

Summary of Leadership Mandates

Recall from earlier the 30 leadership mandates developed in Section II of the book. We list these mandates for reference and re-emphasize how they derive from practical application. Hence, unlike the 30 theoretical principles recently summarized, which require an additional step for practical application, this set of leadership mandates can be applied in practice directly.

1.   Realistic expectations, shared vision, and appropriate people participating full-time represent the preconditions for success that are absent or insufficient most often in KM projects. This is addressed in Ch. VI.

2.   Reliance upon external expertise, narrow technical focus, and animosity toward staff and specialists represent the preconditions for failure that are present or sufficient most often in KM projects. This is addressed in Ch. VI.

3.   Knowledge representation, attention to tacit knowledge, and focus on organizational memory represent unique considerations that merit particular attention in KM projects. This is addressed in Ch. VI.

4. Measurements of how people perceive a KM project (e.g., using measures such as *pessimism, affective commitment,* and *normative commitment)* can indicate KM readiness. This is addressed in Ch. VI.

5. Knowledge audits can help organizations that do not know what they know. This is addressed in Ch. VI.

6. Knowledge value analysis privileges tacit knowledge appropriately. This is addressed in Ch. VI.

7. The greater the use of automation at the beginning of a process, the lower the improvement rate. This is addressed in Ch. VI.

8. Performance improvement reflected by learning curves involves more than just individual knowing and learning. This is addressed in Ch. VI.

9. Knowledge can be lost and found. This is addressed in Ch. VI.

10. Trust cannot be bought. This is addressed in Ch. VI.

11. Using computational models, organizations can be designed and tested virtually, in a manner similar to the design of airplanes, bridges, and computers. This is addressed in Ch. VI.

12. Specialist and generalist knowledge represent (imperfect) economic substitutes for one another. This is addressed in Ch. VI.

13. Knowledge-flow vectors can be used to represent dynamic knowledge requirements. This is addressed in Ch. VII.

14. It is essential to plan how knowledge technologies will be used by people. This is addressed in Ch. VII.

15. The learning curve measures knowledge flows through OJT. This is addressed in Ch. VII.

16. Socialization and acculturation represent viable approaches to enhancing tacit knowledge flows. This is addressed in Ch. VII.

17. Trans-organizational collectivities (e.g., communities) may have greater influence over employee knowledge, culture, and performance than leadership and management do. This is addressed in Ch. VII.

18. Knowledge flows critical to enabling critical workflows center on tacit knowledge. This is addressed in Ch. VII.

19. An organizational process without consistent improvement over time suffers from knowledge clumping. This is addressed in Ch. VII.

20. Members of a team must learn to work with one another before knowing how to work together on a project. This is addressed in Ch. VII.

21. Ten unique knowledge-flow processes are required for military task force efficacy. This is addressed in Ch. VIII.

22. OJT involves knowledge flowing at two different speeds; knowledge application through doing is fast and knowledge creation through learning is slow. This is addressed in Ch. VIII.

23. Given the time-critical nature of warfare, most tacit knowledge must already be in place when the officer first reports for duty. This is addressed in Ch. VIII.

24. Systematic storytelling can increase the reach of this time-honored and effective approach to sharing tacit knowledge. This is addressed in Ch. VIII.

25. Socialization, teamwork, and acculturation must interconnect to enable healthy knowledge-flow circulation. This is addressed in Ch. VIII.

26. Leading by example and evangelism represent viable approaches to enhancing acculturation knowledge flows. This is addressed in Ch. IX.

27. Once one understands a relatively small set of key knowledge-flow processes, he or she can analyze any knowledge flows — healthy or pathologic — in any organization. This is addressed in Ch. IX.

28. The key to self-organization is having people enjoy what they do together. This is addressed in Ch. IX.

29. The ability of different people to work together on teams is just as important as the individual skills and experiences they bring individually. This is addressed in Ch. IX.

30. Leaders who are concerned about acculturation knowledge flows must address participants' beliefs. This is addressed in Ch. IX.

Research Agenda

Through the kind of knowledge-flow theory articulated in this book, we are beginning to understand the dynamics of knowledge better than at any point in history. More than simple or colorful metaphors, knowledge flows represent important phenomena. Through attribution to the processes responsible for knowledge flows, we can identify and explain increasingly well how knowledge moves through an organization. Through the kind of multidimensional coordinate system illustrated previously, we can classify and visualize myriad diverse dynamic knowledge-flow trajectories. Through the kinds of knowledge-flow propositions developed in these pages, we can analyze organizational knowing and learning in a principled manner to an unprecedented extent.

Additionally, through the kinds of application cases studied here, we can learn from the experiences of others and examine directly how various knowledge-flow principles and management interventions apply and contribute to a diversity of organizations. Through our extension of knowledge-flow principles to develop guidance for leaders and managers to assess their own organizations, we can translate theory into practice and inform practice with theory. Through the kinds of leadership mandates induced and developed from application, knowledge about knowledge flows can be applied directly. Through knowing what we know about knowledge flows, we can identify important knowledge gaps and seek interventions to fill such gaps. Through continued research on knowledge flows, we can fill such gaps. Through the ongoing research processes of creating, sharing, and applying the associated knowledge, we can improve further our ability to harness knowledge dynamics. This final section outlines an agenda for such continued research on knowledge flows.

The agenda outlined here makes no claim of completeness. Space prohibits us from articulating a complete agenda. Such agenda will necessarily change through time, anyway. Hence, what may be complete today will become incomplete tomorrow. The agenda outlined here makes no attempt to address the most important deficiencies in our knowledge of knowledge flows. So many important deficiencies remain in this emerging field of knowledge science that space prohibits us from articulating an agenda of the most important topics. Such agenda is unlikely to generate agreement from our community of scholars and practitioners as to its content, anyway. Hence, what may represent our list of most important topics will probably vary from yours.

Instead, the agenda outlined here seeks to articulate the hard problems. It challenges researchers to stop following practitioners around and to stop describing knowledge management as it is today. It exhorts researchers instead to investigate ever more deeply the dynamics of knowledge flows and to extend both theory and practical application through new phenomenological knowledge. It follows the study of dynamic flows in multiple domains of the physical sciences and seeks to understand and model the mechanics of knowledge flows. It follows likewise the engineering of dynamic artifacts in multiple physical domains and seeks to design organizations and processes to enhance knowledge flows. These represent hard problems. Here we ask the questions but do not yet have the answers.

First, researchers need to stop following practitioners around and to stop describing knowledge management as it is today. By most measures — qualitative and quantitative alike — the current practice of KM is ineffective and uninformed. Learning from failure can provide important lessons, but such provision depends critically upon knowing what causes failure and learning how it can be prevented. Little of the current KM research even poses research questions along these lines or employs research methods appropriate for answering such questions. Researchers need to depart from description and move toward explanation and prediction. Descriptive theory is important, but to understand the mechanics of knowledge, one must be able explain how they work. Furthermore, to engineer knowledge flows, one must be able to predict the effects of alternate designs, under various conditions and in diverse environments. Little of the current KM research addresses explanation or prediction.

Explanation requires rich, deep, interpretive research methods to answer research questions posed in terms of "how" and "why," instead of just "what," "who," "where," and the like. This is the case in particular with tacit knowledge flows, which are necessarily human centric. Researchers need to immerse themselves in operational organizations in the field and to investigate how people as individuals, in groups, in organizations, and in even larger collectives know and learn. They need to identify and understand the processes responsible for the corresponding knowledge flows. They need to identify and distinguish the contextual factors that affect the efficacy of various knowledge-flow processes. They need to build upon one another's research and to compare knowledge dynamics across a breadth of different organizations. They need to develop rich theoretical and computational models of knowledge flows that characterize well the fundamental dynamics of such flows. They need to stop focusing on technologies and flows of data and information. This will require a shift in the research foci and methods of most people involved with KM.

Second, KM researchers need to learn from their counterparts in the physical sciences who have investigated, very successfully, dynamic phenomena for decades and even centuries. Clearly, knowledge flows involve people and organizations — not molecules and forces — and are not represented well at present by precise models and mathematical formulae. Several principles from the physical sciences (e.g., *inertia*) appear to have application to dynamic knowledge flows, and several others (e.g., *energy, entropy, density*) offer promise as well. Even if such principles remain metaphorical, they can provide insights into the mechanics of knowledge flows. For the many researchers not knowing where to begin a phenomenological investigation of knowledge flows, seeking to falsify metaphorical relations with physical principles in the domain of knowledge dynamics provides a place to start. One may find that some aspects of various principles pertain well to knowledge flows (among the many that do not) and that such aspects can guide the investigation further.

More importantly, KM researchers have much to learn from their counterparts in the physical sciences in terms of research methods and communicating results. Research in the physical sciences is inherently positivistic, and reductionistic experimentation predominates many fields. Such research is distinct qualitatively from the kinds of interpretive, constructivist field and survey work that is practiced broadly in KM today. Despite this qualitative distinction, however, the two epistemic views and approaches to inquiry are complementary, not conflicting. The positivist can learn from the interpretivist, and vice versa. Experimentation can inform ethnography, and vice versa. Theoretical and computational models can help guide fieldwork, and fieldwork can help inform model development. Hard problems need to be approached across multiple fronts. Harnessing knowledge dynamics remains a hard problem, but researchers remain concentrated within just a few, narrow lines of inquiry.

Third, effective design requires principled knowledge and accurate analysis. Most engineered artifacts benefit from canons of principles developed through the physical sciences. They benefit also from the application of advanced mathematics and, more recently, of computational methods. Knowledge-flow theory is still emerging and is nowhere near as complete in terms of principled knowledge as theory from any of the physical sciences is. But knowledge-flow theory provides an intellectual basis for informed research as well as practical application. Knowledge-flow principles can be used as propositions for different personnel, work-process, organizational, and technological designs. This provides a start, but few KM researchers (or practitioners) to date have taken advantage of the growing number of such principles.

The application of advanced mathematics remains very challenging in the domain of knowledge dynamics. It is doubtful that knowledge flows will ever lend themselves to mathematical representation to the degree that their counterpart physical flows (e.g., fluids, heat, electricity, radiation) do. However, nearly all analytical representations of physical flows employ multidimensional coordinate systems, within which vector mathematics, phase spaces, spectral analyses, and like techniques are hugely informative. Knowledge flows can be described within multidimensional coordinate systems as well. We illustrate this kind of description repeatedly throughout the book — in terms of theory and practice alike. Researchers need to develop further the techniques necessary for representing and manipulating knowledge-flow vectors and trajectories in analytically meaningful ways that can bear down upon design problems in organizations.

The use of computational methods can help. Simulation, for instance, is used broadly in the domain of organizational studies today to assess the performance of systems that defy mathematical representation and analysis. Knowledge flows can be represented via computational models, through which dynamic behaviors can be emulated. Computational methods in the physical sciences are employed widely to address problems in which exact, analytical solutions are unobtainable, and many computational methods employ brute processing power and speed to effect iterative-approximation algorithms to approach hard physical problems in dynamics. Researchers need to embrace computational methods — despite their comparatively primitive level of current development — and work to enhance such methods to address hard problems in the domain of knowledge dynamics.

These represent hard research problems. Addressing them effectively will require considerable change on the part of many KM researchers. Perhaps such change will be too great for the current cadre. Perhaps a new field called *Knowledge Science* will emerge and carve out a niche left poorly addressed by researchers in information science, computer science, organization science, cognitive science, and economics. Such new science will be populated undoubtedly by researchers from the physical sciences, for the agendas and methods are similar. However, such new science will also need to be populated by researchers from the social sciences, for people — in an organizational context — are central to knowledge dynamics.

The prospect of knowledge science emerging from the confusion of current KM research is exciting. The potential of the knowledge developed through such science is awesome. The power to harness knowledge dynamics at quantum new levels awaits. The knowledge required for principled organizational knowing and learning is here today. Although its representation is explicit — and the authors clearly know more about this than they can tell — this book articulates a substantial volume of knowledge about harnessing knowledge dynamics and about principled organizational knowing and learning. Because knowing and learning are mutually reinforcing, path-dependent processes, leaders and managers who learn the knowledge-flow principles today — and apply them to their own organizations — can take a lead over competitors. Over time and through knowledge-based competition, such lead may become insurmountable. Hence, this book offers a contribution toward, as well as insight into, sustainable competitive advantage based on principled organizational knowing and learning. This strikes us as highly appropriate for a book on principled organizational knowing and learning.

References

Alberts, D.S., Garstka, J.J., & Stein, F.P. (1999). *Network centric warfare: Developing and leveraging information superiority* (revised 2nd ed.). Washington, DC: CCRP Publication Series.

Andrews, D.C., & Stalick, S.K. (1994). *Business reengineering: The survival guide.* New York: Yourdon Press Computing Series.

Argote, L., Beckman, S.L., & Epple, D. (1990). The persistence and transfer of learning in industrial settings. *Management Science, 36*(2), 140-154.

Argyris, C., & Schon, D.A. (2004). *Organizational learning.* Reading, MA: Addison-Wesley.

AYSO. (2004). American Youth Soccer Organization. Retrieved on May 18, 2005, from *http://www.soccer.org*

Barney, J.B. (1986). Strategic factor markets: Expectations, luck, and business strategy. *Management Science, 32*(10), 1231-1241.

Bashein, B.J., Markus, M.L., & Riley, P. (1994). Preconditions for BPR success: And how to prevent failures. *Information Systems Management, 11*(2), 7-13.

Bran, J. (2002, November 1). Five minutes with ... NASA. *Knowledge Management Regular, 6*(3). Retrieved on May 18, 2005, from *http://www.kmmagazine.com/xq/asp/sid.0/articleid.338BAE9E-0E28-4B47-B090-55549E920A43/qx/display.htm*

Brown, J.S., & Duguid, P. (1991). Organizational learning and communities-of-practice: Toward a unified view of working, learning, and innovation. *Organization Science, 2*(1), 40-57.

Cheng, C.H.F., & Levitt, R.E. (2001). Contextually changing behavior in medical organizations. In *Proceedings of the 2001 Annual Symposium of the American Medical Informatics Association*, Washington, DC, November 3-7.

Christiansen, T.R. (1993). *Modeling efficiency and effectiveness of coordination in engineering design teams*. Unpublished doctoral dissertation, Department of Civil and Environmental Engineering, Stanford University, CA.

Cleland, D.I., & Ireland, L.R. (2202). *Project management: Strategic design and implementation* (4th ed.). New York: McGraw-Hill.

Clemons, E.K., Thatcher, M.E., & Row, M.C. (1995). Identifying sources of reengineering failures: A study of the behavioral factors contributing to reengineering risks. *Journal of Management Information Systems, 12*(2), 9-36.

Cohen, G.P. (1992). *The virtual design team: An object-oriented model of information sharing in project teams*. Unpublished doctoral dissertation, Department of Civil Engineering, Stanford University, CA.

Cohen, W.M., & Levinthal, D.A. (1990). Absorptive capacity: A new perspective on learning and innovation. *Administrative Science Quarterly, 35*, 128-152.

Cook, S.D.N., & Brown, J.S. (1999). Bridging epistemologies: The generative dance between organizational knowledge and organizational knowing. *Organization Science, 10*(4), 381-400.

Czarniawska, B., & Joerges, B. (1996). Travels of ideas. In B. Czarnaiwska & G. Sevon (Eds.), *Translating organizational change* (pp. 13-48). Berlin: de Gruyter.

Daghfous, A. (2204). Organizational learning, knowledge and technology transfer: A case study. *The Learning Organization, 11*(1).

Darr, E.D., Argote, L., & Epple, D. (1995). The acquisition, transfer, and depreciation of knowledge in service organizations: Productivity in franchises. *Management Science, 41*(11), 1750-1762.

Davenport, T.H. (1993). *Process innovation: Re-engineering work through information technology*. Boston: Harvard University Press.

Davenport, T.H., De Long, D.W., & Beers, M.C. (1998, Winter). Successful knowledge management projects. *Sloan Management Review,* 43-57.

Davenport, T.H., & Stoddard, D.B. (1994). Reengineering: Business change of mythic proportions? *MIS Quarterly, 18*(2), 121-127.

DeFillippi, R.J., & Arthur, M.B. (1998). Paradox in project-based enterprises: The case of film making. *California Management Review, 40*(2), 125-139.

Dierickx, I., & Cool, K. (1989). Asset stock accumulation and sustainability of competitive advantage. *Management Science, 35*(12), 1504-1511.

El Sawy, O.A. (2001). *Redesigning enterprise processes for e-business.* Irwin/McGraw-Hill.

Epple, D., Argote, L., & Devadas, R. (1991). Organizational learning curves: A method for investigating intra-plant transfer of knowledge acquired through learning by doing. *Organization Science, 2*(1), 58-70.

Galbraith, J.R. (1977). *Organization design.* Reading, MA: Addison-Wesley.

Goffman, E. (1961). *Asylums: Essays on the social situation of mental patients and other inmates.* Garden City, NY: Anchor.

Goldstein, D.K. (1986, July). *Hallmark cards* (Case no. 9-186-044). Harvard Business School.

Grace Community Church. (2004). Retrieved on May 18, 2005, from *http://www.redshift.com/~becbobtr/pgcc.html*

Grant, R.M. (1996). Toward a knowledge-based theory of the firm. *Strategic Management Journal, 17*, 109-122.

Grover, V., Jeong, S.R., Kettinger, W.J., & Teng, J.T.C. (1995). The implementation of business process reengineering. *Journal of Management Information Systems, 12*(1), 109-144.

Hammer, M., & Champy, J. (1993). *Reengineering the corporation: A manifesto for business revolution.* New York: Harper Business Press.

Hargadon, A., & Fanelli, A. (2002). Action and possibility: Reconciling dual perspectives of knowledge in organizations. *Organization Science, 13*(3), 290-302.

Harrington, H.J. (1991). *Business process improvement: The breakthrough strategy for total quality, productivity, and competitiveness.* New York: McGraw-Hill.

Holt, D.T., Bartczak, S.E., Clark, S.W., & Trent, M.R. (2004, January). The development of an instrument to measure readiness for knowledge management. In *Proceedings of the Hawaii International Conference on System Sciences*, Hawaii.

Housel, T.J., El Sawy, O., Zhong, J.J., & Rodgers, W. (2001). Measuring the return on knowledge embedded in information technology. In *Proceedings of the International Conference on Information Systems*.

Housel, T.J., & Bell, A.H. (2001). *Measuring and managing knowledge.* Boston: McGraw-Hill.

Ingram, P., & Simons, T. (2002). The transfer of experience in groups of organizations: Implications for performance and competition. *Management Science, 48*(12), 1517-1533.

Jennex, M.E., & Olfman, L. (2004, January). *Assessing knowledge management success/effectiveness models.* In *Proceedings of the Hawaii International Conference on System Sciences*, Hawaii.

Jin, Y., & Levitt, R.E. (1996). The virtual design team: A computational model of project organizations. *Computational and Mathematical Organization Theory, 2*(3), 171-195.

Johansson, H.J., McHugh, P., Pendlebury, A.J., & Wheeler, W.A., III. (1993). *Business process reengineering: Breakpoint strategies for market dominance.* Chichester, UK: Wiley.

Kettinger, W.J., Guha, S., & Teng, J.T.C. (1995). The process reengineering life cycle methodology: A case study. In V. Grover & W. Kettinger (Eds.), *Business process change: Reengineering concepts, methods and technologies* (pp. 211-244). Hershey, PA: Idea Group Publishing.

King, J.L., & Konsynski, B. (1990). *Singapore Tradenet: A tale of one city* (Case no. 9-191-009). Harvard Business School.

KnowledgeWright. (2004). Expert system develop shell. Retrieved on May 18, 2005, from *http://www.amzi.com/products/knowledgewright.html*

Kunz, J.C., Levitt, R.E., & Jin, Y. (1998). The virtual design team: A computational simulation model of project organizations. *Communications of the Association for Computing Machinery, 41*(11), 84-92.

Law, A.M., & Kelton, W.D. (1982). *Simulation modeling and analysis.* New York: McGraw-Hill.

Leavitt, H.J. (1965). Applying organizational change in industry: Structural, technological and humanistic approaches. In J. March (Ed.), *Handbook of organizations.* Chicago: Rand McNally.

Levitt, B., & March, J.G. (1988). Organizational learning. *Annual Review of Sociology, 14*, 319-340.

Levitt, R.E., Thomsen, J., Christiansen, T.R., Junz, J.C., Jin, Y., & Nass, C. (1999). Simulating project work processes and organizations: Toward a micro-contingency theory of organizational design. *Management Science, 45*(11), 1479-1495.

Liebowitz, J. (2004a). *Addressing the human capital crisis in the federal government: A knowledge management perspective.* Amsterdam: Elsevier.

Liebowitz, J. (2004b). A knowledge management implementation plan at a leading US technical government organization: A case study. *Knowledge and Process Management, 10*(4).

Liebowitz, J., Rubenstein-Montano, B., McCaw, D., Buchwalter, J., Browning, C., Newman, B., & Rebeck, K. (2000). The knowledge audit. *Knowledge and Process Management, 7*(1), 3-10.

Loch, C.H., Pich, M.T., Terwiesch, C., & Urbschat, C. (2001). Selecting R&D projects at BMW: A case study of adopting mathematical programming models. *IEEE Transactions on Engineering Management, 48*(1), 70-80.

March, J.G. (1991). Exploration and exploitation in organizational learning. *Organization Science, 2*(1), 71-87.

March, J.G., & Simon, H.A. (1958). *Organizations.* New York: John Wiley.

Massey, A.P., Montoya-Weiss, M.M., & O'Driscoll, T.M. (2002a). Performance-centered design of knowledge-intensive processes. *Journal of Management Information Systems, 18*(4), 37-58.

Massey, A.P., Montoya-Weiss, M.M., & O'Driscoll, T.M. (2002b). Knowledge management in pursuit of performance: Insights from Nortel Networks. *MIS Quarterly, 26*(3), 269-289.

Mintzberg, H. (1980). Structure in 5's: A synthesis of the research on organization design. *Management Science, 26*(3), 322-341.

Mueller, F., & Dyerson, R. (1999). Expert humans or expert organizations? *Organization Studies, 20*(2), 225-256.

NASA. (2004, August 19). Library past announcements. NASA. Retrieved on May 18, 2005, from *http://km.nasa.gov/library/past_announcements.html*

Nissen, M.E. (1998). Redesigning reengineering through measurement-driven inference. *MIS Quarterly, 22*(4), 509-534.

Nissen, M.E. (2002a). An extended model of knowledge-flow dynamics. *Communications of the Association for Information Systems, 8*, 251-266.

Nissen, M.E. (2002b). *Understanding 'understanding' flow for network-centric warfare: Military knowledge-flow mechanics* (NPS Tech. rep. no. NPS-GSBPP-02-001).

Nissen, M.E. (2004a). Dynamic knowledge patterns to inform design: A field study of knowledge stocks and flows in an extreme organization (accepted for publication in the *Journal of Management Information Systems*) (forthcoming 2006).

Nissen, M.E. (2004b). Personal observations and conversations within the AYSO.

Nissen, M.E. (2004c). Personal observations and conversations within the USTA.

Nissen, M.E. (2004d). Personal observations and conversations within the PGCC.

Nissen, M.E. (2005). Toward designing organizations around knowledge flows. In K. Desouza (Ed.), *New frontiers in knowledge management*. Palgrave Mcmillian.

Nissen, M.E., Kamel, M.N., & Sengupta, K.C. (2000, January-March). Integrated analysis and design of knowledge systems and processes. *Information Resources Management Journal, 13*(1), 24-43.

Nissen, M.E., & Levitt, R.E. (2004). Agent-based modeling of knowledge dynamics. *Knowledge Management Research & Practice, 2*(3), 169-183.

Nissen, M.E., & Levitt, R.E. (2005). Knowledge management research through computational experimentation. In D. Schwartz (Ed.), *Encyclopedia of knowledge management*. Hershey, PA: Idea Group Reference.

Nogueira, J.C. (2000). *A formal model for risk assessment in software projects*. Unpublished doctoral dissertation, Department of Computer Science, Naval Postgraduate School, CA.

Nonaka, I. (1994). A dynamic theory of organizational knowledge creation. *Organization Science, 5*(1), 14-37.

Nonaka, I., & Takeuchi, H. (1995). *The knowledge-creating company: How Japanese companies create the dynamics of innovation*. New York: Oxford University Press.

Pfeffer, J., & Sutton, R.I. (1999). Knowing 'what' to do is not enough: Turning knowledge into action. *California Management Review, 42*(1), 83-108.

Pindyck, R.S., & Rubinfeld, D.L. (1998). *Microeconomics* (4th ed.). Upper Saddle River, NJ: Prentice Hall.

Polanyi, M. (1967). *The tacit dimension.* London: Routledge and Keoan Paul.

Postrel, S. (2002). Islands of shared knowledge: Specialization and mutual understanding in problem-solving teams. *Organization Science, 13*(3), 303–320.

Sameulson, P.A. (1974). Complementarity: An essay on the 40th anniversary of the Hicks-Allen Revolution in demand theory. *Journal of Economic Literature, 12*(4).

Saviotti, P.P. (1998). On the dynamics of appropriability, of tacit and of codified knowledge. *Research Policy, 26*, 843-856.

Senge, P.M. (1990). *The fifth discipline: The art and practice of the learning organization.* New York: Doubleday.

Spender, J.C. (1996). Making knowledge the basis of a dynamic theory of the firm. *Strategic Management Journal, 17*, 45-62.

Stein, E.W., & Zwass, V. (n.d.). Actualizing organizational memory with information systems. *Information Systems Research, 6*(2).

Stoddard, D.B., & Jarvenpaa, S.L. (1995). Business process redesign: Tactics for managing radical change. *Journal of Information Management Systems, 12*(1), 81-107.

Stoddard, D.B., & Meadows, C.J. (1992). *Capital Holding Corporation: Reengineering the direct response group* (Case no. 9-192-001). Harvard Business School.

STSC. (2000). *Guidelines for successful acquisition and management of software intensive systems* (version 3.0). Hill AFB, UT: Software Technology Support Center.

Szulanski, G. (1996). Exploring internal stickiness: Impediments to the transfer of best practice within the firm. *Strategic Management Journal, 17*, 27-43.

Talebzadeh, H., Mandutianu, S., & Winner, C.F. (1995). Countrywide loan-underwriting expert system. *AI Magazine, 16*(1), 51-64.

Thompson, J.D. (1967). *Organizations in action: Social science bases in administrative theory.* New York: McGraw-Hill.

Thomsen, J. (1998). *The Virtual Team Alliance (VTA): Modeling the effects of goal incongruency in semi-routine, fast-paced project organizations*. Unpublished doctoral dissertation, Department of Civil and Environmental Engineering, Stanford University, CA.

Tuomi, I. (1999). Data is more than knowledge: Implications of the reversed knowledge hierarchy for knowledge management and organizational memory. *Journal of Management Information Systems, 16*(3), 103-117.

Turban, E., & Aronson, J. (1998). *Decision support systems and intelligent systems*. Upper Saddle River, NJ: Prentice Hall.

USTA. (2004). United States Tennis Association. Retrieved on May 18, 2005, from *http://www.usta.org*

VDT. (2004). The Virtual Design Team Research Group. Retrieved on May 18, 2005, from *http://www.stanford.edu/group/CIFE/VDT/*

von Hippel, E. (1994). 'Sticky information' and the locus of problem solving: Implications for innovation. *Management Science, 40*(4), 429-439.

Walsh, J.P., & Ungson, G.R. (1991). Organizational memory. *Academy of Management Review, 16*(1), 57-91.

Weick, K.E., & Roberts, K.H. (1993). Collective mind in organizations: Heedful interrelating on flights decks. *Administrative Science Quarterly, 38*, 357-381.

Wright, T. (1936). Factors affecting the cost of airplanes. *Journal of Aeronautical Science, 4*(4), 122-128.

Yelle, L.E. (1979). The learning curve: Historical review and comprehensive survey. *Decision Sciences, 10*, 302-328.

Glossary

This glossary is included to facilitate ready reference to terms and concepts presented in the book that may be unfamiliar to the reader. Clearly, definitions and interpretations other than those included here exist and make sense as well, but the definitions and interpretations to follow are consistent with the presentation throughout the book. Almost every item includes a pointer to the chapter in which the associated terms and concepts are discussed.

Abundance. One of two dimensions used to characterize the knowledge hierarchy (see Ch. II). In any organization, data are more abundant than information is, which is in turn more abundant than knowledge is.

Action. The manifest accomplishment of some mental, social, or physical activity such as decision making, communication, or work (see Ch. I). The term *action* is used to differentiate the concept *knowledge* from *information*: knowledge enables direct action (e.g., correct decisions, appropriate behaviors, useful work), whereas information provides meaning and context for such action (e.g., decision criteria, behavior norms, work specifications).

Actionability. One of two dimensions used to characterize the Knowledge Hierarchy (see Ch. II). In any organization, knowledge is more actionable than information is, which is in turn more actionable than data are.

Apprentice. A person who works with a skilled master or craftsman to learn a skill or craft. Apprenticeship represents a technique for experts to share tacit knowledge (see Ch. I).

Appropriation. A term connoting one's ability to assert ownership over some asset, generally with the intent to extract *economic rent* (e.g., monetary payment) from it. The term *appropriation* is used to differentiate tacit knowledge from its explicit counterpart in terms of greater competitive advantage (see Ch. I).

Articulable knowledge. Knowledge that can be described through words, diagrams, formulae, computer programs, and like means. The term *articulable* is used to differentiate explicit knowledge from its tacit counterpart (see Ch. II).

Articulation. The action of describing knowledge through words, diagrams, formulae, computer programs, and like means. Tacit knowledge resists articulation and transfer (see Ch. I).

Artificial intelligence. This field of computer science focuses on developing computational devices (e.g., expert systems and software agents) that emulate the behaviors of people who are considered to be intelligent. Unlike most information technologies, many artificial intelligence applications address knowledge — as opposed to information — directly and are performative in nature (see Ch. IV).

Backcasting. A modification of forecasting techniques through the process of "predicting," *ex-post*, known organizational outcomes using only information that was available at the beginning of a project. This technique is used to validate computational models (see Ch. VI).

Barrier to market entry. An impediment that makes it difficult for some rival firm to compete in a particular market. Barriers to market entry can be financial (e.g., high capital costs), positional (e.g., large market share and brand loyalty), geographical (e.g., the best location), knowledge-based (e.g., inimitable knowledge), and based on other advantages (see Ch. I).

Business Process Re-engineering. A philosophy and set of tools and methods conceived originally as an approach for radical change to effect dramatic performance improvements in organizations. This organizational phenomenon in the 1990s provided a broad-based impetus and set of techniques to enable organizations to perform better with fewer resources (see Ch. I). Re-engineering research has addressed several important questions pertaining to managing change (see Ch. VI). As with most knowledge management projects today, the abundance of re-engineering projects focused on information technology.

Case-based reasoning. An artificial intelligence technique that uses aspects of stored case descriptions to guide computational inference pertaining to problem solving associated with similar cases. Organizational applications such as technology help desks demonstrate benefits of this approach (see Ch. IV).

Chat. The common name for the *Internet relay chat protocol* that enables users to exchange near-synchronous, near-duplex, textual messages between computers. This information technology application is used for distributed, synchronous, text-based communications, often in the place of telephone or radio conversations. Chat differs from e-mail in that it supports synchronous communication, whereas e-mail messages are asynchronous (see Chs. II and IV).

Competency trap. This term *competency trap* (Levitt & March, 1988) is used to describe a situation in which an organization develops considerable competency in some area, only to find itself unable to develop one or more alternate competencies when necessitated by either management strategy or environmental shifts (see Ch. I). Competency traps can develop through unbalanced focus on exploitation of extant knowledge over exploration to develop new knowledge (see Ch. V).

Competitive advantage. This concept is discussed generally in economic terms such as earning superior rents, gaining larger market share, raising barriers to market entry, locking out competitors, and locking in customers (see Ch. I). It pertains more generally to the ability of one organization to outperform its competitors.

Competitive disadvantage. This is the opposite of competitive advantage. It pertains generally to the ability of an organization's competitors to outperform it. Where knowledge fails to flow well, even to enable ordinary workflows, the organization may experience competitive disadvantage, as it fails to perform even its routine work effectively (see Ch. I).

Competitive potential. This refers to the potential for competitive advantage. By the term *potential*, we imply that a firm has the capability to attain competitive advantage but may not have done so yet through manifest action (see Ch. I).

Competitive resource. In a resource-based view, an organization competes on the basis of the unique set of resources it possesses and puts to use. Economic inputs such as *land*, *labor*, and *capital* represent traditional resources employed in this view. *Knowledge* represents more than just another resource along these lines because it can enable sustainable competitive advantage (see Ch. I).

Computational modeling. This information technology application represents an extension of simulation (see Ch. IV). Computational models are used extensively in the physical sciences (e.g., to represent the dynamics of phenomena such as fluid flows, heat transfers, and resilience of structures) and progressively more often in the social sciences (e.g., to represent the dynamics of money flows, economic transfers, and communication structures). Models from both sciences provide a basis for designing physical artifacts (e.g., airplanes, bridges, computers) and for making decisions about social systems (e.g., finance, trade, broadcasting) by representing such artifacts and systems via models and by simulating their dynamic behaviors under various conditions (see Ch. VI).

Context. Context refers to the situation, environment, and perspective of actions such as cognition, conversation, and work. Context can make data intelligible and enable them to convey meaning as information (see Ch. II). The term *context* is used along with *meaning* to operationalize the concept *information*.

Core competencies. The capabilities that can enable competitive advantage for an individual, group, or organization. Many organizations shed peripheral capabilities to focus their attention on the core set that is most relevant strategically (see Ch. V).

Core rigidities. The duality associated with core competencies that restrict the range of activities that can be performed well by an organization (see Ch. V).

Critical path. The sequence of tasks, activities, and/or events in a project that determine the shortest possible schedule for completion. The *critical path* concept is used extensively in project management for planning and analysis. Because knowledge is required for the performance of work, knowledge flows can be viewed clearly as lying on the critical paths of the workflows they enable (see Ch. I).

Data. Data are operationalized best as interpreted signals that can reduce uncertainty or equivocality. Relationships and distinctions between *data*, *information*, and *knowledge* are important (see Ch. II).

Database. A class of information technology applications for the organized storage and retrieval of data. Databases can be massive and sophisticated. As conveyed by their name, databases address data, not information or knowledge (see Chs. II and IV).

Data mining. The use of statistical and inferential pattern-matching techniques to identify regularities in databases that are imperceptible to most people. The discovery of new patterns and regularities in data represents a form of knowledge creation (see Chs. II and IV).

Data warehouse. A very large, generally decision-support database that is used to collect, organize, and retrieve data from multiple, generally operational databases. Data warehouses are often used in conjunction with data mining (see Ch. IV).

Database query. The use of interactive techniques for a user to extract desired subsets and summaries of data from a database. Database queries are often used to answer factual or statistical questions.

Declarative knowledge. The class of knowledge that is expressed as facts or assertions. The term *declarative knowledge* is often used in contrast with *procedural knowledge* (see Ch. II).

Diagnose. The deductive sequence of tasks associated with identifying a problem or pathology. The term *diagnose* is often used in a medical context of identifying diseases. This term also makes sense in the context of identifying problems or pathologies suffered by an organization. *Knowledge clumping* represents one such pathology addressed in particular in this book (see Ch. I).

Discussion board. An information technology application that enables multiple, simultaneous, asynchronous textual conversations between geographically distributed participants. Generally, each unique conversation is labeled with a title and separated from other conversations as distinct *threads*. This groupware application offers infrastructural support for knowledge work and enhances the environment in which knowledge artifacts are created and managed (see Ch. II).

Discussion thread. A unique, segmented, and labeled conversational topic associated generally with discussion boards, network news groups, and e-mail lists (see Ch. II).

Document repository. An information technology application for the organized storage and retrieval of documents. A document repository is equipped generally with some kind of search engine that uses keyword matching and like techniques to locate and retrieve documents of potential interest to users. The document repository is analogous to the database in terms of function and use. The document repository addresses documents, whereas the database addresses data (see Chs. II and IV).

Doing. A form of knowing focused on accomplishing work activities (see Ch. I). The term *doing* is used often for contrast with *learning* (see Ch. V).

E-mail. Electronic mail is an information technology application that enables the asynchronous exchange of textual messages across computer networks. The e-mail application complements its chat counterpart, the latter of which enables synchronous, networked communication (see Chs. II and IV).

Education. A formal approach to knowledge flow in which students enroll in organized courses offered by institutions such as universities, colleges, and vocational schools. Generally, an instructor leads the course, which consists of prearranged readings, assignments, lectures, laboratory experiments, discussions, and other learning activities. The term *education* is often used in the same context as *training* (see Ch. I) and for contrast with other knowledge-flow processes such as *on-the-job training (OJT), trial and error, direct experience*, and others that connote the informal accumulation of experience-based knowledge (see Ch. III).

Ephemeral competitive advantage. Competitive advantage that can be obtained but not sustained over time. The term *ephemeral competitive advantage* is often used for contrast with *sustainable competitive advantage* (see Ch. I).

Ephemeral knowledge. Knowledge that can be created or acquired but not retained or preserved over time (see Ch. I).

Equivocality. A state of ignorance pertaining to context, in which the causes of observable or putative effects or results cannot be identified, or in which decision makers lack sufficient knowledge of their situation to even know which questions to ask. The terms *equivocality* and *uncertainty* are often used in the context of data (see Ch. II).

Experience. The accumulation of knowledge associated with direct interaction with some object, process, or system in the world (see Ch. I). The term *experience* is often used in connection with the performance of work activities. The performance of people and organizations improves generally as a result of experience and can often be measured using learning curves (see Ch. VI).

Experience-based knowledge. Knowledge created and accumulated through experience (see Ch. I). Such knowledge is generally tacit and slow to accumulate (see Ch. III).

Expert. A person recognized as possessing qualitatively higher levels of skill and experience in some domain than most people possess. The term *expert* is often used to describe a person who has accumulated very large stocks of knowledge and for contrast with *novice* (see Chs. I, IV, and V).

Expert system. An information technology application from the field of artificial intelligence that seeks to emulate the performance of human experts. Expert system applications address knowledge directly and are performative in nature. This provides a contrast with the supportive nature of most information technologies (see Ch. IV).

Explicit knowledge. Knowledge that has been articulated through words, diagrams, formulae, computer programs, and like means. The term *explicit knowledge* is used widely for contrast with *tacit knowledge*, which cannot be or has not been articulated, and with *implicit knowledge*, which can be but has not been articulated (see Ch. II).

Explicitness. The relative ability to articulate knowledge. *Explicitness* describes the nature of knowledge along a dimensional construct with tacit and explicit endpoints. It represents one of the four dimensions used in this book to classify and visualize knowledge flows (see Ch. III).

Exploitation. The application of extant knowledge for organizational performance and pursuit of competitive advantage (see Ch. I). The term *exploitation* is often used for contrast with *exploration* (March, 1991). Exploitation involves principally the form of knowing called *doing* and the application or refinement of existing knowledge, whereas exploration involves principally the form of knowing called *learning* and the creation or acquisition of new knowledge (see Ch. V).

Exploration. The search for new knowledge for organizational performance and pursuit of competitive advantage (see Ch. I). The term *exploration* is often used for contrast with *exploitation* (March, 1991). Exploration involves principally the form of knowing called *learning* and the creation or acquisition of new knowledge, whereas exploitation involves principally the form of knowing called *doing* and the application or refinement of existing knowledge (see Ch. V).

Externalization. One of four knowledge-flow processes associated with the Spiral Model (Nonaka, 1994) of knowledge flows. The term *externalization* refers generally to knowledge formalization from tacit to explicit form (see Ch. III).

Flow principles. Systematic and general principles pertaining to fluid movements such as exhibited by water, air, heat, and electricity. Flow principles are used to describe, explain, and predict the dynamics of such fluids. Flow principles can be used also to describe, explain, and predict the dynamics of knowledge (see Ch. III).

Gedanken **experiment**. *Gedanken* means "thought." Gedanken experiments refer to mental simulations (see Chs. I, II, and IV).

General knowledge. Knowledge that pertains more to high-level patterns and relationships than to low-level details. The term *general knowledge* is often used for contrast with *specialist knowledge*. To some extent, general and specialist knowledge can be substituted for one another (see Ch. VI).

Groupware. A class of information technology applications that offer infrastructural support for knowledge work and enhance the environment in which knowledge artifacts are created and managed. Common organizational applications include e-mail, chat, discussion boards, and like technologies (see Ch. IV).

Ignorance. The lack of knowledge in some domain or area. The adjective *ignorant* is often used for contrast both with both *knowledgeable* and *stupid*. The former contrast connotes that the ignorant person lacks knowledge (see Ch. I). The latter contrast connotes that the ignorant person is capable of learning to overcome ignorance (see Ch. V). Groups and organizations can be ignorant, knowledgeable, or stupid.

Imitable. Capable of imitation. Where knowledge that enables some kind of competitive advantage is imitable, the corresponding advantage is likely to be ephemeral. Competitors will try to imitate the organizational processes, technologies, products, and services that provide for competitive advantage. Organizational capabilities predicated on explicit knowledge are more imitable generally than those predicated on tacit knowledge are (see Ch. I).

Implicit knowledge. Knowledge that is articulable but has not been articulated yet through words, diagrams, formulae, computer programs, and like means. The term *implicit knowledge* is used widely for contrast with *tacit knowledge*, which cannot be or has not been articulated, and with *explicit knowledge*, which can be and has been articulated (see Ch. II).

Information. Information is operationalized best as providing meaning and context for action. Relationships and distinctions between *data, information,* and *knowledge* are important (see Ch. II).

Inimitable. Incapable of imitation. Where knowledge that enables some kind of competitive advantage is inimitable, the corresponding advantage is likely to be sustainable. Competitors may try but will fail to imitate the organizational processes, technologies, products, and services that provide for competitive advantage. Organizational capabilities predicated on tacit knowledge are more inimitable generally than those predicated on explicit knowledge are (see Ch. I).

Instruction. This knowledge-flow process is associated with formal classroom education or training (see Ch. I). It focuses more on the knowing activity *learning* than on *doing* and is used often for contrast with experience-oriented knowledge-flow processes such as *on-the-job training* (*OJT*), *trial and error*, and the like (see Ch. V).

Intelligent tutoring. An information technology application from artificial intelligence that uses models of students to facilitate and tailor pedagogical decisions and actions such as lesson plans, tests, and reinforcement activities (see Ch. IV).

Internalization. One of four knowledge-flow processes associated with the Spiral Model (Nonaka, 1994) of knowledge flows. The term *internalization* refers generally to knowledge refinement from explicit to tacit form (see Ch. III).

Intranet. An information technology application comprised of computer networks and services that are based on Internet standards and protocols but restricted to use by people within an organization. Most such applications are Web-based (see Ch. IV).

Knower. The entity associated with knowing, either learning or doing (see Chs. II and V).

Knowing. Knowing involves knowledge in action. Learning and doing represent two forms of knowing (see Ch. V).

Knowing-doing gap. A knowing-doing gap (Pfeffer & Sutton, 1999) manifests itself in part when organizations "know better" than to do what they do and in part when organizations "know how" to do something they do not do (see Ch. V).

Knowledge. Knowledge is operationalized best as enabling direct action. Relationships and distinctions between *data, information,* and *knowledge* are important (see Ch. II).

Knowledge acquisition. Gaining new knowledge through learning. Knowledge acquisition represents a form of knowledge creation. The knowledge acquired need not be "new" to the entire world (e.g., knowledge developed through scientific discovery). Rather, such knowledge needs only to be new in the context of its coordinates (e.g., to an individual or organization, at a particular point in space or time; see Ch. V).

Knowledge application. Using existing knowledge through doing. Knowledge application involves putting knowledge into action. *Knowledge application* represents the fifth stage of the knowledge life cycle (see Ch. III).

Knowledge audit. The Knowledge Audit (Liebowitz et al., 2000) is a diagnostic activity focused on identifying organizational problems with potential to be addressed via knowledge management (see Ch. VI).

Knowledge-based theory of the firm. An extension of the resource-based view that privileges the power of knowledge for competitive advantage (see Ch. I).

Knowledge capture. Gaining new knowledge through learning. Knowledge capture represents a form of knowledge creation. The knowledge captured need not be "new" to the entire world (e.g., knowledge developed through scientific discovery). Rather, such knowledge needs only to be new in the context of its coordinates (e.g., to an individual or organization, at a particular point in space or time; see Ch. V).

Knowledge chunks. Discrete units of knowledge acquired through learning. A chunk can be a low-level unit such as a fact, medium-level unit such as a procedure, or high-level unit such as a pattern. The psychological term *chunking* refers to the cognitive process associated with memory and recall. The accumulation of many knowledge chunks is associated with expertise (see Ch. I) and expert systems development (see Ch. IV).

Knowledge clump. Knowledge that collects at some isolated coordinate (e.g., in an individual or organization, at a particular point in space or time; see Ch. III). Knowledge clumps are symptoms of flow pathologies in the organization.

Knowledge consumer. A person or organization on the receiving end of knowledge flows and that is learning new knowledge. The term *knowledge consumer* is often used synonymously with *knowledge receiver* and for contrast with *knowledge producer/source* (see Ch. II).

Knowledge creation. Gaining new knowledge through learning. *Knowledge creation* represents the first stage of the knowledge life cycle (see Ch. III). The knowledge created need not be "new" to the entire world (e.g., knowledge developed through scientific discovery). Rather, such knowledge needs only to be new in the context of its coordinates (e.g., to an individual or organization, at a particular point in space or time; see Ch. V).

Knowledge differential. The difference in levels of knowledge stocks between two or more different individuals or organizations. Knowledge differential can provide a basis for competitive advantage (see Ch. I).

Knowledge directionality. A vector representation of dynamic knowledge, in which the corresponding flow has a distinguishable source and receiver (see Ch. II).

Knowledge dissemination. Sharing knowledge broadly. Knowledge dissemination represents a form of knowledge sharing, associated generally with explicit knowledge and broad organizational reach (see Ch. III).

Knowledge dynamics. The study of how knowledge moves with respect to time. Phenomenological research methods are most prevalent in this study at present.

Knowledge engineer. A technological intermediary responsible for the development of expert systems (see Ch. IV).

Knowledge-flow process. The sequence of organizational activities responsible for producing and propagating knowledge flows (see Ch. III).

Knowledge-flow theory. The canon of principles and techniques from knowledge dynamics pertaining to the phenomenology of knowledge flows.

Knowledge-flow visualization. The graphical representation of knowledge flows that uses a multidimensional vector space to delineate dynamic movements of knowledge (see Ch. III). The four dimensions *explicitness*, *reach*, *life cycle*, and *flow time* are used in this book for visualization of knowledge flows.

Knowledge flow. A dynamic movement of knowledge between coordinates (e.g., between individuals or organizations, or points in space or time; see Ch. III).

Knowledge flow time. The amount of time required for knowledge to flow between coordinates (e.g., individuals or organizations, or points in space or time). *Knowledge flow time* represents one of the four dimensions used in this book to classify and visualize knowledge flows (see Ch. III).

Knowledge flow vector. A graphical representation of knowledge flows in which arrows are used to depict dynamic motion (see Ch. III).

Knowledge formalization. Making tacit knowledge take explicit form. *Knowledge formalization* represents the third stage of the knowledge life cycle (see Ch. III).

Knowledge hierarchy. The knowledge hierarchy (Nissen, 2002a) provides a conceptualization of interrelations between knowledge, information, and data (see Ch. II).

Knowledge hoarding. The practice of not sharing knowledge (see Ch. I).

Knowledge inertia. The tendency of knowledge at rest to remain at rest. Knowledge that has clumped will remain clumped unless some kind of managerial intervention is taken (see Ch. III).

Knowledge inventory. A construct to measure the level of knowledge stock in a person or organization. An organization's knowledge inventory both enables and inhibits what actions it can take (see Chs. I and V). The term *knowledge inventory* is often used synonymously with *knowledge level*.

Knowledge level. A construct to measure the knowledge inventory possessed by a person or organization (see Chs. I and V). The term *knowledge level* is often used synonymously often with *knowledge inventory*.

Knowledge life cycle. A dimensional construct to characterize the kind of activity associated with knowledge flows. *Knowledge life cycle* represents one of the four dimensions used in this book to classify and visualize knowledge flows (see Ch. III).

Knowledge management. The practice of leveraging knowledge for competitive advantage. Most knowledge management programs to date have focused on technology (see Ch. IV).

Knowledge management system. A suite of information technology applications and organizational routines employed for knowledge management. Most knowledge management systems employed to date have focused on technology (see Ch. IV).

Knowledge management tools. A set of information technology applications employed for knowledge management (see Ch. IV).

Knowledge power. The capability of harnessing dynamic knowledge for competitive advantage (see Ch. I).

Knowledge producer. A person or organization on the sending end of knowledge flows and that is sharing existing knowledge. The term *knowledge producer* is often used synonymously with *knowledge source* and for contrast with *knowledge consumer/receiver* (see Ch. II).

Knowledge receiver. A person or organization on the receiving end of knowledge flows and that is learning new knowledge. The term *knowledge receiver* is often used synonymously with *knowledge consumer* and for contrast with *knowledge producer/source* (see Ch. II).

Knowledge refinement. Learning over time from experience. *Knowledge refinement* represents the sixth stage of the knowledge life cycle. It connects *knowledge application* with *knowledge creation* to complete a cycle of knowledge flows (see Ch. III).

Knowledge sharing. Inducing knowledge to flow between different people or organizations. *Knowledge sharing* represents the fourth stage of the knowledge life cycle (see Ch. III).

Knowledge stocks. A concept to characterize the level of knowledge accumulated by a person or organization. *Knowledge inventory* and *knowledge level* represent two measures intended to operationalize the concept *knowledge stocks*. Knowledge flows and knowledge stocks interrelate tightly and dynamically (see Ch. V).

Knowledge source. A person or organization on the sending end of knowledge flows and that is sharing existing knowledge. The term *knowledge source* is often used synonymously with *knowledge producer* and for contrast with *knowledge consumer/receiver* (see Ch. II).

Knowledge technology. Technology used for knowledge management. Information technologies are employed most widely at present for knowledge management (see Ch. IV).

Knowledge transfer. Sharing knowledge locally. Knowledge transfer represents a form of knowledge sharing, associated generally with tacit knowledge and broad organizational reach (see Ch. III).

Knowledge uniqueness. The strong distinction between the concepts *knowledge* and *information/data* (see Ch. II).

Knowledge value analysis. Knowledge Value Analysis (Housel & Bell, 2001) employs principles such as *information entropy* in attempt to measure the return on investments in acquiring and sharing knowledge (see Ch. VI).

Learning. Learning refers to knowledge in motion. It is used most often to characterize the creation or acquisition of new knowledge. The term *learning* is often used for contrast with *doing* (see Ch. V).

Learning curves. An empirical technique that blends theory with practice to measure knowledge flows (see Ch. VI). Knowledge-based performance at the individual, group, and organizational levels improves at a measurable and predictable rate through task repetition and refinement.

Learning rate. The speed at which learning is accomplished. *Learning rate* is inversely proportional to *knowledge flow time* (see Ch. I).

Local knowledge. Knowledge of proximal conditions. Much tacit knowledge is local in nature, meaning it can be difficult to share broadly (see Ch. III).

Locking in customers. Raising switching costs that prohibit customers from pursuing products or services from rival competitors (see Ch. I).

Locking out competitors. Raising barriers to entry that prohibit new competitors from challenging an organization (see Ch. I).

Management interventions. Actions taken by leaders and managers to change aspects of an organization that are seen as problematic or pathological (see Ch. I).

Market share. The fraction of a market segment that is controlled by a particular competitor (see Ch. I).

Meaning. The significance of information. *Meaning* implies that a message has caused some cognitive change in the receiver's understanding. This term is used along with *context* to operationalize the concept *information* (see Ch. II).

Mentoring. A knowledge-flow process in which an experienced or otherwise-knowledgeable person helps a less-experienced or -knowledgeable person to learn in a work setting. Mentoring is a part of apprenticeship and contrasts with both the knowledge-flow processes *on-the-job training/trial and error* and *formal education/training* (see Ch. III).

Metadata. Data about data in a database. Metadata are used to describe characteristics of the data that are organized and stored within a database. Examples include the names of fields, types of values various data can take on, and relationships between different database tables (see Ch. II).

Multimedia. An information technology application that enables textual, graphical, audio, and other modes of data to flow across a network and to be presented simultaneously, in an integrated manner (see Ch. II).

Novice. A person recognized as possessing qualitatively lower levels of skill and experience in some domain than most people possess. The term *novice* is often used to describe a person who has accumulated very small stocks of knowledge and for contrast with *expert* (see Chs. I, IV, and V).

Observation. Physically watching some task, activity, or process performed, often with the intent of learning how to perform such task, activity, or process (see Ch. II).

On-the-job training. Direct experience with some work task, activity or process, generally with the implication that some kind of experience-based learning is taking place. *On-the-job training (OJT)* is used widely as a euphemism for *trial and error*, a relatively slow and error-prone but pervasive knowledge-flow process employed by organizations (see Chs. I and III).

Organization. A collective of people who coordinate their actions for some common purpose.

Organizational change. A program of planned alteration of the structure, processes, technologies, or other aspects of an organization (see Ch. VI).

Organizational learning. Learning at the organizational level of reach. Organizational learning is a form of knowing that relates most closely with knowledge flows and is oriented principally toward exploration. In contrast, organizational memory is a form of knowing that relates more closely with knowledge stocks or inventories and is oriented principally toward exploitation (see Ch. V).

Organizational memory. Memory and retrieval at the organizational level of reach. Organizational memory is a form of knowing that relates most closely with knowledge stocks or inventories and is oriented principally toward exploitation. In contrast, organizational learning is a form of knowing that relates more closely with knowledge flows and is oriented principally toward exploration (see Ch. V).

Organizational performance. How closely the results of an organization's actions fit its goals. Performance of one organization can be absolute in terms of its internal goals or can be relative in terms of competitors' performance (see Ch. I).

Organizational reach. A dimensional construct to characterize the level of social aggregation associated with knowledge flows. *Organizational reach* represents one of the four dimensions used in this book to classify and visualize knowledge flows (see Ch. III).

Organizational routines. Systems, procedures, habits, and patterns of activity in organizations that produce outputs and represent knowledge application at the organizational level of reach (see Ch. III).

Path-dependent. The longitudinal nature of organizational experience that results from making choices. Once one metaphorical path has been chosen, one or more alternate paths cannot be taken at the same time. An organization develops a set of capabilities based on activities it has experienced over time, but it also fails to develop alternate sets of capabilities based on activities it has not experienced over time. Path-dependency relates to both *core competencies* and *core rigidities* in terms of organizational learning (see Ch. V).

Pathology. A serious problem or illness. *Knowledge clumping* represents a common organizational pathology (see Ch. I).

Performative applications. A class of information technology applications that focus directly on knowledge and are able to perform work in lieu of people. The term *performative* is used often for contrast with *supportive* applications (see Ch. I).

Precedence relations. A necessary sequential ordering. Various knowledge flows are interrelated tightly through precedence relations; that is, some chunks of knowledge must complete their flows before others can begin effectively. Workflows are related by precedence as well (see Ch. III), and many knowledge flows are precedent to the workflows they enable (see Ch. I).

Procedural knowledge. The class of knowledge that is expressed as processes or procedures. The term *procedural knowledge* is often used in contrast with *declarative knowledge* (see Ch. II).

Qualitative reasoning. A class of information technology applications from artificial intelligence that seek to represent and support inference pertaining to common sense knowledge. This represents a contrast with expert systems, which seek to represent and support inference pertaining to expert knowledge (see Ch. IV).

Redesign. Planned organizational change, generally on a relatively large scale. The term *redesign* is often used to describe the key analytical activity associated with business process re-engineering (see Ch. VI).

Research. A knowledge-flow process focused on systematic discovery of new knowledge. Research focuses on exploration through learning new knowledge but also involves exploitation through application of existing knowledge (see Ch. III).

Resource-based view. In a resource-based view, an organization competes on the basis of the unique set of resources it possesses and puts to use. Economic inputs such as *land, labor*, and *capital* represent traditional resources employed in this view. *Knowledge* represents more than just another resource along these lines because it can enable sustainable competitive advantage (see Ch. I).

Search engine. An information technology application that uses keyword matching and like techniques to locate and retrieve documents of potential interest to a user. Search engines commonly accompany document repositories, intranets, and Web portals, and they are invaluable for finding information on the Internet (see Ch. II).

Semantic. Having to do with meaning. Knowledge is required to establish a semantic structure to represent information (see Ch. II). The term *semantic* is used frequently to distinguish information technologies that focus on information from those that focus on data (see Ch. IV).

Semantic Web. A class of information technology applications, many involving artificial intelligence, that combine and integrate diverse techniques to enable computers to accomplish autonomously many information work tasks that can be accomplished at present only by people (see Ch. IV).

Shell tools. A class of information technology applications involving artificial intelligence that are used to develop expert systems (see Ch. IV).

Shopping bots. A class of information technology applications, many involving artificial intelligence, that are used to automate several aspects of information work associated with shopping (see Ch. IV).

Signals. Physical patterns that may be interpreted to constitute data. All flows of knowledge, information, and data reduce ultimately to signals in the physical realm (see Ch. II).

Single-loop learning. Single-loop learning (Argyris & Schon, 1978) represents organizational learning that focuses on improving performance with respect to a static goal; that is, an organization can learn to do the wrong thing very well and not realize that its competency is suited well to the environment no longer. The term *single-loop learning* is often used synonymously with *competency traps* (Levitt & March, 1988) and for contrast with *double-loop learning*, the latter of which pertains to learning how and when to adjust organizational goals (see Ch. I).

Situated knowledge. Knowledge that is proximal to the knower and context. Situated knowledge implies that one must be at a particular space-time coordinate to learn. Such knowledge tends to be tacit and local, making it difficult to share broadly (see Ch. I).

Socialization. One of four knowledge-flow processes associated with the Spiral Model (Nonaka, 1994) of knowledge flows. The term *socialization* refers generally to knowledge sharing in tacit form (see Ch. III).

Software agents. A class of information technology applications, many involving artificial intelligence, which are used to automate several aspects of information work. Shopping bots represent a kind of software agent. Software agents play a prominent role in the Semantic Web (see Ch. IV).

Specialized expertise. Knowledge that pertains more to low-level details than to high-level patterns and relationships. The term *specialist knowledge* is often used for contrast with *general knowledge*. To some extent, general and specialist knowledge can be substituted for one another (see Ch. VI).

Standard operating procedure. A formal, generally written routine for performing a set of work tasks in the organizational context. Standard operating procedures reflect explicit knowledge used to support organizational routines (see Ch. I).

Sticky knowledge. Sticky knowledge (von Hippel, 1994) represents tacit experience that is difficult to transfer across organizational units (see Ch. I).

Supportive applications. A class of information technology applications that focus indirectly on knowledge to support people who perform work tasks. The term *supportive* is often used for contrast with *performative* applications (see Ch. I).

Sustainable competitive advantage. Competitive advantage that can be obtained and sustained over time. The term *sustainable competitive advantage* is often used to contrast with *ephemeral competitive advantage* (see Ch. I).

Tacit knowledge. Knowledge that cannot be or has not been articulated through words, diagrams, formulae, computer programs, and like means. The term *tacit knowledge* is used widely for contrast with *explicit knowledge*, which has been articulated in explicit form, and with *implicit knowledge*, which can be but has not been articulated (see Ch. II).

Tactic. A set of actions based upon knowledge. The term *tactic* is often used when describing competitive military combat actions (see Ch. I).

Taxonomy. An organized hierarchy of concepts. Taxonomies are used broadly to classify concepts such as different kinds of life, different kinds of rocks, and like tangible concepts. Taxonomies are used also to classify different kinds of knowledge, information, and data (see Ch. II).

Teaching. This knowledge-flow process is associated with formal classroom education or training (see Ch. I). It focuses more on the knowing activity *learning* than on *doing* and is often used for contrast with experience-oriented knowledge-flow processes such as *on-the-job training* (*OJT*), *trial and error*, and the like (see Ch. V).

Tradeoff. The requirement for a decision maker to give up some of one thing of value in order to obtain more of another valued item. Tradeoffs manifest themselves broadly in decision making when resources are constrained (see Ch. III).

Training. A formal approach to knowledge flow in which students enroll in organized courses offered by human resource departments and like units within organizations. Generally, an instructor leads the course, which consists of prearranged readings, assignments, lectures, laboratory experiments, discussions, and other learning activities. The term *training* is often used in the same context as *education* (see Ch. I) and for contrast with other knowledge-flow processes such as *on-the-job training* (*OJT*), *trial and error, direct experience*, and others that connote the informal accumulation of experience-based knowledge (see Ch. III).

Trial and error. Direct experience with some work task, activity, or process, generally with the implication that some kind of experience-based learning is taking place. The term *trial and error* is used sparingly as a substitute for *on-the-job training (OJT)*, a relatively slow and error-prone but pervasive knowledge-flow process employed by organizations (see Chs. I and III).

Uncertainty. A state of ignorance pertaining to fact, in which the values of particular states or variables are unknown, but in which decision makers have sufficient knowledge of their situation to know which questions to ask. The terms *uncertainty* and *equivocality* are used often in the context of data (see Ch. II).

Video teleconferencing. An information technology application enabling synchronous, remote, multimedia communications, generally through multiplexed audio and visual channels (see Ch. II).

Web portal. An information technology application that organizes data and information in an intranet environment. Web portals generally include multiple tools and services such as databases, document repositories, search engines, and like facilitators of information work. Web portals are very prominent at the present in knowledge management projects (see Chs. II and IV).

Work. The context of purposeful action in an organization. Work drives performance and depends upon knowledge (see Ch. I).

Work process. The sequence of activities associated with a workflow and required to produce work in the organization (see Ch. I).

Workflow. A dynamic movement of work through an organization. Workflows drive performance dynamically and depend upon knowledge flows (see Ch. I).

Workflow system. An information technology application focused on supporting information workflows (see Chs. I and IV).

Appendix

This appendix is included for reference to help the interested reader to see the complete set of rules used to develop the small expert system described in Chapter IV. This appendix includes the whole file in textual form, which should facilitate the reader's understanding of the components that comprise a simple expert system. The interested reader can use this appendix to further build his/her own simple expert system.

As a guide, the expert system code to follow is divided into several parts, each part beginning with the symbol "%" followed by a short descriptor of its content. For instance, the third line of the code is: "% folder." This starts the first part, which is the folder section. This particular expert system does not utilize extensively the folder feature of the shell tool.

The second part begins with "% knowledgebase." This is where the problem-solving goal ("goals = [technology_use]") is expressed, where the main action of the expert system is specified, and where some HTML formatting is accomplished.

The third part begins with "% fact." This is where declarative, factual information is stored. If this expert system had been loaded with pre-existing facts, then such declarative chunks would be included here. Such facts are used in many systems for aspects of the world that remain constant or at least very stable. This particular expert system does not utilize facts. The reasons are twofold. First, few aspects of asynchronous instructional tools remain constant, so facts entered in this section would have to be updated frequently. Second and more importantly, this small, simple illustrative application gathers all of its necessary factual information from users, and it was programmed with many facts "hardwired" into the rules that follow. This does not represent first-class programming practice but suffices to develop the expert system for demonstration.

The fourth part begins with "% question." This is the part that guides the expert system's interrogative interaction with the user, hence, where it acquires factual information to use for inference and decision making. For instance, the first question, labeled "prompt = text("5. What computer skills do you expect students to have?")," is asking about student computer skills. Notice the program offers a predetermined set of choices, labeled: "choices = ["none", "browsing", "programming"]." Of course, alternate approaches can be pursued as well.

The fifth part begins with "% sql." This small, simple, illustrative expert system does not utilize the SQL feature.

The sixth part begins with "% rule_set." This is where procedural, explicit knowledge is stored. The two rules included in the figure discussed in Chapter 4 are taken from this part. This is where the inferential problem-solving and decision-making logic of the expert system is programmed.

The seventh and eighth parts begin with "% rules_table" and "% data_table," respectively. As noted, in connection with some other parts, this small, simple, illustrative expert system does not utilize these features.

The ninth part begins with "% text." This is where prescripted textual messages are included. As with the questions previously addressed, such textual messages are presented interactively with the user.

***

```
knowledgewright_jig(basic, 11).

knowledgewright_license(academic_personal, '[]').


% folder

:- indexed folder(1,0,0).


% knowledgebase

:- indexed knowledgebase(1,0,0).

knowledgebase(main, /, [
   description = "Implements part of the Bates & Poole (2003) SECTIONS Model for selecting and using
education technology.",
   goals = [technology_use],
   date_format = 'm/d/y',
   odbc = "",
   charset = "",
   question_separator = "<P>",
   menu_separator = "<BR>",
   value_separator = "<P>",
   question_top = text("<HTML><HEAD></HEAD><BODY><FORM METHOD=""POST"" ACTION=""/cgi-
bin/kwcgibasic.exe" + system(cgi_parameters) + """>"),
   question_bottom = text("<P><INPUT NAME=""Submit"" TYPE=""Submit""
VALUE=""Submit""></INPUT> <INPUT TYPE=""Reset""
VALUE=""Reset""></INPUT></FORM></BODY></HTML>"),
   output_top = text("<HTML><HEAD></HEAD><BODY>"),
   output_continue = text("<FORM METHOD=""POST"" ACTION=""/cgi-bin/kwcgibasic.exe" +
system(cgi_parameters) + """><INPUT NAME=""Submit"" TYPE=""Submit""
VALUE=""Continue""></INPUT></FORM>"),
   output_bottom = text("</BODY></HTML>")
   ]).


% fact

:- indexed fact(1,0,0).


% question

:- indexed question(1,0,0).

question(student_skills, /, [
   prompt = text("5. What computer skills do you expect students to have?"),
   question_type = menu_single_choice,
   question_style = listbox,
   choices = ["none", "browsing", "programming"],
   'rule-display_choices' = [["rule_text", "display_text"]],
```

```
    answer_type = text,
    length = 20,
    height = 1,
    default = "",
    ask_also = '[]'
    ]).

question(student_priorDL, /, [
    prompt = text("7. What prior approaches to learning are students likely to have?"),
    question_type = menu_single_choice,
    question_style = listbox,
    choices = ["classroom only", "classroom and VTE", "classroom and media", "classroom and
webbased"],
    'rule-display_choices' = [["rule_text", "display_text"]],
    answer_type = text,
    length = 20,
    height = 1,
    default = "",
    ask_also = '[]'
    ]).

question(student_demographics, /, [
    prompt = text("2. What are the likely demographics of the students you will be teaching?"),
    question_type = menu_single_choice,
    question_style = listbox,
    choices = ["resident students", "professionals ashore", "officers at sea"],
    'rule-display_choices' = [["rule_text", "display_text"]],
    answer_type = text,
    length = 20,
    height = 1,
    default = "",
    ask_also = '[]'
    ]).

question(equipment_cost, /, [
    prompt = text("6. Will students be able to justify the marginal cost of technology required for the
course?"),
    question_type = menu_single_choice,
    question_style = listbox,
    choices = ["no", "yes"],
    'rule-display_choices' = [["rule_text", "display_text"]],
    answer_type = text,
    length = 20,
    height = 1,
    default = "",
    ask_also = '[]'
    ]).

question(student_access, /, [
    prompt = text("3. To which technologies are students likely to have regular access?"),
    question_type = menu_single_choice,
    question_style = listbox,
    choices = ["T1+", "DSL or cable", "modem", "other", "none"],
    'rule-display_choices' = [["rule_text", "display_text"]],
    answer_type = text,
    length = 20,
```

```
   height = 1,
   default = "",
   ask_also = '[]'
   ]).



% sql

:- indexed sql(1,0,0).



% rule_set

:- indexed rule_set(1,0,0).

rule_set(access, /, [
   description = "",
   type = single_value,
   rules = [[conditions, value], [student_access = "modem", text("low bandwidth")], [student_access = "DSL
or cable", text("high bandwidth")], [student_access = "T1+", text("high bandwidth")], [student_access =
"other", text("low bandwidth")], [student_access = "none", text("no bandwidth")]]
   ]).

rule_set(cost, /, [
   description = "",
   type = single_value,
   rules = [[conditions, value], [equipment_cost = "no", text("not cost-effective")], [equipment_cost = "yes",
text("cost-effective")]]
   ]).

rule_set(feasible, /, [
   description = "",
   type = single_value,
   rules = [[conditions, value], [cost = "not cost-effective", text("infeasible")], [access = "low bandwidth" and
cost = "cost-effective", text("feasible")], [access = "high bandwidth" and cost = "cost-effective",
text("feasible")], [access = "no bandwidth" and cost = "cost-effective", text("feasible")]]
   ]).

rule_set(technology, /, [
   description = "",
   type = single_value,
   rules = [[conditions, value], [feasible = "feasible" and access = "low bandwidth", text("use minimal
graphics & interaction via technology")], [feasible = "feasible" and access = "high bandwidth", text("use full
graphics & interaction via technology")], [default, text("current technology does not appear to support your
plan")]]
   ]).

rule_set(class_type, /, [
   description = "",
   type = single_value,
   rules = [[conditions, value], [student_demographics = "resident students", text("an enhanced, mediated,
or web-based course")], [student_demographics = "professionals ashore" and access \= "no bandwidth",
text("a web-based course")], [student_demographics = "officers at sea" and access \= "no bandwidth",
text("a web-based course")], [default, text("your current course plan appears infeasible")]]
```

```
   ]).


% rules_table

:- indexed rules_table(1,0,0).


% data_table

:- indexed data_table(1,0,0).


% text

:- indexed text(1,0,0).

text(technology_use, /, [
   description = "",
   type = text,
   file = "",
   text = text("Given the information you have provided, SECTIONS Advisor recommends: " + class_type
+ "; " + technology + ".
Key factors in this recommendation include: " + access + ", " + student_demographics + " and " + cost + ".
Thank you for using SECTIONS Advisor.
")
   ]).
```

About the Author

Mark E. Nissen, PhD, is associate professor of information science and management at the Naval Postgraduate School, USA. His research focuses on knowledge dynamics. He approaches technology, work, and organizations as an integrated design problem, with recent research concentrating on the phenomenology of knowledge flows. Dr. Nissen's publications span knowledge management, information systems, project management, organization studies, and related fields. In 2000, he received the Menneken Faculty Award for Excellence in scientific research, the top research award available to faculty at the Naval Postgraduate School. In 2001, he received a prestigious Young Investigator Grant Award from the Office of Naval Research. From 2002 to 2003, he spent his sabbatical year in the Stanford Engineering School. Dr. Nissen serves as regional editor (Americas) for the journal, *Knowledge Management Research & Practice*. Before his information systems doctoral work at the University of Southern California, he acquired more than a dozen years of management experience in the aerospace and electronics industries.

Index

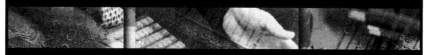
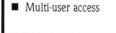